The Best of
Windows Vista®:
The Official Magazine

A real-life guide to
Windows Vista and your PC

PUBLISHED BY
Microsoft Press
A Division of Microsoft Corporation
One Microsoft Way
Redmond, Washington 98052-6399

Copyright © 2008

Library of Congress Control Number: 2008927274

Printed and bound in the United States of America.

1 2 3 4 5 6 7 8 9 QWT 3 2 1 0 9 8

Distributed in Canada by HB Fenn and Company Ltd.

A CIP catalogue record for this book
is available from the British Library.

Microsoft Press Books are available through booksellers and distributors worldwide. For further information about international editions, contact your local Microsoft Corporation office or contact Microsoft Press International directly at fax 425) 936-7329. Visit our web site at **www.microsoft.com/ mspress**. Send comments to **mspinput@microsoft.com**.

All images in this book are supplied by Jupiter Images (UK) Ltd (www.jupiterimages.com) or Future Publishing Ltd.

With grateful thanks to the following people and organizations for their contributions to the content of this book:
Garden Organizer Deluxe (PrimaSoft PC, Inc, 2008), Crysis (Crytek, EA, 2008), Gavin Reynoldson, Alun Rogers, Linda Jones, Alison Schillaci, Lynn Cormack, Peter Boston, Mark Moran, Patricia Kenar, Jake Ludington, Philip Collie, Conan, Joanna Wrickmasinghe.

Acquisitions Editor: Juliana Aldous
Developmental Editor: Sandra Haynes
Project Editor: Valerie Woolley
Technical Editor: Neil Mohr, Future Publishing
Operations Editor: Jo Membery, Future Publishing

Body Part No: X14-95074

Discover...
Windows Vista®

Welcome

to the ultimate guide to using Windows Vista!
The latest version of Windows truly is amazing and the team that
puts together *Windows Vista: The Official Magazine* has, in conjunction
with Microsoft, put together this book about how you and Windows Vista
can help improve every aspect of your life, not just your digital one.

Introduction

Inside this book you'll find easy-to-follow, step-by-step guides to using every aspect of Windows Vista. You'll discover how to get the most from the impressive-looking interface and how to tailor the layout to your particular liking. Once you're comfortable with the basics, you can move on to the many in-built features; from the new Security Center, the Parental Controls, to the varied and exciting Media Center options. Then you'll discover just how Windows Vista, and its integrated applications, can help in all areas of your life – including organizing exciting events, creating cards and even getting fit.

Get Started

If you're new to Windows Vista, want to know how to get around the new interface, or just want to see if you're missing any fundamentals, our Get Started guide takes you around all the essential elements of Windows Vista; from key features to integrated applications.

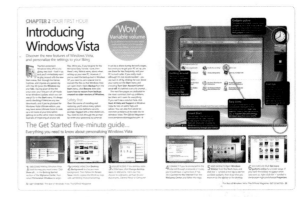

Explore

Once you're up and running, it's time to start exploring every feature that Windows Vista has to offer. Here you'll find an in-depth look at each area and, in turn, discover how to get the most from Windows Vista while you're online, working, organizing, or just chilling out and playing games.

Do More

Armed with a thorough knowledge of the workings of Windows Vista, it's time to start having fun with it. The Do More tutorials enable you to organize your life and have fun with your PC, while getting your family, friends and colleagues involved with events, parties and gifts.

Contents

Get Started

Explore

Contents

Contents

Do More

Contents

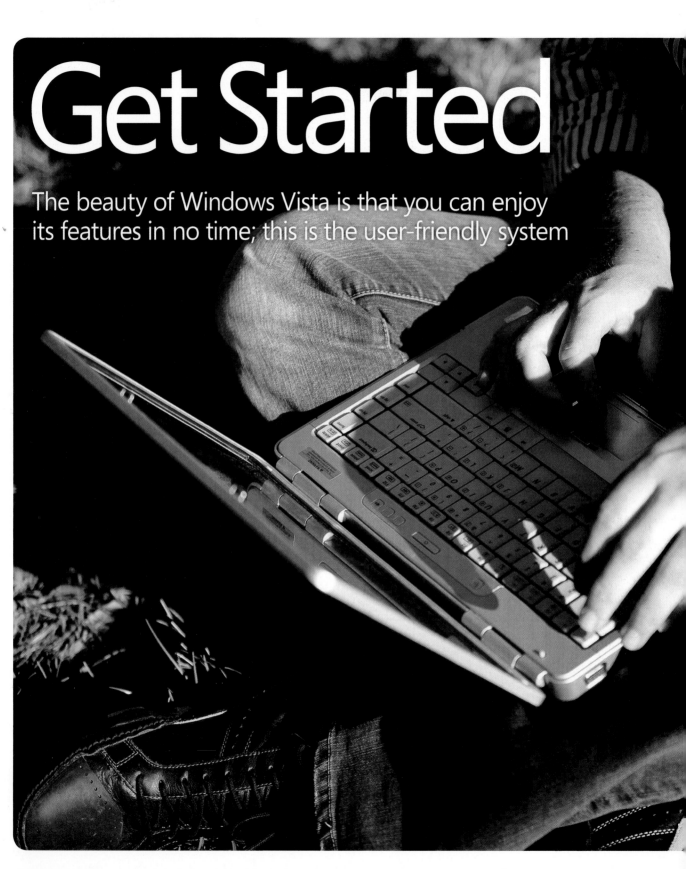

Get Started

The beauty of Windows Vista is that you can enjoy its features in no time; this is the user-friendly system

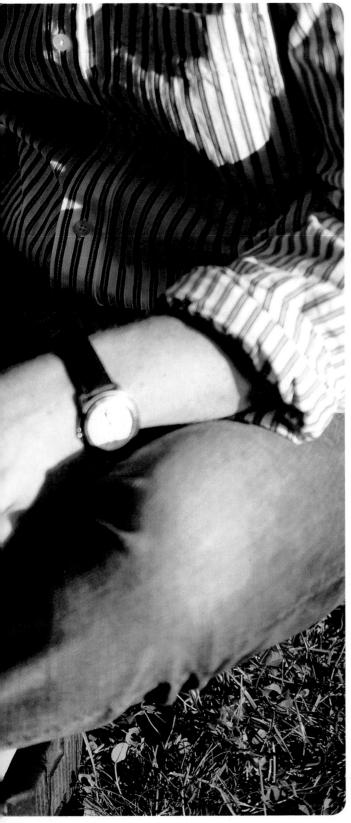

"Wow"

12 reasons why you'll love Windows Vista

A before-and-after guide to the most outstanding improvements in this latest Microsoft operating system

(1) The whole new interface just looks amazing

Before
■ Windows XP proved that operating systems didn't have to be made of flat, gray boxes, but the bright colors were deemed a 'Fisher-Price' look by many. To make things worse, it then became an eight-year-old Fisher-Price look... Even plastic doesn't last that well.

After
■ The Windows Aero interface manages to be both eye-catching

and unobtrusive. Much of this is down to the Aero Glass transparency effects on window borders and menus – you can now see exactly what's where on the desktop. And the frosted look gives it a futuristic feel, but without ever getting in the way.

There's a whole bunch of new effects, such as Flip3D, which shows every running application in a scrollable 3D stack of windows. You can actually see movies and games still cheerfully playing back, but in thumbnail form.

(2) Simple but powerful Photo Gallery functions

Before
■ Despite how popular digital photography quickly became, the treatment of images in Windows XP was pretty basic. It was possible to view thumbnails but this was limited and badly understood.

You had the option to view, copy or print new pictures when you plugged in a memory card, but anything more than that required costly third-party software – unless you wanted to edit photos with the very basic Windows Paint...

After
■ Photos are now treated like VIPs. The core function of the new Windows Photo Gallery tool should be reasonably clear, but it's the new way that you can arrange things that makes it great – organizing photos by tags you assign to them rather than their location. So, you can tag a bunch of related photos scattered across your hard drive with 'dog's wedding anniversary' and find them all listed under that, rather than only being able to group them together if they are all in the same folder. There are also some basic photo-fixing tools, plus the

BIGGER PICTURE Now you can order prints online or even make movies from your pics

options to burn pictures to CD/DVD or upload them to the web. And the way image files are displayed is much improved, with a whole selection of different modes and thumbnail views available.

(3) Foolproof to set up

Before
■ The Windows XP set-up was rather time-consuming and unnecessarily complicated – and it couldn't even be left alone to finish once you'd started it off, because it paused repeatedly to ask you lots of tedious questions about languages and networking.

After
Insert DVD, press Install, turn brain off. The set-up process in Windows Vista is no more taxing than installing a game, and no longer stops halfway through to ask you an asinine question about which currency symbols to use at which times.

(4) Speed up in a flash

Before
■ Windows XP became noticeably slower as time went by and you accrued more applications and files, eventually requiring either a complete reinstall or a hardware upgrade to get it to perform as it originally did. This was either complicated and time-consuming, or else expensive – or both.

After
■ Windows Vista offers an easy way to eke a bit more life out of a laboring machine, and all without taking the side off of the case. ReadyBoost means an instant adrenaline infusion, and all it takes is plugging in a ReadyBoost-compatible flash drive or digital camera memory card.

Because these can read and write data very quickly, they can act as surrogate memory, meaning the PC can do more things at once without grinding to a halt. It's like using steroids, but without the expense, health risks or any fear of being banned from the Olympics.

SPEED UP You decide how much space on your USB drive is required for ReadyBoost

(5) You can get Windows Media Center built in

Before
■ Everyone liked the Windows Media Center interface, but no one liked having to buy an expensive special version of Windows XP on top of the one they already owned if they wanted to use it. Or worse, having to buy a whole new computer, because Media Center wasn't, technically speaking, available on its own.

After
■ Windows Media Center is now a component part of the Windows Vista Home Premium and Ultimate editions. Its advanced from-your-own-sofa television recording, scheduling and time-shifting capabilities mean that, for many of us, all other forms of recording TV and movies will quickly become obsolete. It's also a great way of managing a bewilderingly huge music and photo library – again, all from sedentary comfort.

ENTERTAINMENT TIME Windows Media Center turns your PC into an easy-to-use, complete home entertainment system

⑥ All you need for top class gaming

Before

In Windows XP, there was no management of your games – instead, they were treated as common or garden applications, with no help at all with the complexities of running them, and each had its own subfolder in the Start menu, rather than them all being in one place. And the fact that Windows XP was released long before the graphics card market became quite as complicated as it is now meant that it was often frustratingly difficult to work out whether a given game would even play on your system, as for many gamers the names given to graphics cards might as well be in a foreign language. Additionally, PC games were beginning to trail in the dust of next-generation consoles.

After

DirectX – the part of Windows that handles games – has been upgraded to version 10, exclusively available with Windows Vista. It means both improved graphics for upcoming stuff and better performance for existing games. In DirectX 10's wake, consoles look like the day before yesterday's news. Windows Vista also offers safe passage through the problem of working out whether a given game will run on your PC. The new Performance Index tool checks out what hardware is in your system, then assigns a number to it that you can compare to the one on the back of a game box. If your PC's number is equal or better, you can play it – kind of like a rigged lottery, but with better graphics.

⑦ Parental controls

Before

In Windows XP, there was no way to prevent children from playing violent videogames or looking at unsuitable or dangerous web sites (newspapers carried regular reports of how easy it was for criminals to communicate with children online). Unless, that is, you splashed out on some expensive extra software that was often of debatable merit.

The previous version of Internet Explorer did allow some modification of what web content was and wasn't allowed, but it was still complicated to do and very limited in its scope.

It was also difficult to limit what programs your children – or any user for that matter – could use with their account and how long they should be able to use the PC for, or access the internet in the first place.

After

At last, you can ease back on some of the worry about what your little rugrats are up to on the computer. Windows Vista has a collection of very straightforward ways to keep non-patronizing tabs on your kids' computing, such as setting strict time limits on how long they can use the PC for, what age-rating of game they're allowed to play, or restricting specific sites and types of site so they can't ever clap innocent eyes on them. This is all easily and simply tied into the individual User Accounts that you can create and set-up with Windows Vista, not only providing a personal space for your children, but a space that you can place responsible limits on as well.

(8) The super-handy little Windows Sidebar

Before
■ Because it pre-dated the widespread use of broadband internet, Windows XP didn't anticipate just how much online information we would ultimately need to manage on a daily basis.

It required you to laboriously load multiple applications if you wanted to quickly access everyday information such as scheduling, contacts, inboxes, headlines from your favorite web sites and weather reports, along with having a separate window for every web site! This was time-consuming, and required you to manage an irritating number of windows.

After
■ **Handily, all the essentials (and plenty of entertaining non-essentials) of the modern PC experience have been crammed into one neat little column that resides discreetly on the desktop. Headlines from web sites, your inbox, the local weather, a TV guide, a photo gallery, a notepad, Sudoku – pretty much everything that you care to mention has either already had a 'gadget' made for it, or will do very soon. Microsoft has created a handy gallery of gadgets so it's easy to browse, select and install exactly what you need.**

MOVEABLE FEASTS Sidebar gadgets can also be detached and dragged across to the desktop if you want to up the scale

(9) Supremely fast file-searching facilities

Before
■ The search function in Windows XP was slow and had become outdated. The task of finding a specific document – or whatever it was you were looking for – required Windows XP to trawl the entire PC, which took ages and tended to throw up lots of irrelevant system files. Everyone loved that little time-waster, eh...

After
■ The new operating system has a constantly-updated database, which keeps tabs on every file as it's created, changed or deleted. Whenever you type in a search term (whether it's a filename, the sender of an email, name of a song, or a million other possibilities), the results will be presented instantly – as you type.

(10) Mobile computing

Before
■ Windows XP was always built with laptops in mind, but the market share and technology has changed dramatically since its release. Today, laptops are outselling desktop systems, and the technology inside them has totally changed. While Windows XP can work efficiently on these new laptops, it is not able to give a huge amount of control to the user about how it should take advantage of these new technologies or provide very good feedback on how much power it uses.

After
■ Available in premium editions, the new Windows Mobility Center puts efficient laptop power usage at the heart of Windows Vista. There are now three configurable power plans that enable users to opt for difference levels of performance or battery life. Alongside this a new battery meter makes it easier to track how much longer a laptop can run for. Also, a number of mobile-centric features have been implemented to make connecting to networks on the move easier and safer.

11 The best networking

Before

Windows XP always offered networking capabilities, but it was developed during a time where most homes still only used a single computer without any wired or wireless network, and at a time when even broadband was rare. Because of this, the networking features, information and diagnostics were hard to understand and use for the majority of home users, being overrun with complex information and dialog boxes. This is without even considering wireless networking, which at the time was in its embryonic stages of development. Today most homes have broadband alongside either a wireless or wired network (or a combination) and home users need the tools to set up and manage these.

After

To make everyone's life easier, an entire new Network and Sharing Center has been introduced that puts you in control of your network and its connectivity. It provides a simple-to-understand visual breakdown of your entire network, where you can check the connection status, view network devices and the computer, as well as troubleshoot problems. This information is provided via the Network Map that lets you instantly see if the network can find the internet, and provides a summary of all this information. For solving problems the new Network Diagnostics and Troubleshooting enables you to do just that in easy-to-understand reports and advice.

Windows Vista is also designed to work with the latest wireless networks and offers the latest in security support for WPA2. Meaning it's far easier and safer to use in conjunction with wireless hotspots.

(12) A secure safety net for you to perform over

Before

Windows XP contained some serious security problems. And while they were regularly fixed, you still had to apply large downloads to prevent some hacker remotely rifling through your system or causing it to fail. Not to mention the need for third-party applications if you wanted to stop your system being overrun with spyware, malware and viruses every time you went online. This was time consuming to manage and confusing for new users to understand.

After

Security is a major focus this time around. As well as it being designed in a fundamentally different way to Windows XP – meaning that the most significant vulnerabilities simply no longer exist – Windows Vista keeps a beady eye open for online threats at all times, giving you a gentle nudge if it spots anything out of the ordinary. The new Security Center, meanwhile, documents just what's been going on. It can give your system a thorough scour for anything that shouldn't be there, then restore it to squeaky-clean status and let you know via an easy-to-understand interface.

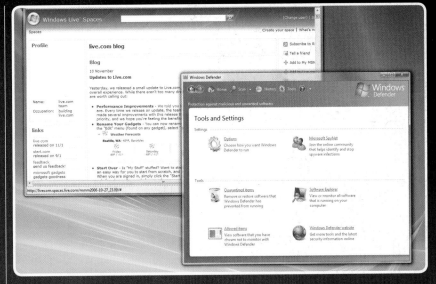

Introducing Windows Vista

Discover the new features of Windows Vista, and personalize the settings to your liking

The first excitement Windows Vista offers is its glossy new look – load it up, and you'll immediately want to play around with the new Start menu, flick through the Games Explorer, and impress any passers-by with Flip 3D (press the **Windows** key and **Tab**). Having given all this the once-over, your first port of call needs to be Windows Update, which you can search for in the **Start** menu. It's always worth checking if there are any new downloads, and if you've plumped for Windows Vista Ultimate edition, you may have some Ultimate Extras to soak up a bit more of your time before getting on to the rather more mundane business of importing all of your old

files. Mind you, if you've gone for the Windows Easy Transfer route, then there's very little to worry about when setting up your new PC. However, if you've used the backup tool in Windows XP, you need to use a special tool to convert the files so that Windows Vista can open them. Open **Backup** from the **Start** menu, click **Restore**, then click **Learn how to restore from backups created on older versions of Windows**.

Safety first

Over the course of installing and restoring, you'll notice many system options are now behind a security prompt, flagged with a little shield icon. You need to click through the prompt (or enter your password) to continue.

It can be a chore during the early stages, but once you've got your PC set up, you see these far less frequently, and your PC is much safer. If you really must – although it's not recommended – you can turn it off by clicking the icon above your name on the **Start** menu and choosing **Turn User Account Control on or off**. It's behind a security prompt...

The next few pages are dedicated to the most common start-up problems, but there isn't room for everything. If you can't see a solution here, click **Start → Help and Support** in Windows Vista for lots of useful help and advice. You can also find advice on common problems at the web site for *Windows Vista: The Official Magazine* – www.windowsvistamagazine.com.

"Wow" Variable volume

To set different levels for your music and email alerts, click the speaker icon, then **Mixer** – and you can adjust the volume of the system alerts so they don't disturb your listening

The Get Started five-minute guide...

Everything you need to know about personalizing Windows Vista

1 WELCOME Making Windows Vista look the way you want is easy. Click **Show all...** in the **Getting Started** section of the **Welcome Center**, then select **Personalize Windows** to begin.

2 CHANGE VIEW Click **Desktop Background** to choose a new background. Then follow the **Screen Saver** link to replace the Windows logo with something more entertaining.

3 ADJUST ICONS If the desktop looks a little bare, click **Change desktop icons** to add some. Here you may choose to add icons, perhaps to your documents, Control Panel or Computer.

Recycle Bin

Gadgets galore
The Sidebar by default contains three gadgets: a clock, slide show and an applet for displaying downloaded headlines. Right-click one and select **Add gadgets** to add more.

Getting around
Navigate around Windows Vista folders using the **Back** and **Next** buttons, clicking the words in the address bar, or by entering a location in the **Search bar** ('backup', for example).

Tool tips
The system tray isn't a separate area any more, but you'll still find various icons tucked away at this end of the taskbar. Hover the mouse cursor over each one for a tool tip describing what it does.

Easy icons
Icons you'll need early on are conveniently displayed in the Welcome Center. Click **Add new users** to create a new user account, say, or **Transfer files and settings** to import data from your old PC.

Smart Start
The old green Start button of Windows XP has been replaced by the smaller, more attractive Start orb. Click here, or press the **Windows** key on your keyboard, to start browsing through your menus.

4 CONNECT If you're connected to the internet through a network or router, you should have a connection; if not, click **Connect to the Internet** from the Welcome Center and follow the steps.

5 ADD GADGETS Open **Windows Sidebar** from the **Start** menu and click the '+' symbol at the top to see the available gadgets, then drag what you want on to the sidebar or the desktop.

6 GO FURTHER Click **Get more gadgets online** for a wider range. If you want the Sidebar to appear when you start up, right-click the '+' symbol in the bottom-right and choose **Properties**.

CHAPTER 2 YOUR FIRST HOUR

The Welcome Center

Now that you're used to Windows Vista, it's time to start exploring all the nooks and crannies of customizing this good-looking operating system

You've switched on your Windows Vista PC, so now it's time for you to become acquainted with your shiny new operating system. As well as looking radically different to Windows XP, Windows Vista works differently, too. In this section, you'll find your way around the interface and discover how you can tweak it to fit your own particular preferences.

Welcome indeed

The first thing you'll see when you run Windows Vista is the Welcome Center – and it should make you feel very welcome indeed. Not only is it there when Windows Vista loads, but you'll also spot it on the Start menu and find it in Control Panel. To prevent the Welcome Center from loading every time you switch on your PC, you can uncheck the **Run at startup** box to kill

it, but don't do that just yet, because you can learn some key things about Windows Vista just by looking at it.

Basics first

At the top of the Welcome Center there's some basic information about your computer and the current version of Windows Vista, and that information is accompanied by a link to more details (this opens the **System and Maintenance → System** application). Below this you'll find links to User Accounts, Easy Transfer and other features; while only six icons are displayed, there's also a hyperlink that you can use to show all available items. If you click on this, the Welcome Center expands to show you some further destinations including Windows Media Center and the Ease of Access Center. This is very much part of the Windows Vista style; by default you're shown a

limited selection of key information, and related features are just a click away.

Below the 'Get started with Windows' pane you'll find Offers from Microsoft for many of its latest products.

User access

Before closing the Welcome Center there's one last thing to try. Click on **Show more details** in the top panel, and look for the link in the Computer Name section that says **Change settings**. When you click this, up pops a User Account Control window asking you to confirm or cancel your actions – and until you choose an option, your entire system freezes. Welcome to User Access Control, which is telling you to proceed with caution. If you find this a little too intrusive, it is possible to turn this off. You can find out more about the User Access Control – how to use it and what the benefits are – on page 46.

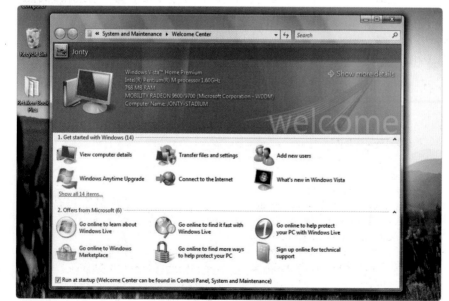

YOU'RE VERY WELCOME The Welcome Center is the first thing you see when you launch Windows Vista; it's an easily navigable window to introduce you to the system

In real life...
Very accessible

Paul Douglas, Editor, *Windows Vista: The Official Magazine*
By its very nature, the default interface requires a good degree of hand-eye coordination. New users or anyone with a physical impairment may find it necessary to adjust the basic input controls. This could be as simple as slowing down the mouse speed, changing how large the on-screen text is displayed or requesting Visual Notifications rather than audio ones. Thankfully, Windows Vista is fully set up for any of these options, and more.

The Ease of Access Center

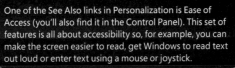

Ease of Access Center
One of the See Also links in Personalization is Ease of Access (you'll also find it in the Control Panel). This set of features is all about accessibility so, for example, you can make the screen easier to read, get Windows to read text out loud or enter text using a mouse or joystick.

Narrator
This is an updated version of the Microsoft text-to-speech tool, which is designed to read aloud menus, window contents and keystrokes as you type.

Magnifier
The Magnifier is a floating or docked pane that magnifies the active area of the screen. With the souped-up vector-based graphics in Windows Vista, this is now a genuinely useful high-resolution tool, whereas in previous versions of Windows you'd often find that text suffered under magnification.

High contrast
This enables you to select alternative non-Aero color schemes that make the on-screen content considerably easier to read.
   Elsewhere in the Ease of Access Center are links to mouse and keyboard settings, Sound Sentry (visual notifications for sound events), speech recognition and more.

On-screen keyboard
As with Windows XP, you can use the mouse or a joystick to type instead of using a keyboard.

Improved access
Windows Vista groups related features in one place to make them easy to navigate.

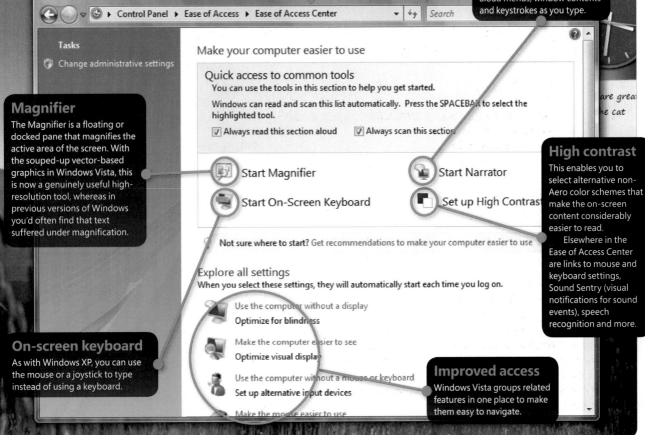

Introducing the Address Bar

It hides more power than you might imagine, so use it wisely...

Windows Vista uses 'breadcrumb' navigation. Look at the contents of the address bar: System and Maintenance is to the left of the Welcome Center, the current location, indicating their relationship. The Welcome Center is located within System and Maintenance.
   To open System and Maintenance, point at the name in the Address bar – it glows blue – and click. The window changes to System and Maintenance and you're in the heart of the toolkit. The breadcrumb in the

address bar is now Control Panel, as it's the parent of System and Maintenance. To get back to the Welcome Center, click the back arrow left of the address bar. It's essentially a web browsing approach, with address bar breadcrumbs, hyperlinks and arrows.
   If you point at the arrow between any two connected entities in the address bar, you get a drop-down menu providing links to key features within the parent. If you click the double chevron at the far left of the address bar, you can trace through the

NIFTY NAVIGATION The address bar is now an interactive navigational tool, with clickable buttons and drop-down menus

hierarchy and jump to key locations, including your user profile. Finally, you'll see a search box beside the address bar. Search is everywhere in Windows Vista.

The Start menu

What's really on the menu with Windows Vista? It's time to hit Start and see what's on offer

It's time to hit the Start button; the gateway to the Start menu itself. As in Windows XP, there's a Pinned Programs section at the top of the left menu. This retains permanent links to programs while the rest of the left menu updates dynamically. Pinned Programs comes with internet (Internet Explorer 7) and email (Windows Mail) links by default, but you can add other programs here by right-clicking it and selecting **Pin to Start Menu**. You can also drag and drop folder shortcuts here.

In Windows Vista the left side of the menu displays the programs you've used most recently, with the most commonly used programs at the top. A subtle change from Windows XP – where the menu displays only the most commonly used programs – but an important one: how often have you installed a new program in Windows XP then waited an age for it to appear on the Start menu? That's when you might resort to pinning programs, but the Windows Vista approach pretty much guarantees Start menu shortcuts are more relevant to your current habits.

On the other hand, it could be a giveaway that you've been playing games instead of working, so you may prefer to deactivate this. Right-click the **Start** button, select **Properties** and uncheck **Store and display a list of recently opened programs**. You can do the same for recently opened files, too.

Dynamic updates

The All Programs menu has had a much-needed facelift. In previous versions of Windows, All Programs spawned a fly-out menu that took over the desktop. In Windows Vista, All Programs opens within the left side of the Start menu with a vertical scroll bar. When you click a folder icon within All Programs, it expands the contents of the folder in a drop-down list, so the Start menu always updates dynamically. Click the **Back** button at the bottom of **All Programs** to return to the Start menu view.

On the right side of the menu you'll find shortcuts; nothing too radical here, apart from dropping the word 'My' from 'My Computer' and 'My Documents'.

The Start menu can be customized by right-clicking the **Start** button, **Properties**, then **Customize** in the **Start Menu** tab. For instance, you can convert the Control Panel to a menu rather than a link. Here, because the link is the right side of the Start menu, you do get a fly-out menu. You can also ditch the Windows Vista menu's behavioral pattern completely by reverting to a Classic – Windows XP – menu style.

NEW, IMPROVED Start looks a bit like it did in Windows XP but it behaves in a very new way

"Wow" It's a classic

Some people like holding on to the past... To get the classic Start menu back, right-click the taskbar and select **Properties ➜ Start menu tab ➜ Classic Start menu ➜ OK**

Search is central

The basics are as important as the clever stuff...

The Start menu hooks you up to Search Everywhere and Search the Internet options. The former launches a standard search window; the latter fires up Internet Explorer and conducts, by default, a Windows Live web search. Switch between them with the arrow keys. Given the overwhelming integration of search within Windows Vista, you might expect a permanent search field. However, if you hit the **Windows** key or click the **Start** button, a live cursor appears in the search field, so you can type your search terms. Using the Windows key as a search button tells you something about the importance of search within Windows Vista.

MAKE ROOM The All Programs menu displays on the left of the Start menu, leaving the desktop clear

Personalize your PC

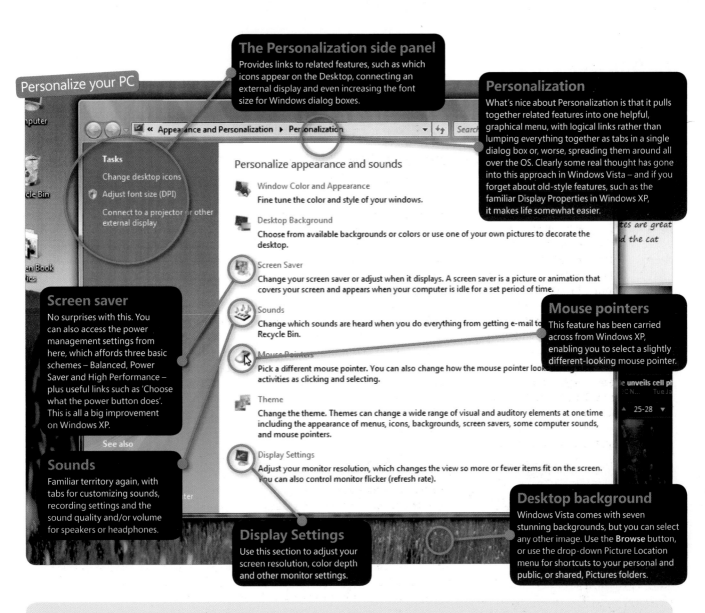

The Personalization side panel
Provides links to related features, such as which icons appear on the Desktop, connecting an external display and even increasing the font size for Windows dialog boxes.

Personalization
What's nice about Personalization is that it pulls together related features into one helpful, graphical menu, with logical links rather than lumping everything together as tabs in a single dialog box or, worse, spreading them around all over the OS. Clearly some real thought has gone into this approach in Windows Vista – and if you forget about old-style features, such as the familiar Display Properties in Windows XP, it makes life somewhat easier.

Screen saver
No surprises with this. You can also access the power management settings from here, which affords three basic schemes – Balanced, Power Saver and High Performance – plus useful links such as 'Choose what the power button does'. This is all a big improvement on Windows XP.

Mouse pointers
This feature has been carried across from Windows XP, enabling you to select a slightly different-looking mouse pointer.

Sounds
Familiar territory again, with tabs for customizing sounds, recording settings and the sound quality and/or volume for speakers or headphones.

Display Settings
Use this section to adjust your screen resolution, color depth and other monitor settings.

Desktop background
Windows Vista comes with seven stunning backgrounds, but you can select any other image. Use the **Browse** button, or use the drop-down Picture Location menu for shortcuts to your personal and public, or shared, Pictures folders.

Windows Themes

Add a little extra color into your life through a new theme...

You can adjust the transparency of windows in the default Glass theme and also change the overall tint. Both color changes and transparency effects can be previewed live just by clicking on the appropriate boxes and moving the transparency slider to suit your taste.

If you find that your computer struggles with transparency, or if you just don't like it, click the **Classic Appearance** link and opt for **Windows Vista Basic** rather than **Aero**. You'll now have flat windows

but the same overall look, feel and color scheme. Incidentally, if Windows Vista has decided on your behalf that your PC lacks the graphical oomph to run Glass, you cannot force it to try.

You may think that Themes should be part of the Windows Color and Appearance section, but it's not used that often as Windows Vista ships with the two official themes, and it's only used to select high-contrast modes to make on screen text more legible, so it makes sense to keep it out of the way in favour of frequently-used features.

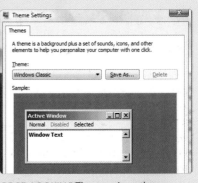

GOOD LOOKING The new Aero theme looks great but you can go classic

The Windows Sidebar

One of the most visual new aspects of Windows Vista is also one of the most practical; the Windows Sidebar offers amazing potential for customization

It's time to take a close look at the Windows Sidebar on the desktop, home to gadgets. Although the Sidebar eats into desktop space, it does get covered by any open windows. However, if you love your gadgets so much that you can't bear to lose sight of them, right-click the **Sidebar** icon in the **Notification** area of the taskbar, click **Properties**, and check the box **Sidebar is always on top of other windows**. You now have a permanent feature on the desktop, much like the taskbar. Windows have to cede screen space accordingly. This is not nearly as daft as it sounds so long as a) you're running a widescreen monitor, and b) you have genuinely useful gadgets in the Sidebar to justify the loss of space.

Alternatively, when windows or programs are masking the Sidebar, you can bring hidden gadgets to the foreground simply by clicking the Sidebar icon or by pressing **Windows** and the **Space** bar. The Sidebar itself remains fully transparent so gadgets

float over whatever else is happening on screen. When you point at a gadget, a standard mini toolbar fades into view. Its three buttons enable you to close the gadget, to access its options menu, and to drag it to a different spot on the Sidebar – or indeed off the Sidebar and on to the desktop, whereupon you can place it wherever you like.

It's possible to have a Sidebar void of any attached gadgets whatsoever, with them all floating around the desktop. However, closing the Sidebar removes even detached gadgets from the desktop.

So handy

Some gadgets have their own handy little toolbars that appear when you point at them. For instance, the Slide Show gadget has buttons for skipping backwards and forwards through images, which are themselves culled from the Windows Photo Gallery.

To add new gadgets, click the '+' sign at the top of the **Sidebar**. You'll find a small collection of gadgets already

installed on your computer, such as a sticky note application and a live weather feed. But for the real fun, hit the **Online** link and see what third-party developers have in store. Some of these are deceptively simple and instantly useful, such as digital radio players that eliminate the need to go near a browser. Think of gadgets as little programs in themselves; a logical extension to RSS feeds, sucking in live content from web-based destinations without requiring you to pay a direct visit.

ADDED VALUE Windows Vista offers a few basic gadgets – go online to see the full catalog and start building up your collection

New views for Windows Vista

All-new ways to view files and folders make finding stuff easier and faster

Folder icons have been overhauled to take advantage of the 3D capabilities of Windows Vista. Essentially, they display live thumbnails of the files inside (depending on file type). This is only useful when folder icons are large enough to reveal the details, so click **Views** on a window's toolbar and experiment. Extra Large Icons, for example, are huge but the level of detail is exceptional. In addition to

the superb new icons, you also get the familiar **List**, **Details** and **Tiles** views. As with folders, your files can be displayed as live thumbnails. Click **Organize** to customize the way in which a window displays folders and files. The **Details** pane appears at the bottom of the window and displays basic file information – such as filename and date created – and, where relevant, document metadata and tags.

SNEAK PEEKS Folder icons show you what's inside using 3D thumbnails rather than giving you mere filenames

Improve your PC's performance

Manage startup programs

This fires up the Software Explorer element of Windows Defender, Microsoft's anti-spyware program. Here you can disable programs that start automatically with Windows, especially those that do so without your knowledge.

Experience Index

The Windows Experience Index monitors performance by rating key hardware features. To check this, go to **Control Panel → System and Maintenance → Performance Information → Tools**. Your Index rating is displayed automatically, but be sure to refresh it if you change or add any hardware or drivers. As a resource, the Windows Experience Index is very helpful and elsewhere Windows Vista is positively overflowing with performance-related tools. These can all be accessed in the left pane of the **Performance Information and Tools** window.

Performance Information and Tools

Tasks

- Manage startup programs
- Adjust visual effects
- Adjust indexing options
- Adjust power settings
- Open Disk Cleanup
- Advanced tools

Rate and improve your computer's performance

Not sure where to start? Learn how you can improve y

Your computer has a Windows Experience Index base score of **3.4**

Component	What is rated	Subscore	Base score
Processor:	Calculations per second	3.4	
Memory (RAM):	Memory operations per second	3.9	
Graphics:	Desktop performance for Windows Aero	3.6	
Gaming graphics:	3D business and gaming graphics performance	3.6	
Primary hard disk:	Disk data transfer rate	3.9	

3.4

Determined by lowest subscore

View and print details

Learn more about the scores online

View software for my base score online

Adjust visual effects

As in earlier versions of Windows, you can disable some of the eye-candy for the sake of speedier performance. The one-click **Adjust for best performance** kicks Windows Vista into Aero Basic mode, shorn of transparency, 3D effects and animation. It's worth experimenting with the various options to get the best balance between prettiness and power.

Open Disk Cleanup

The familiar **Disk Cleanup** tool looks for useless temporary files, old installation files and other detritus, with a view to freeing up disk space.

Adjust power settings

This gives you three configurable power schemes. They're much more relevant to laptop users than to desktop owners, but they're still useful for setting options such as getting your PC to sleep after a specified period of inactivity.

Adjust indexing options

Given that indexing is used by search, and given that search is everywhere in Windows Vista, it would be a shame to turn this off. Indexing monitors filenames, file contents (where possible) and metadata (where available); there is a performance hit using the default settings but it's slight and worth putting up with.

Advanced tools

Advanced really does mean advanced...

Among the links on the left side of the Performance Information and Tools you'll find Advanced tools. This option opens an expansive window dedicated to performance. There's some overlap with the main menu, such as links to Disk Defragmenter and Task Manager and, at the top of the window, you'll be warned of any known issues.

Another link here invites you to 'Generate a system health report'. This opens the Reliability and Performance Monitor, which produces a diagnostic report that flags performance bottlenecks and trouble spots, and shows you how to resolve them.

There's a lot to get your teeth into, but this is pretty advanced territory. There's also a dedicated link straight to the Reliability and Performance Monitor in the Advanced Tools menu, but this launches it in a live resource monitoring mode. This is a useful way of keeping an eye on processor, memory, disk and network activity, replete with graphs. It's far better than

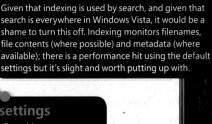

PEAK PERFORMANCE The sidebar in the Performance Information and Tools menu hooks up to all manner of helpful utilities

anything we've seen in Windows before because all of these graphs can be configured to show exactly what you want them to.

The new way to look after all your files

Windows Vista is designed to make your day-to-day life easier.
Check out the new-look Windows Explorer and easy file system

It's often easier to find things on the internet than on your own computer. While internet search engines, such as Windows Live Search, can find almost anything no matter how obscure, on a typical PC you'd need to remember not just what you're looking for but what you called it and where you put it. However, with Windows Vista, things are very different – if it's on your PC, Windows Vista will find it.

There are two ways to explore your hard disk: you can browse it or search it. The former's best when you know what you're looking for; the latter's better when you need something in a hurry.

In Windows Vista, browsing your hard disk couldn't be easier. To see your folders, just click on the **Start** button; in the right-hand panel you'll now see links to key places on your hard disk. If you click on your name you'll be taken to your home folder, which contains folders such as documents, pictures, music and so on. If you're looking for a specific folder, just click on its name – so if you want to open your Documents folder, for example, click on **Documents**; if you want to open the Pictures folder, click on **Pictures**, and so on.

For old-timers the Computer and Network links give you direct access to the files and folders stored respectively either on your computer's hard drives or shared on other PCs connected to your local network – helpful if you know exactly where

something is. Windows Vista makes browsing much smarter and much more powerful than ever before, but that's not the only trick it has up its sleeve. The built-in search engine is a thing of wonder – here's what it can do...

EXPLORE Windows Vista Explorer offers more options and better features

Browsing with Windows Explorer
The logical way to explore your files

1 GOING HOME Every user on your computer has a home folder, which stores all their various files and folders. In order to access your home folder, click on **Start** and then your user name.

2 QUICK CLICKS Double-click a folder to see its contents. To return to your home folder, click on the back arrow (top left of the window) or click on your user name in the Address Bar.

3 EASY ACCESS It's easy to move to different folders when browsing. In the address bar, click the down arrow (to the left of user name). You'll see a list of folders; click the one you want to look at.

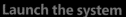

The new Windows Explorer

Launch the system
Click **Start → Computer** to launch the Explorer for Windows Vista – a big improvement over earlier versions. For example, you can now just drag folders into the Favorite Links pane on the left to create shortcuts to them.

Extra options
Common options such as View Settings, and tasks from sharing to Burn Files, are now available from this toolbar. Can't see the setting you need? Press the **Alt** key, and an extra menu bar appears.

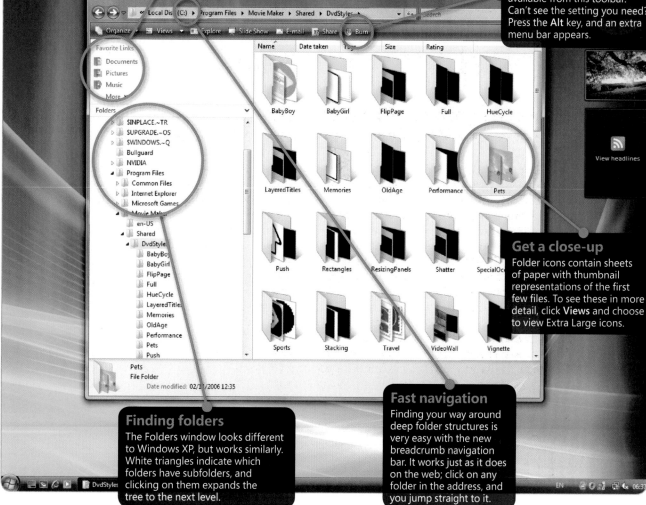

Get a close-up
Folder icons contain sheets of paper with thumbnail representations of the first few files. To see these in more detail, click **Views** and choose to view Extra Large icons.

Finding folders
The Folders window looks different to Windows XP, but works similarly. White triangles indicate which folders have subfolders, and clicking on them expands the tree to the next level.

Fast navigation
Finding your way around deep folder structures is very easy with the new breadcrumb navigation bar. It works just as it does on the web; click on any folder in the address, and you jump straight to it.

4 EASY ORDER If you hover the mouse over a column heading, you see a drop-down arrow. Click this to filter files; if you choose '0-9', you'll only see file names beginning with these numbers.

5 MULTIPLE You can apply multiple filters; you might use the Name heading to show file names beginning with a digit, and then the Date heading to see only files created on a specific day.

6 SAVE FOR LATER If you think you're going to use your filters again, you can save them as a search folder. Simply click on **Save Search** in the toolbar and give your search a relevant name.

The new interface

So you're up and running it's now time to start exploring all the new and powerful features that are available in all of the new applications and services

Not only is Windows Vista a secure, user-friendly new system, it also comes crammed full of great new applications, services and tools that will transform the way you use your PC. From the all-new optimized interface, to internet browsing, enjoying photos and music, to writing emails and organizing your social life and business contacts, Windows Vista can help. Before plunging deep into each element of Windows Vista, here's a guide to the essential areas.

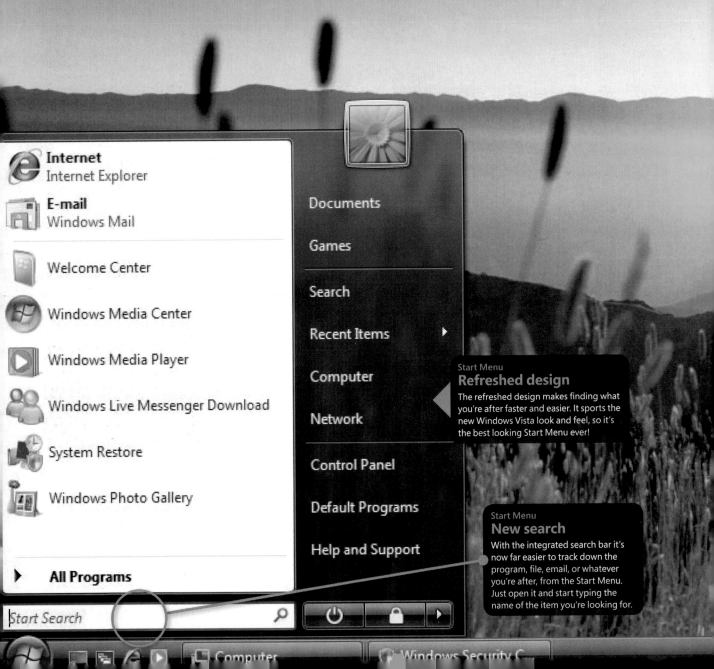

Internet
Internet Explorer

E-mail
Windows Mail

Welcome Center

Windows Media Center

Windows Media Player

Windows Live Messenger Download

System Restore

Windows Photo Gallery

▶ **All Programs**

Documents

Games

Search

Recent Items ▶

Computer

Network

Control Panel

Default Programs

Help and Support

Start Search

Start Menu
Refreshed design
The refreshed design makes finding what you're after faster and easier. It sports the new Windows Vista look and feel, so it's the best looking Start Menu ever!

Start Menu
New search
With the integrated search bar it's now far easier to track down the program, file, email, or whatever you're after, from the Start Menu. Just open it and start typing the name of the item you're looking for.

Computer   Windows Security C...

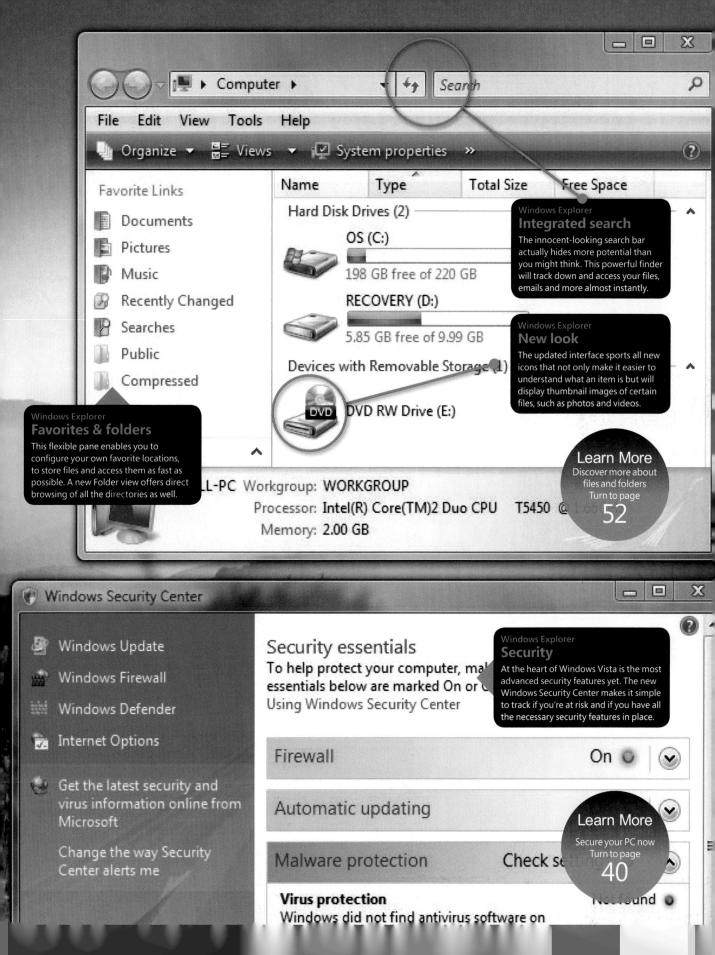

Computer ▾ | ↻ | Search

File   Edit   View   Tools   Help

📑 Organize ▾   ▤ Views ▾   🖳 System properties   »   ⑦

Name	Type	Total Size	Free Space

Hard Disk Drives (2)

OS (C:)
198 GB free of 220 GB

RECOVERY (D:)
5.85 GB free of 9.99 GB

Devices with Removable Storage (1)

DVD RW Drive (E:)

Windows Explorer
Integrated search
The innocent-looking search bar actually hides more potential than you might think. This powerful finder will track down and access your files, emails and more almost instantly.

Windows Explorer
New look
The updated interface sports all new icons that not only make it easier to understand what an item is but will display thumbnail images of certain files, such as photos and videos.

Favorite Links
- 📄 Documents
- 🖼 Pictures
- 🎵 Music
- 📂 Recently Changed
- 🔍 Searches
- 📁 Public
- 🗜 Compressed

Windows Explorer
Favorites & folders
This flexible pane enables you to configure your own favorite locations, to store files and access them as fast as possible. A new Folder view offers direct browsing of all the directories as well.

LL-PC Workgroup: **WORKGROUP**
Processor: **Intel(R) Core(TM)2 Duo CPU   T5450 @ 1.66**
Memory: **2.00 GB**

Learn More
Discover more about files and folders
Turn to page
52

🛡 Windows Security Center

- 🖥 Windows Update
- 🧱 Windows Firewall
- 🛡 Windows Defender
- 🔧 Internet Options

🌐 Get the latest security and virus information online from Microsoft

Change the way Security Center alerts me

Security essentials
To help protect your computer, ma[...]
essentials below are marked On or [...]
Using Windows Security Center

Windows Explorer
Security
At the heart of Windows Vista is the most advanced security features yet. The new Windows Security Center makes it simple to track if you're at risk and if you have all the necessary security features in place.

Firewall	On ●	⌄
Automatic updating		⌄
Malware protection	Check set[...]	⌄

Virus protection   Not found ●
Windows did not find antivirus software on

Learn More
Secure your PC now
Turn to page
40

Enjoy music and images

Powerful media accessories will help you to get the most from your collections of digital photos, music, video and much more

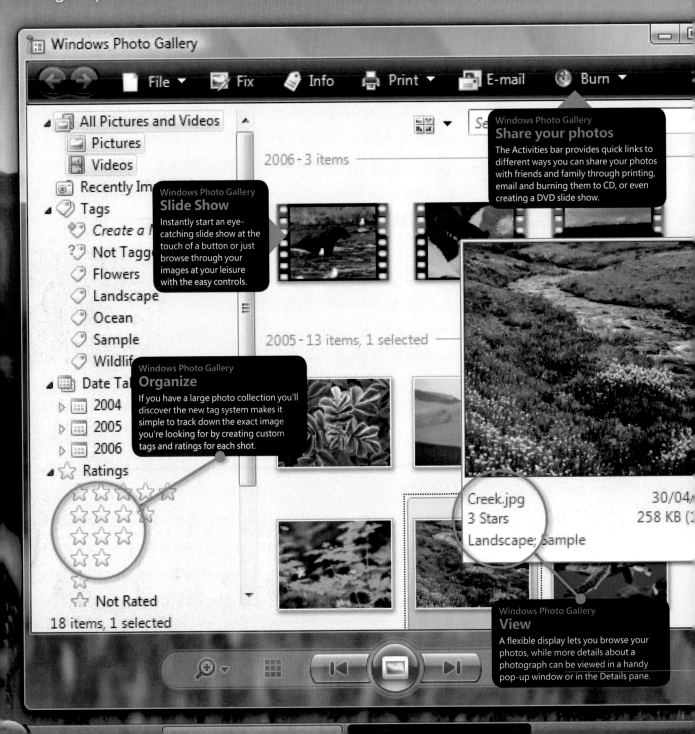

Windows Photo Gallery

File ▾   Fix   Info   Print ▾   E-mail   Burn ▾

All Pictures and Videos
- Pictures
- Videos
- Recently Im
- Tags
  - Create a
  - Not Tagg
  - Flowers
  - Landscape
  - Ocean
  - Sample
  - Wildlif
- Date Ta
  - 2004
  - 2005
  - 2006
- Ratings

Not Rated
18 items, 1 selected

2006 - 3 items

2005 - 13 items, 1 selected

Windows Photo Gallery
Share your photos
The Activities bar provides quick links to different ways you can share your photos with friends and family through printing, email and burning them to CD, or even creating a DVD slide show.

Windows Photo Gallery
Slide Show
Instantly start an eye-catching slide show at the touch of a button or just browse through your images at your leisure with the easy controls.

Windows Photo Gallery
Organize
If you have a large photo collection you'll discover the new tag system makes it simple to track down the exact image you're looking for by creating custom tags and ratings for each shot.

Creek.jpg   30/04/
3 Stars   258 KB (
Landscape; Sample

Windows Photo Gallery
View
A flexible display lets you browse your photos, while more details about a photograph can be viewed in a handy pop-up window or in the Details pane.

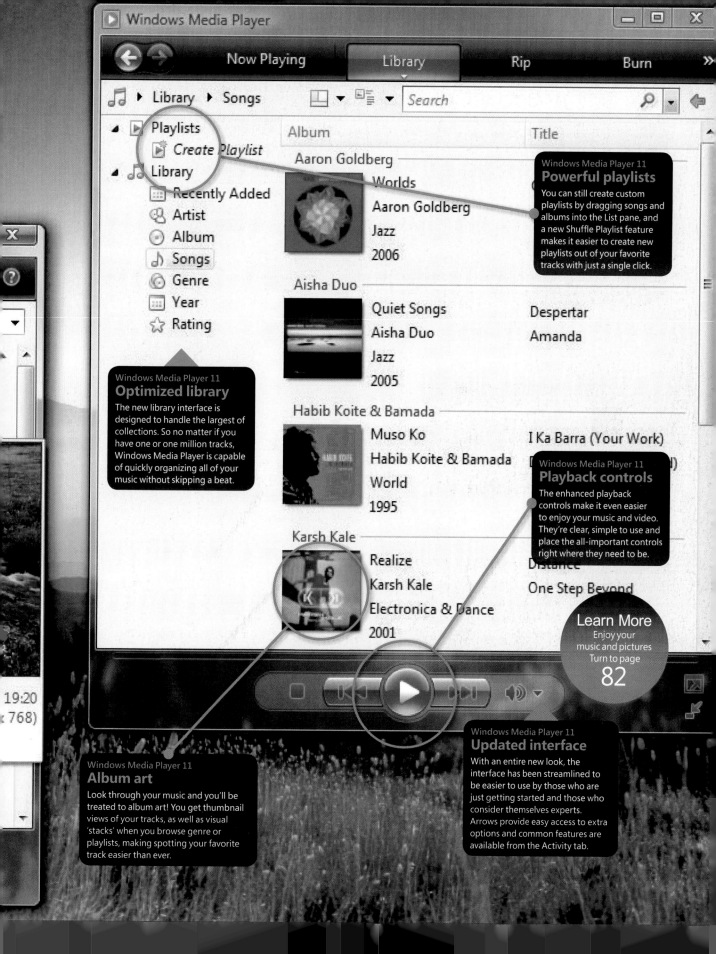

Windows Media Player

Now Playing | **Library** | **Rip** | **Burn**

♫ ▶ Library ▶ Songs — Search 🔍

▲ ▶ Playlists
  📄 *Create Playlist*
▲ ♫ Library
  ▦ Recently Added
  👥 Artist
  ◉ Album
  ♪ Songs
  ◎ Genre
  ▦ Year
  ☆ Rating

Album | **Title**

Aaron Goldberg
Worlds
Aaron Goldberg
Jazz
2006

Aisha Duo
Quiet Songs — Despertar
Aisha Duo — Amanda
Jazz
2005

Habib Koite & Bamada
Muso Ko — I Ka Barra (Your Work)
Habib Koite & Bamada
World
1995

Karsh Kale
Realize
Karsh Kale — One Step Beyond
Electronica & Dance
2001

Windows Media Player 11
Powerful playlists
You can still create custom playlists by dragging songs and albums into the List pane, and a new Shuffle Playlist feature makes it easier to create new playlists out of your favorite tracks with just a single click.

Windows Media Player 11
Optimized library
The new library interface is designed to handle the largest of collections. So no matter if you have one or one million tracks, Windows Media Player is capable of quickly organizing all of your music without skipping a beat.

Windows Media Player 11
Playback controls
The enhanced playback controls make it even easier to enjoy your music and video. They're clear, simple to use and place the all-important controls right where they need to be.

Learn More
Enjoy your music and pictures
Turn to page 82

Windows Media Player 11
Album art
Look through your music and you'll be treated to album art! You get thumbnail views of your tracks, as well as visual 'stacks' when you browse genre or playlists, making spotting your favorite track easier than ever.

Windows Media Player 11
Updated interface
With an entire new look, the interface has been streamlined to be easier to use by those who are just getting started and those who consider themselves experts. Arrows provide easy access to extra options and common features are available from the Activity tab.

19:20
x 768)

Get more done

Discover the feature-rich productivity applications that come with
Windows Vista, helping you organize and run your life more smoothly

Windows Calendar
Calendar subscriptions
The popular iCalendar format is fully supported. This makes it simple to import and subscribe to online calendars. So you can import common holidays, match dates for your favorite soccer club or even calendars shared by other people.

Windows Calendar
Appointments
Never miss another meeting, date or birthday. Creating appointments is easy; just set the time and the duration – you can even set a reminder. Add notes to make sure you don't forget those extra details and you can create appointments that reoccur on a regular basis.

Windows Calendar
Shared calendars
Not only can you create multiple sets of calendars, you can share them among multiple users on the same computer. So if you, your partner, flatmate or children have accounts, you can all access shared calendars either on a full access or read-only basis.

Windows Calendar
View
Depending on just how busy you are, you can view your calendar in traditional day, week and month views; giving you more or less detail on your up-and-coming appointments.

Windows Calendar
Tasks
So Windows Vista will remind you about that all-important meeting, but what about all the preparation you need to do? Windows Calendar enables you to build appointment task lists, each with its own priority, deadline and progress.

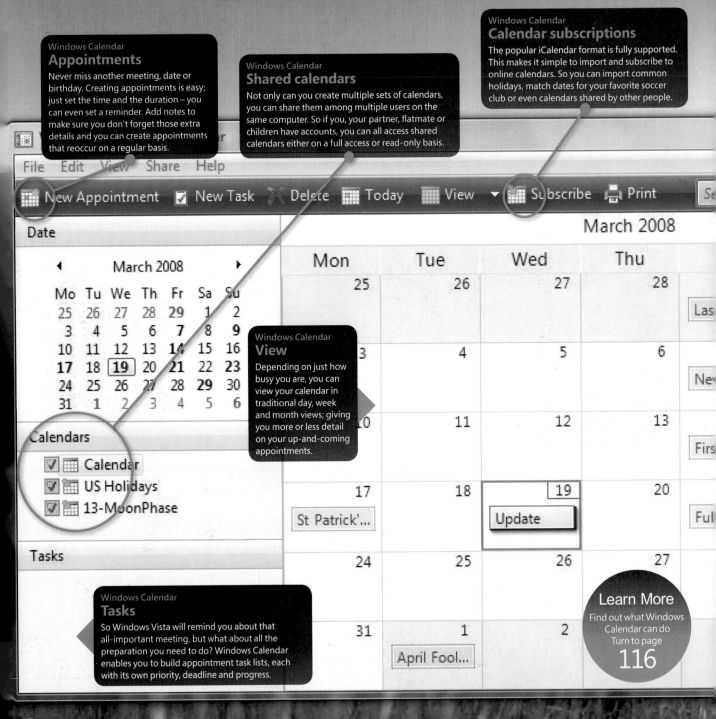

Learn More
Find out what Windows Calendar can do
Turn to page
116

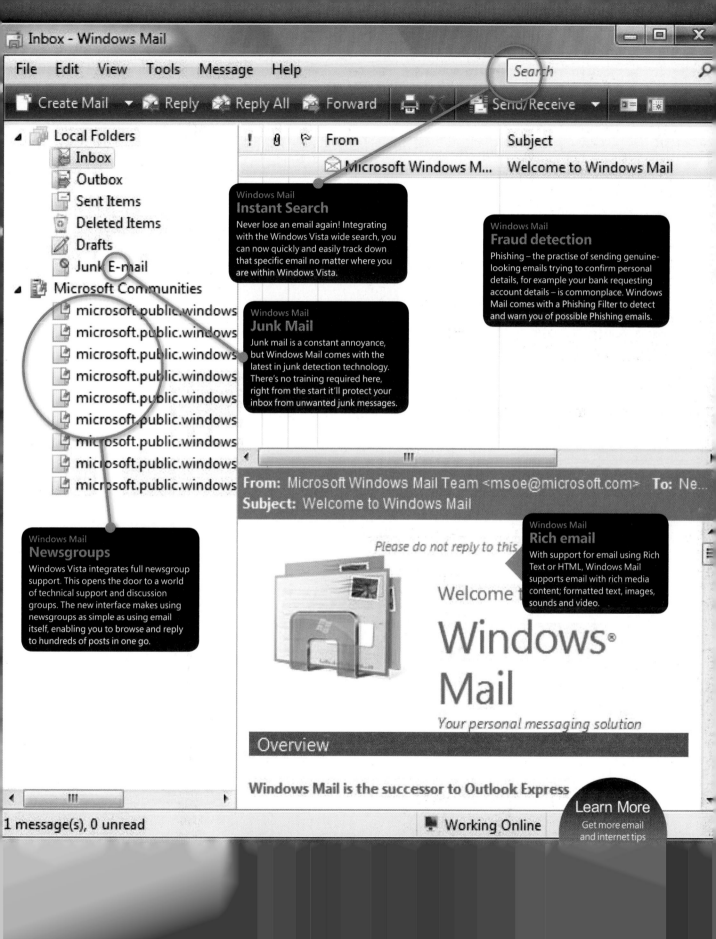

Explore

It's time to get to grips with every vital area of Windows Vista, one step at a time, from security to system tools...

Keeping your system safe and secure online

Windows Vista offers the most protected Windows platform yet, giving you the ultimate in PC peace of mind

Security might not seem as sexy as the Aero Glass interface or the Windows Vista cool multimedia tools, but it's one of the most important reasons for upgrading.

When Windows XP was designed, most of us didn't have always-on broadband connections – and then when we got them, assorted net nasties were quick to go on the attack. Web sites attempted to install malicious software, spammers created avalanches of infected emails, and if you connected an unprotected PC to the internet, it would be full of damaging infections in a matter of minutes.

Microsoft did its best to thwart the attacks, but no sooner did it fix one

problem than another one popped up in its place. The answer was clear; instead of patching Windows, Microsoft needed to completely rethink the way Windows worked. And with Windows Vista, that's exactly what happened.

Self-protection

Not all the problems came from outside, though. If you're a fan of gory PC gaming, you'll be vividly aware that some games aren't suitable for young children. And, as anyone who uses the internet knows, offensive and utterly unsuitable content is only ever a few clicks away. As more and more of us have moved our PCs from a small study room to the main front room, the need for parental controls has grown.

In Windows Vista there are six key tools that keep your system safe and secure: Windows Security Center, which enables you to control security options; User Account Control (UAC), which stops software (and other users) from doing things without your permission; Parental Controls, which keep the kids safe and keep the system safe from your kids; Windows Defender, which hunts and kills malicious software; Windows Firewall, which is designed to stop anything dodgy getting on your system in the first place; and last but not least, BitLocker, which keeps your private files private. Together they offer rock-solid security and peace of mind. Over the next few pages you'll discover how to use them to keep you – and your system – safe. ◀

In real life...
Safe and snug

Nick Odantzis, Writer, *Windows Vista: The Official Magazine* Windows Vista helps to allay a host of typical PC-use fears. It's such a well thought-out system that really protects on all counts. From first lines of defense, such as the Firewall, to phishing alerts to the customizable Parental Controls, there's an omnipresent approach to protection that encompasses all areas of Windows itself, your life online and the information stored on the computer.

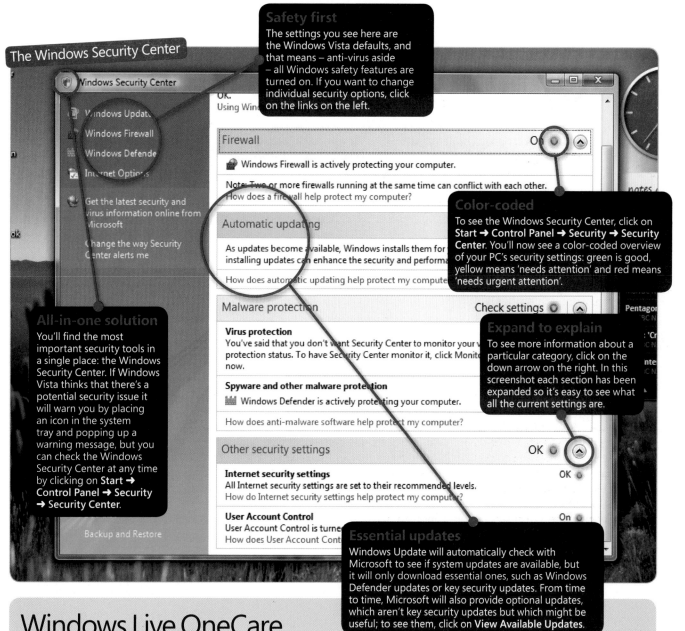

The Windows Security Center

Safety first
The settings you see here are the Windows Vista defaults, and that means – anti-virus aside – all Windows safety features are turned on. If you want to change individual security options, click on the links on the left.

Color-coded
To see the Windows Security Center, click on **Start → Control Panel → Security → Security Center**. You'll now see a color-coded overview of your PC's security settings: green is good, yellow means 'needs attention' and red means 'needs urgent attention'.

All-in-one solution
You'll find the most important security tools in a single place: the Windows Security Center. If Windows Vista thinks that there's a potential security issue it will warn you by placing an icon in the system tray and popping up a warning message, but you can check the Windows Security Center at any time by clicking on **Start → Control Panel → Security → Security Center**.

Expand to explain
To see more information about a particular category, click on the down arrow on the right. In this screenshot each section has been expanded so it's easy to see what all the current settings are.

Essential updates
Windows Update will automatically check with Microsoft to see if system updates are available, but it will only download essential ones, such as Windows Defender updates or key security updates. From time to time, Microsoft will also provide optional updates, which aren't key security updates but which might be useful; to see them, click on **View Available Updates**.

Windows Live OneCare

For hassle-free, continuous PC protection, go to onecare.live.com

There's no doubt that Windows Vista is the most secure version of Windows so far, but there is still more you can do to protect yourself, your children and your data – both on and offline.

Working quietly in the background on your computer, Microsoft Windows Live OneCare is an always-on PC-care service that protects against viruses, spyware, hackers,

and other unwanted intruders. This online service is ever-evolving and features such as multi-PC management, printer sharing support, and centralized backup of up to three PCs covered under the same OneCare subscription are already available.

Providing all-in-one protection in a single convenient package, Windows Live OneCare offers anti-virus and anti-spyware scanners, a two-way firewall

and anti-phishing technology, which together offer protection from viruses, worms, Trojans, hackers, phishing and other threats. These run continuously and can be automatically updated, too.

With additional performance management to keep your PC in tip-top condition – along with Backup and Restore plus Instant Help features – it's an invaluable package.

Stop spyware with Windows Defender

Protect your PC from unwanted programs and malware with the help of this vigilant tool

In some ways owning a PC is like owning a pet – it takes a lot of looking after. If left to its own devices it could get into all sorts of trouble. This is where a guiding hand comes in useful and, as part of Windows Vista, you get Windows Defender, a program that will help you and your PC defend against malicious or unwanted programs.

You've probably heard of spyware and adware, which are programs that sneak on to your system and snoop on your personal data, blast you with adverts and generally fill your PC with nonsense. They're often hard to detect and difficult to remove, which is why Windows Defender is so handy. It does two important things – it gets rid of

unwanted programs from your PC, and it stops them getting into your system in the first place. You can launch the program by clicking on **Windows Defender** in Windows Security Center.

Fully integrated

Windows Defender works with Internet Explorer 7 to help you decide whether new software should or should not be installed; it provides always-on protection that monitors key system locations and watches for changes that signal the presence of spyware.

It works by combining a number of useful and very clever strategies. Superior scanning and removal technologies use up-to-date spyware definitions created by Microsoft, with

help from Windows Defender users who submit reports of potential new spyware.

At all stages, Windows Defender is simple to use and comes with preconfigured settings to help you set up a stable platform and then continue to stay secure. An improved user interface gives you more control over your software. Common tasks such as scanning, blocking, and removing unwanted software are easier than ever, and a Software Explorer helps you understand which software and services are running on your computer and stops or disables 'rogue' software. Windows Defender automatically handles many common tasks and interrupts or alerts you only in the case of serious issues that require immediate action.

Windows Defender

Secure your system against spyware and other internet nasties

1 LAST SCAN When you launch Windows Defender, it tells you when it last scanned your system. If you want Windows Defender to scan automatically, click **Tools** in the toolbar.

2 OPTIONS The Tools and Settings screen enables you to see what software's running and what files are quarantined. Want to check the scanning settings? Click on **Options**.

3 SELF-DEFENSE Windows Defender will check for updates then scan your system at 2am every day. If you want to change the time, use the fields for **Frequency** and **Approximate Time**.

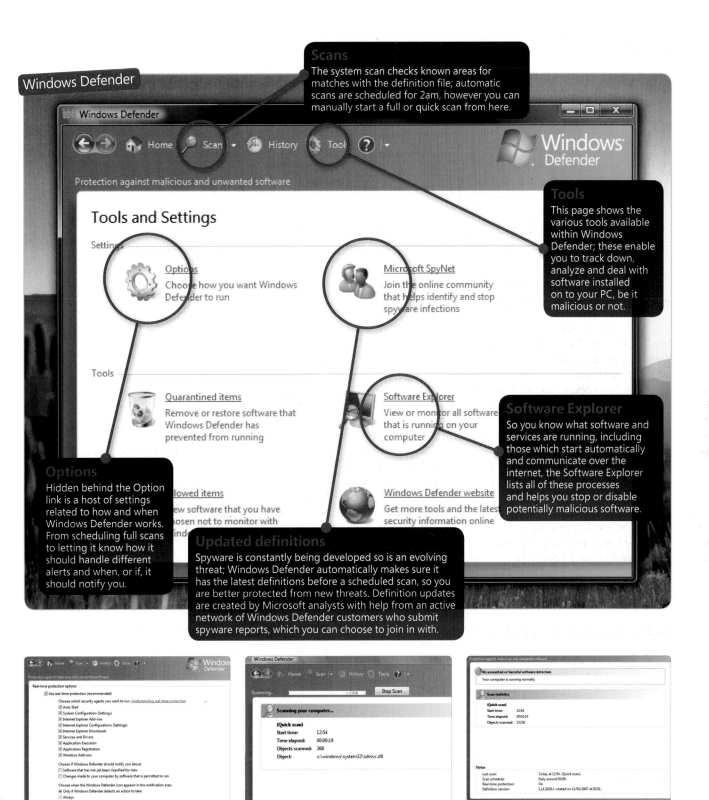

Scans
The system scan checks known areas for matches with the definition file; automatic scans are scheduled for 2am, however you can manually start a full or quick scan from here.

Tools
This page shows the various tools available within Windows Defender; these enable you to track down, analyze and deal with software installed on to your PC, be it malicious or not.

Tools and Settings

Settings

Options
Choose how you want Windows Defender to run

Microsoft SpyNet
Join the online community that helps identify and stop spyware infections

Tools

Quarantined items
Remove or restore software that Windows Defender has prevented from running

Software Explorer
View or monitor all software that is running on your computer

Software Explorer
So you know what software and services are running, including those which start automatically and communicate over the internet, the Software Explorer lists all of these processes and helps you stop or disable potentially malicious software.

Options
Hidden behind the Option link is a host of settings related to how and when Windows Defender works. From scheduling full scans to letting it know how it should handle different alerts and when, or if, it should notify you.

Allowed items
View software that you have chosen not to monitor with Windows Defender

Windows Defender website
Get more tools and the latest security information online

Updated definitions
Spyware is constantly being developed so is an evolving threat; Windows Defender automatically makes sure it has the latest definitions before a scheduled scan, so you are better protected from new threats. Definition updates are created by Microsoft analysts with help from an active network of Windows Defender customers who submit spyware reports, which you can choose to join in with.

4 MORE POWER Real-Time Protection (on by default) checks on crucial elements of Windows and warns of attempts to change them: only disable if using another anti-spyware package.

5 ON-DEMAND Scan at any time by clicking **Scan** in the toolbar. The process takes a few minutes because it peers into every corner of your PC to make sure you're spyware-free.

6 THE NEWS Once the scan has completed, Windows Defender will tell you the results. If your PC is free from nasties, you'll see the 'Your computer is running normally' message.

Prevent hackers with Windows Firewall

Keep hackers at bay and arm yourself against online attacks with this simple but thorough defense system

The news is always rife with how another hacker has attacked some computer system in the world. It's not as if these hackers are physically attacking systems, they're attempting to gain access via the internet. To stop this sort of malicious attack, the Windows Firewall is a critical first line of defense.

You might be wondering how it's possible for someone to gain access to a computer over the internet. In order to communicate with other computers, PCs have various ports – so, for example, chat software might use one port, file sharing software another, network printing yet another, and so on. Ports are a bit like real-world doors – if you don't

keep them locked, there's always the possibility that an unwanted intruder will sneak in. Windows Firewall addresses the problem by locking any ports you're not using, and by doing so it can prevent some of the nastier kinds of online attacks from affecting your PC. It's switched on by default and you can see its settings by clicking on **Windows Firewall** in Windows Security Center

Properly configured, the Windows Firewall can stop many kinds of malware before they can infect your computer or other computers on your network. Windows Firewall, which comes with Windows Vista, is turned on by default and begins protecting your computer as soon as Windows starts. The Windows Firewall Control Panel is designed to be

easy to use, with several configuration options and a simple interface.

Clever is the word

More advanced than the Windows Firewall in previous versions of Windows, the firewall in Windows Vista helps protect by restricting other operating system resources if they behave in unexpected ways – a common indicator of the presence of malware. For example, if a component of Windows that is designed to send network messages over one port on your PC tries to send messages by way of a different port due to an attack, Windows Firewall can stop that message leaving your computer, thereby preventing the malware from spreading to other users.

In real life...
Putting a block on your open ports

Paul Douglas, Editor, *Windows Vista: The Official Magazine* For the majority of time you won't be troubled by Windows Firewall, but there might be the odd occasion when you'll have to delve a little deeper to fix a problem or adjust the limits given to a certain program. Go to the **Exceptions** tab, which will show you a list of network services – such as File and Printer Sharing – plus all the programs that have been given access through the Firewall. If you're having problems with a single

program or service, it's possible that the Windows Firewall is blocking it. So if Remote Desktop, or a similar service, won't seem to function it's worth checking here to see if it has been approved or not. Scan the list of tick boxes and the related name, if you see the service or program as being unchecked then tick the relevant box and see if that fixes the problem. Using the **Add program** button, it's also possible to add individual programs, and restrict access for these to the local network or individual IP addresses.

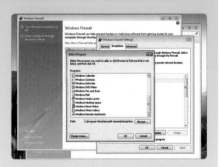

EXTRA PROGRAMS You can add programs yourself, as well as configuring individual ports and restricting access to the local network or specific IP addresses

Slamming the internet front door

"If your name's not down, you're not getting in!"

 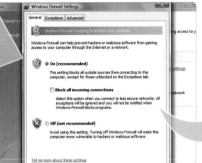 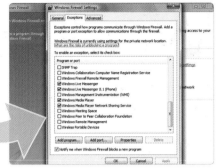

1 LOCKED Windows Firewall blocks incoming connections. If a program attempts a connection, Firewall will ask whether it should be allowed. If yes, Firewall can remember your answer; if no, the program will remain blocked.

2 STRONG SECURITY Click **Change Settings** to see more options. If you're in a potentially insecure environment such as an airport or other public place, the **Block all** option is worth using for maximum security.

3 GUEST LIST Unless you've selected **Block all**, Windows Firewall blocks connections from programs you haven't added to exceptions. Check **Notify me...** in the Exceptions tab so that you can override any decisions you want to.

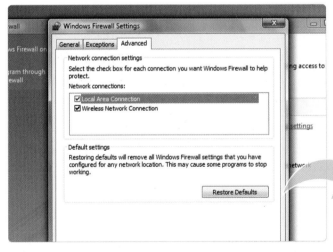

4 DIFFERENT STROKES Windows Firewall can have different settings for different connections. In this screen it's keeping an eye on our local network, but if we installed a wireless networking card we'd be able to set different rules for our wireless network – without changing our local network settings.

The Windows Firewall blocks certain connections; check Notify me so that you can override any decisions

5 IN ACTION When it comes to general use, you'll probably hear nothing from Firewall – it'll just happily monitor things. If you run a new program that tries to access the internet in an unusual way, that's when an alert will be generated and you'll need to decide if the program should have access.

Those different settings...

The ability to vary settings in Windows Firewall is handy if you use your PC in different locations: Windows Firewall will detect which network connection you're using and use the appropriate settings to protect.

Protecting you and your data

Keeping files safe from prying eyes and limiting access to your PC is now easy to sort out

Windows XP had a major Achilles heel; by default, when you installed it you had administrator access. As an administrator you have total control over your system, which means you can change system settings, install software and make any modifications you wish. Unfortunately that access was exploited – if you were running in administrator mode and a bit of malicious software crept on to your system, it too had administrative access, which meant it could cause chaos.

If you've ever suffered from malware, for example when your PC blasts you with unwanted adverts or your browser home page gets changed without your knowledge, then you've seen the

problem in action. In Windows Vista, a new feature called User Access Control – UAC – provides the solution by preventing any system changes from happening without your knowledge. For example, if a program attempts to change your internet settings, a UAC message will pop up. You've then got a choice – you can click **Continue** and accept the changes, or click **Cancel** to prevent the changes from being made.

Stress free

This will save all manner of headaches, because if any software tries to do anything at all with your PC, you'll have to give it permission. In theory, this should enable you to spot any potentially malicious activity on your

computer and put a stop to it.

UAC works in two ways. If you're logged in as the computer administrator (which, as the owner of the PC, you probably will be), system changes no longer happen silently. Instead, the UAC warning will pop up and nothing will happen if you don't click **Continue**. Again the idea here is to stamp out unauthorized activity. If you're not the computer administrator, UAC is more demanding. Instead of the Continue and Cancel buttons, you'll be asked for the administrator password. If you don't have it, the changes won't happen – even if you want them to.

That means that UAC doesn't just protect you from malicious software, but also from any other members of

How BitLocker works at keeping all of your

How you can keep your data secret with any PC and a USB flash drive

1 MISSING CHIP Normally a PC requires a special feature called a TPM chip to use BitLocker; for computers that lack this click on **Start** and type 'gpedit.msc' into the search box.

2 CHANGE POLICY Press **Enter**, then click **Continue** if the User Account Control dialog box pops up. Click **Local Computer Policy → Administrative Templates → Windows Components.**

3 ADVANCED OPTIONS Double-click **BitLocker Drive Encryption**, then click **Control Panel Setup: enable advanced startup options**. This will bring up the advanced start-up dialog.

"Wow" Enhanced protection

For Service Pack 1, BitLocker has even greater security including support for new encryption standards and multi-drive protection!

OUT OF CONTROL It is possible to disable the UAC system, but it is not really advisable

your family fiddling with your system settings, which can be almost as big a headache as a virus!

Data protection

For companies, data security is a big problem; a lost or stolen PC might contain sensitive information that, in the wrong hands, could be very damaging. BitLocker is designed to eliminate this threat, and you'll find it in Windows Vista Enterprise and Ultimate editions. The idea behind it is simple. It uses a system called encryption to scramble the data on your hard disk; once the data is encrypted it can't be accessed by other people – even if they use hacking tools or run a different operating system. You have access, but other people don't. 🪟

Using BitLocker to lock up your PC

A handy prompt to check that you're doing the right thing

BitLocker Drive Encryption is a data protection feature available in Windows Vista Enterprise and Ultimate, and is Microsoft's response to the problem of protecting data.

BitLocker has been designed to work with PCs that include a TPM (Trusted Platform Module) chip; if your PC has such hardware you can log on when BitLocker is running. If you don't have a TPM chip you can still use BitLocker, but you'll need a USB flash drive. Your BitLocker password will be installed on this drive, and you'll need to insert the drive every time you boot your PC.

Although many firms now offer TPM-enabled hardware, such PCs are still quite rare – in the tutorial below you'll see how to use BitLocker with a USB flash drive. Before you start, make sure you're logged on as the system administrator.

BitLocker prevents a thief who boots another operating system or runs a software hacking tool from breaking Windows Vista file and system protections or performing offline viewing of the files stored on the protected drive.

By combining drive encryption and integrity checking of early boot components (which helps to ensure that data decryption is performed only if those components appear unmolested and in the original computer), BitLocker can provide a seamless, secure, and manageable data protection solution available for both business and personal users.

START SCRAMBLING BitLocker enables you to protect the data on entire drives

vital data safe and secure

4 ENABLE USB Click **Enabled** and make sure the **Allow BitLocker without a compatible TPM** box is also ticked. This means you'll be able to use BitLocker with your USB flash drive. Click **OK**.

5 APPLY CHANGES Click on the **Start** menu and type 'gpupdate.exe' in the Search box. Press **Enter**; wait for 'User Policy update has completed successfully' message. BitLocker is ready to use.

6 GET LOCKING Click on **Start →** **Control Panel → Security →** **BitLocker Drive Encryption**. You may notice that BitLocker is switched off; to turn it on, click **Turn On BitLocker**.

Set up your PC so it's safe for all the family

It's great that children are so computer literate, but you still need to keep tabs on what they're up to...

So you've secured your system against malicious online attacks, it's time to think about the children. There very well might be content on your computer that you don't want them to see, such as details of the family finances or important work documents. You might enjoy the odd game of Doom 3 but be less keen for your seven-year-old to play it.

Even if you're not sharing a system you probably want to make sure your children don't stumble on to any unsuitable internet sites. The good news is that the Parental Control features in Windows Vista cover all of these issues, and they couldn't be easier to use.

The real worry for parents, though, is what their children use the computer for. It's bad enough that they've already borrowed 'Soldier Trainer: Attack, Attack' from the cool kid in the playground, and are now learning marksmanship behind your back, without the added worry of what web sites they're visiting and who they're talking to online.

Breathe easier

There's no substitute for sitting with your kids and teaching them to use a computer responsibly but, in the longer term, when you can't always be in the room with them, Windows Vista will let you breathe a bit more easily.

In the Home Basic, Home Premium and Ultimate editions you can set up monitored accounts for every youngster in your family from the Control Panel, using the Parental Controls button. From here you can create User Accounts, within which your child can fully personalize their desktop and settings. However, what they can view, read and play is controlled by filters for games and web content that you set up.

The very young

The Web Filter option is particularly useful for very young children, because you can make an exclusive access list of suitable sites, and limit your child's browsing to these.

Try a dedicated kids' TV web site as a starting point, many of them have a section for grown-ups, with helpful guidelines about how to give your kids computing time responsibly – and it'll be an entertaining start for your child's first foray into PC use. ⊞

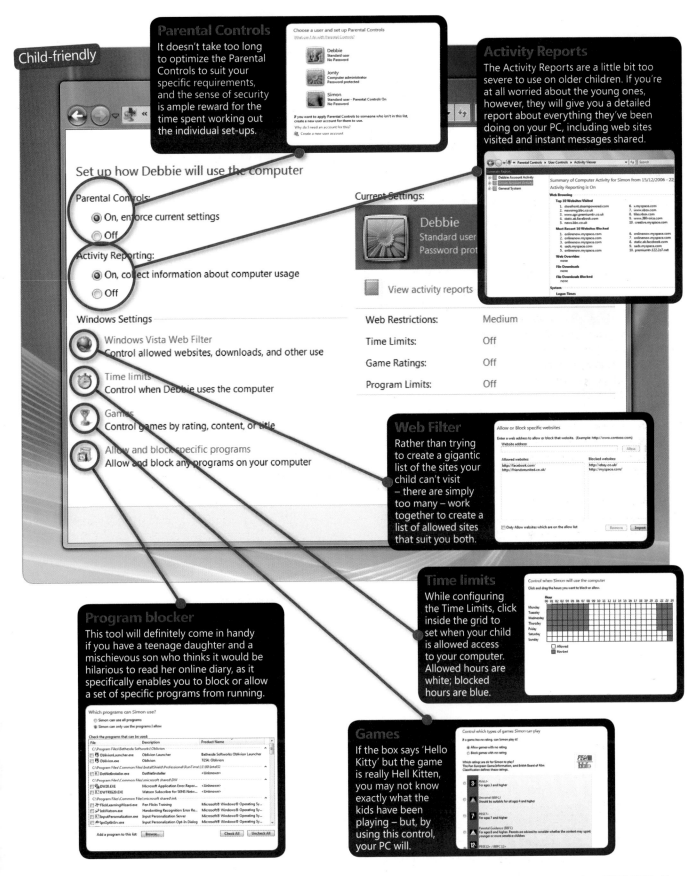

Parental Controls

It doesn't take too long to optimize the Parental Controls to suit your specific requirements, and the sense of security is ample reward for the time spent working out the individual set-ups.

Choose a user and set up Parental Controls
What can I do with Parental Controls?

Debbie
Standard user
No Password

Jonty
Computer administrator
Password protected

Simon
Standard user - Parental Controls On
No Password

If you want to apply Parental Controls to someone who isn't in this list, create a new user account for them to use.
Why do I need an account for this?
Create a new user account

Activity Reports

The Activity Reports are a little bit too severe to use on older children. If you're at all worried about the young ones, however, they will give you a detailed report about everything they've been doing on your PC, including web sites visited and instant messages shared.

Set up how Debbie will use the computer

Parental Controls:
- ● On, enforce current settings
- ○ Off

Activity Reporting:
- ● On, collect information about computer usage
- ○ Off

Windows Settings

Windows Vista Web Filter
Control allowed websites, downloads, and other use

Time limits
Control when Debbie uses the computer

Games
Control games by rating, content, or title

Allow and block specific programs
Allow and block any programs on your computer

Current Settings:

Debbie
Standard user
Password prot

View activity reports

Web Restrictions:	Medium
Time Limits:	Off
Game Ratings:	Off
Program Limits:	Off

Web Filter

Rather than trying to create a gigantic list of the sites your child can't visit – there are simply too many – work together to create a list of allowed sites that suit you both.

Program blocker

This tool will definitely come in handy if you have a teenage daughter and a mischievous son who thinks it would be hilarious to read her online diary, as it specifically enables you to block or allow a set of specific programs from running.

Time limits

While configuring the Time Limits, click inside the grid to set when your child is allowed access to your computer. Allowed hours are white; blocked hours are blue.

Games

If the box says 'Hello Kitty' but the game is really Hell Kitten, you may not know exactly what the kids have been playing – but, by using this control, your PC will.

Using User Accounts to protect your children

With youngsters being so computer literate, it's vital to get to grips with the comprehensive systems built into Windows Vista

While the majority of children sit at a PC to carry out school research or look for innocent amusement with no problems at all, we're all too aware that an alarming number of minors receive unwanted sexual comment online or by text message, making it a worrying situation for parents. Web sites like MySpace, Bebo and Facebook offer thousands of profiles; often showing a child's name, age, location and more, that can be used by undesirables.

So what's the solution? Well, whatever your opinion of social networking, the extreme popularity of web sites like these means that they are likely to be a permanent fixture on the internet agenda for the forseeable future. We need to accept that these social arenas will attract our youngsters and we need to do what we can to protect them while they're surfing for sites or catching up with friends over the internet.

Safe to surf

Tightening controls is one of the solutions, and something that various child protection agencies are working hard to bring into practise. Ideally, child safety software should be part of every new PC built today.

As we've seen on the previous pages, one of the big advantages of Windows Vista is that it comes with built-in Parental Controls (**Start → Control Panel → User Accounts and Family Safety → Parental Controls**), which help you to limit access and make the internet a safer place. You can create an account for each child, with Parental Controls activated, and then select what restrictions to put in place. You can use the standard settings to block them from visiting certain web sites or using programs, or you can create a customised list.

What's even more reassuring is that these safety measures are all so simple to set up and put into action. ⊞

Parental Controls

Keep the kids safe – and away from your secret files

1 ACCESS Create a new account to let someone else access your PC. Launch **Control Panel**, click **User Accounts and Family Safety**, then click **User Accounts**. It's a good idea to have a separate account for each family member.

2 SET LIMITS Click **Create a New Account** and enter the user's name. Give that person a standard user account (unless you want them to have the power to uninstall software and change your Windows Vista settings, that is).

3 EDIT THE ACCOUNT The next step is to set a password for the account. Click on the new account name and then click **Create a Password**. Now only the person you've assigned this account to will be able to access it.

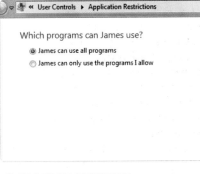

4 SET STANDARDS The account in this example is a standard one (you can only set Parental Controls for standard accounts, not administrator ones). To see the Parental Controls, click on the account name.

5 JUST CLICK ON As you can see, the Parental Controls for this account are switched off by default. Switching them on is simple – just click on the **On, enforce current settings** button under Parental Controls.

6 REPORTS Activity Reporting is now on. So whenever this user is logged in it will record what programs they've used, what games they've played and whether they've tried to do things you've blocked them from doing.

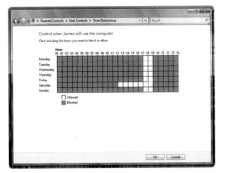

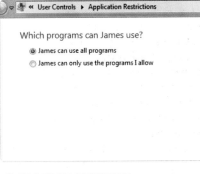

7 STOP THE CLOCK If you click on **Time Limits** you'll see an empty grid; you can block times by coloring them in with the mouse. If the user attempts to log on to your PC during a blocked period, Windows will turn them away.

8 SURF SAFE Click **Windows Vista Web Filter** and you can specify whether the user can access the entire internet, or if they should be kept away from certain sites and downloads. For max security you can create an **Allow** list of safe sites.

9 PROGRAM PROTECT You can stop users launching certain programs – handy if you don't want others to see your finances in Microsoft Money. Click **Allow and Block Specific Programs** to see a list of the software on your PC.

10 ESSENTIALS ONLY You now have two options: let the user launch any program or restrict them to specific software. If you choose the latter, any programs you don't tick in the list won't be available to that user.

11 GORE-FREE GAMING From the Parental Controls menu, click on **Games** and you'll see this screen. You can choose to block games altogether, block or allow specific games, or limit games by age rating.

12 AGE APPROPRIATE Restricting games according to age rating is one of the easiest ways to ensure that children don't play inappropriate games. Click on **Set Game Ratings** and then choose the classification.

Prime searching

Windows Vista is designed to never lose anything again, so how easy is it to find elusive files?

We've all experienced it: you need to find something in a hurry and while you can remember what it was about, you've no idea when you did it, what program you did it in, what you called it or where you put it. Considering we now store virtually our entire lives on our PCs, finding a document, video or photo is like looking for a needle in a haystack. Windows Vista solves the problem in style though.

The Windows Vista search engine is fast, flexible and incredibly effective, and if it can't find something, it probably doesn't exist! There are three ways to search: when you're browsing, you can use the Search box in the top right-hand corner of the window; the **Search** box in the Start Menu; or you can click **Start ➜ Search** to open the Search folder to carry out very complex searches..

When you type text in a search box, Windows Vista looks for any occurrence of that text – for example, if you typed 'john', it would look for files called 'john', documents containing the word 'john' and files created by a user called 'john'. You can specify searches a bit more by adding prefixes, such as:
Name:john This searches only for files whose name includes the word 'john'.
Modified: 2007 This searches only for files that were changed in 2007.

You can also use search operators such as AND, OR and NOT, as well as the greater than and less than symbols:
Summer AND Vacation – Windows Vista will show you files containing the word 'summer' and 'vacation'. Files containing just one of the words won't be listed.
Summer NOT Vacation – will come up with files that include the word 'summer' but don't include the word 'vacation'.
Summer OR Vacation – will show you files that contain either the word 'summer' or the word 'vacation'.
Summer Vacation – will only show

you files containing the phrase 'summer vacation'.
date: < 01/01/08 – will only show you files created before the January 1 2008
size: > 4MB – will only show you files bigger than 4MB.

You can create very complex searches, but wouldn't it be great if you could use plain English instead? You can. Open the Control Panel, click **Appearance and Personalization** and then **Folder Options**. Now, click on the **Search** tab and then tick the **Use natural language search** box. Click on **OK**, and you can now search in plain English – so, for example, you might search for 'documents by bert 2005'. ⊞

Using the search box

Get the most from those magic boxes that pop up

1 QUICK HITS Click **Start** menu. Type your criteria in the search box; the results appear as you type. Windows Vista searches files and browsing history, but you can carry out an internet search.

2 QUICK PICS You'll notice an extra toolbar at the top; this enables you to filter results. Click on **Document** to hide results that aren't documents, **Picture** hides files that aren't pictures.

3 BIG PIC Expand the search's scope by clicking **Advanced Search**. The options slide into view, enabling you to choose a different location and use more complex search criteria.

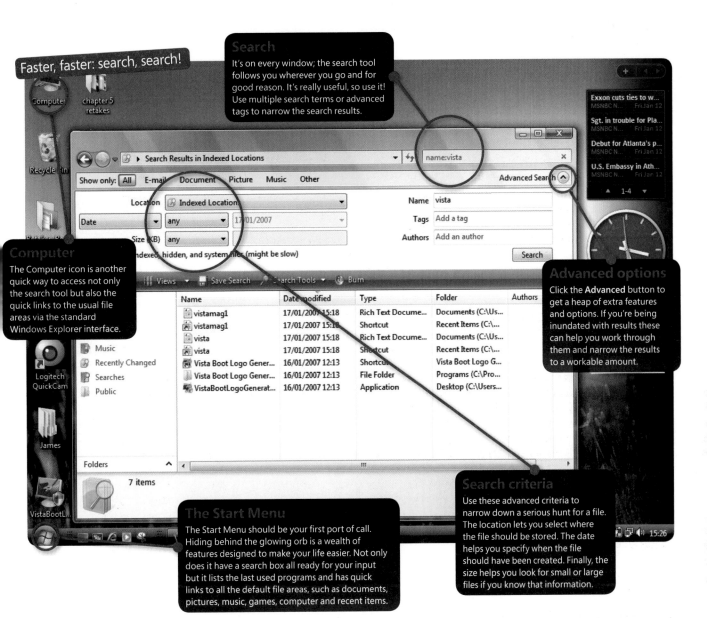

Faster, faster: search, search!

Search

It's on every window; the search tool follows you wherever you go and for good reason. It's really useful, so use it! Use multiple search terms or advanced tags to narrow the search results.

Computer

The Computer icon is another quick way to access not only the search tool but also the quick links to the usual file areas via the standard Windows Explorer interface.

Advanced options

Click the **Advanced** button to get a heap of extra features and options. If you're being inundated with results these can help you work through them and narrow the results to a workable amount.

The Start Menu

The Start Menu should be your first port of call. Hiding behind the glowing orb is a wealth of features designed to make your life easier. Not only does it have a search box all ready for your input but it lists the last used programs and has quick links to all the default file areas, such as documents, pictures, music, games, computer and recent items.

Search criteria

Use these advanced criteria to narrow down a serious hunt for a file. The location lets you select where the file should be stored. The date helps you specify when the file should have been created. Finally, the size helps you look for small or large files if you know that information.

4 SIMPLE SEARCH Open the Search folder and you get the screen shown here. Either type your search terms in the box at the top, or click the **Advanced Search** arrow to show additional options.

5 NARROW DOWN You get the same drop-down menus and fields as when you clicked **Advanced Search** in a folder – but this time, Search will look at all your files rather than a single folder.

6 BURN BABY BURN The toolbar above the results includes useful features including Burn (to burn the files to CD or DVD). Save your search criteria to the Searches folder by clicking **Save Search**.

Find files quickly and easily

Let's go a step further to see just how powerful the Windows Vista detective team is...

When hard drives were tiny and we only saved work stuff, finding things was easy. Now, though, hard disks are huge and we stuff them with songs, photos, videos and emails – so you're asking quite a lot of your PC when you ask it to find a particular file. Hurrah, then, for the search system in Windows Vista. It's bad news for U2 – *I have found what I'm looking for* would be a rotten song – but it's great news for everyone else, because you'll never lose another file – from that important spreadsheet to those holiday snaps – ever again. As you'll discover, it's easy to make file finding even faster when you know what type of file it is or another key detail using the advanced search features. 🪟

"Wow"
Never ending

Whenever you wander off and leave your PC idle, Windows Vista updates its search index so it always knows what's in your files and you can find stuff instantly

SEARCH FASTER The Windows Vista Search makes it easy to find what you're after

Limit your search to speed it up

By searching for a specific type of file you can speed up your file hunts

1 FIND A KIND In Search (**Start ➔ Search**) is a toolbar labeled 'Show only' which limits a search. To look for a file in Windows Media Player library, click **Music** then type your search criteria.

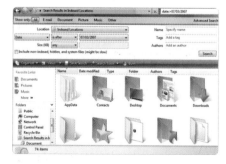

2 DO IT BY DATE Click on the **Advanced Search** button and use the Date field to limit your search to only files changed on, before or after a specific date.

3 BIG PIC Expand the search's scope by clicking **Advanced Search**. The options slide into view, enabling you to choose a different location and use more complex search criteria.

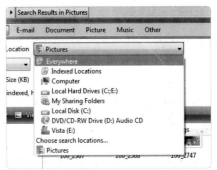

4 CHOOSE THE CULPRIT You can also limit your search to a specific author – handy if you've got multiple accounts on your PC. To do this, click the **Advanced Search** button, and enter the author's name in the Authors field.

5 FOLDER SEARCH You can limit your search to a particular folder, for when you know roughly where something is. Simply navigate to the folder you want to search and type your criteria in the search box in the top-right corner.

6 SEARCH ALL Often the file(s) you're looking for will be in obvious places. However, you might need to search your entire hard drive or a removable drive. Click **Advanced Search**, then **Location** to tell Windows Vista where to look.

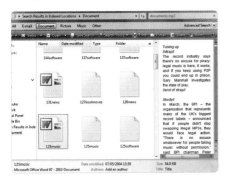

7 TRACK ALL THOSE TAGS Tags enable you to add extra valuable information to files, and Windows Vista can search for those tags. Go to **Advanced Search** and type the tag or tags you want to find in the Tags field.

8 SORTING YOUR RESULTS Sorting your results can help make things clearer. Click on column headings to sort by that field or use the drop-down arrow at the right of the column heading to apply sort criteria.

9 PILE THE FILES You can also stack your results into piles. Click on the drop-down arrow at the right of a column heading and choose the **Stack By** option to create stacks of returns based on that column.

10 PREVIEW FILES You can see a file's contents without leaving Search. Click on **Organize → Layout** and tick the **Preview Pane** box. In the case of Microsoft Word docs, this means you can read the file without opening it.

11 SAVE YOUR SEARCH Once you've fine-tuned your search criteria, you can save it for future use by clicking on Save Search. Anytime you want to run it go to **Username → Searches** and double-click on your search folder.

12 TALK PLAIN In Control Panel → Appearance & Personalization → Folder Options → Search you can switch on natural language searching. This means you can use plain language, such as 'charges overdraft'.

Exploring the Index

The Index is a catalog of files that Windows Vista updates whenever there is the capacity to do so

When you search in Windows Vista you're not actually searching your hard disk, you're searching the Index. This is much faster than looking through your entire hard disk whenever you're looking for something.

The Index doesn't keep track of every single file on your computer, though. That's because your PC is packed with system files, hidden files and other components you probably never look at. Instead, the Index looks at the folders you actually use; your Home folder, your Pictures folder, and so on.

That doesn't mean you don't need to tweak the Index. You might not want it to scan your browser history, or you might keep important files in folders the Index doesn't scan. The walkthrough below shows how to customize the Index to your exact requirements. You can access the Index in two ways – from the Search folder or by clicking **Start →**

Control Panel → System and **Maintenance → Indexing Options.**

Since the invention of the PC, we've stored our stuff in the same way we'd store paperwork; we create different folders for different things and then store files in each folder. So your Work folder might have subfolders for contracts, research, letters, etc.

There's nothing wrong with this method but, just like the real-world, filing has its limits. Not everything falls into one category and one category only, and this is particularly apparent when you're storing digital photos.

Enter tags... These allow you to attach as many different terms to a file as you like. You can then search for those tags, so for example you might search for 'Fred' and 'family', or you might search for a single 'the kids' tag. With Windows Vista, you can do the same with the files on your hard disk. As you'll see, it couldn't be easier – or more effective. ⊞

In real life...
Tag everything

Simon Arblaster, Disc Editor, *Windows Vista: The Official Magazine*

The real power of tagging comes through being as thorough as possible with each and every one of your files. If you're tagging a picture, you might start with when the picture was taken – 'June 2008', 'summer', 'holiday' – but you should also include what's in the picture, such as 'fred', 'dog' and more general items such as 'tree', 'outdoor' and so on. The idea being that if you need that particular picture of your dog Fred running round the tree back in June 2008, you can find it in an instant.

Tag, you're it!

Forget about old-fashioned filing; unleash the power of tagging

1 ADD A TAG At the bottom of the window you'll see information about the currently selected file. If you click on **Add a tag**, you can add tags to the file without having to open it.

2 TAG TEAM You can apply tags to multiple documents simultaneously, provided the files are taggable. Select the files and enter the appropriate info. Click **Save** to add the tags to all the files.

3 FAST FIND To find tagged items, go to **Advanced Search** in Search and enter tag details. Here, the search is for 'vista' and 'work' tags, and Windows Vista has found the relevant files.

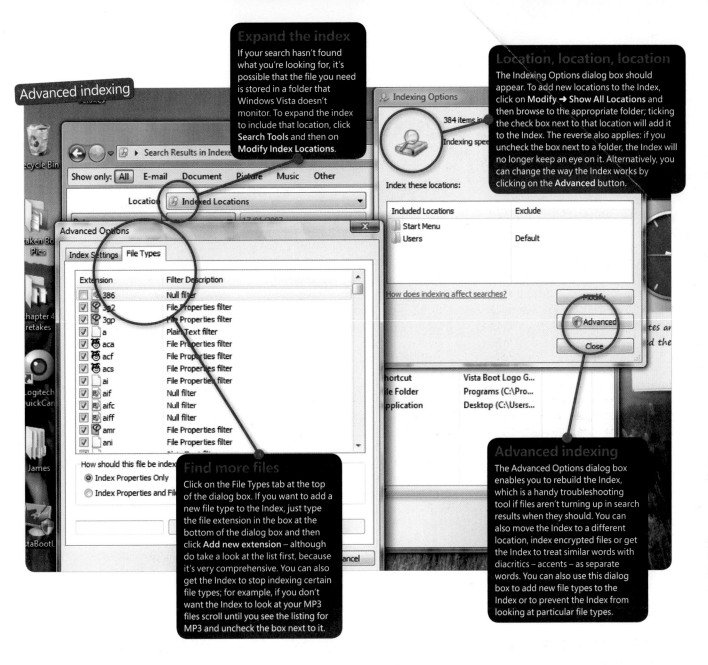

Advanced indexing

Expand the index
If your search hasn't found what you're looking for, it's possible that the file you need is stored in a folder that Windows Vista doesn't monitor. To expand the index to include that location, click **Search Tools** and then on **Modify Index Locations**.

Location, location, location
The Indexing Options dialog box should appear. To add new locations to the Index, click on **Modify → Show All Locations** and then browse to the appropriate folder; ticking the check box next to that location will add it to the Index. The reverse also applies: if you uncheck the box next to a folder, the Index will no longer keep an eye on it. Alternatively, you can change the way the Index works by clicking on the **Advanced** button.

Find more files
Click on the File Types tab at the top of the dialog box. If you want to add a new file type to the Index, just type the file extension in the box at the bottom of the dialog box and then click **Add new extension** – although do take a look at the list first, because it's very comprehensive. You can also get the Index to stop indexing certain file types; for example, if you don't want the Index to look at your MP3 files scroll until you see the listing for MP3 and uncheck the box next to it.

Advanced indexing
The Advanced Options dialog box enables you to rebuild the Index, which is a handy troubleshooting tool if files aren't turning up in search results when they should. You can also move the Index to a different location, index encrypted files or get the Index to treat similar words with diacritics – accents – as separate words. You can also use this dialog box to add new file types to the Index or to prevent the Index from looking at particular file types.

4 RAPID RESULTS Double-click a stacked tag to see files. This will show as a search result. Save the results using **Save Search**; search again and Windows Vista will find files with the selected tag.

5 TAG PICTURES Tags get even smarter when used with images. If you want to apply tags to multiple images, you need to use the mouse in order to select those files you want to tag.

6 SEE MORE Click **See More Details** to view or add tags to selected files. Move your mouse over the gray stars to change them to gold; click on the rating you want then **Save** to apply changes.

Do things quicker in Windows Vista

Are you using your PC to its full potential? Here are 11 ways to optimize the way you use Windows Vista

1 Schedule
If your PC is left on when not in use, you can schedule common tasks to occur. Go to the Start Search menu, type in 'Task Scheduler' and hit **Enter**. Once the Scheduler is open, select tasks and edit the time they occur and how long they last, along with other options. The tasks you'll probably want to run most often are Defrag and System Restore.

2 Integration
You can save time on reading emails and news by integrating them into your email program. Do this by downloading the recently released Windows Live Mail

ALL IN ONE Save time and stress by combining all your emails and feeds in one program

at get.live.com. From here you can add mail accounts, send instant messages and get RSS feeds delivered.

3 Streamline
To make it quicker to open programs or folders you use on a regular basis, you need them to be easy to access. The desktop is the most obvious place,

NAME DROPPING Add tags to your files to make them quicker and easier to find in future

although desktop icons require a double click. An even faster way is to put them on the quick launch toolbar at the bottom of the screen or, if space is tight, you can put them in the Start Menu. Simply left-click on a folder or program and drag it where you want it to go.

4 Synchronize devices
If you're constantly adding new songs, pictures or videos to your PC, and you want them on your MP3 or portable media player as well, then you want to set up a sync partnership. When your device is plugged in and set up, Sync Center will detect whether new files have

PERFECT HARMONY Set up a partnership to ensure your MP3 player is always in sync

been added to your PC and add them to your device. To do this, go to **Start → All Programs → Accessories → Sync Center**.

5 Tag your files
If you've got a lot of photos or music stored on your PC, you'll want to be able to find them quickly and easily. You can tag files by left-clicking them and adding or changing the text in the bottom of the window they're open in. You can also tag multiple files by selecting them all, right-clicking one of the highlighted files, clicking on **Properties** in the drop-down menu, and selecting the Details tab.

6 Start up in seconds
When you shut down your PC it can take a few minutes to power down – and then even more time to start up again. You can avoid this process by using the Sleep function. Just open the Start Menu and click on the power button. This will save your current session and put your PC into a low-power state. All you need to do to start it back up is click the power button on your computer's case.

7 Use the Start search
To really save time using your PC, you need to master Start search. When you've got a lot of files, programs or emails to sift through, you can find them quickly by opening the Start search menu and typing into the box. The less you type, the more options you get (for example, type 'cal' and you'll get calculator, calendar, etc). You can also save your searches, so you can find things again in a hurry.

8 Renaming files

When you've got a huge amount of files you'd like to rename, instead of altering them one by one, you can rename them all in just a few clicks. Hold **Ctrl** and left-click each file, or left-click and drag to select all the files. Then press **F2**, type in a common name to use for all the files, press **Enter** and all the files will be given the same name, with the exception of a number at the end.

9 Disable UAC

User Account Control (UAC) is the in-built security prompt designed to safeguard against potentially damaging changes. It's a great feature, but it slows you down a bit. If you'd prefer not to have it popping up, turn it off by typing 'User Accounts' into the Start menu search, and clicking on **Turn User Account Control on or off**. Of course, this is not recommended, but it is there.

10 Change users

When you've got a whole family using just one computer, you'll probably have set up individual accounts. To swap between these accounts, just press **Ctrl**, **Alt** and **Delete** on your keyboard, and select **Switch user** to change.

CTRL, ALT + DEL A quick way to lock your PC while you're away or to switch between users

11 Add gadgets

You don't have to open Internet Explorer each time you want to check on the weather or look at your eBay account. Instead, use Windows Sidebar gadgets by right-clicking on the Sidebar and selecting **Add gadgets**. To get more gadgets, go to http://gallery.live.com to download and install what you want.

10 keyboard shortcuts

Control your computer at the touch of a button or two

Quit application
One of the most useful shortcuts you'll ever know. To quickly close a window, you can use this command to close them without using the mouse. When you're on the desktop, it even opens the box to allow you to shut down or restart your PC.

Copy and paste
To copy and paste text from one file to another, just highlight the text, press **Ctrl and C**, then open the second file and press **Ctrl and V**.

Rename
When you've selected an item, pressing **F2** will allow you to rename it without having to left-click it twice with a gap in between, hoping that you don't open it instead.

Auto web address
Instead of writing a whole web site address (such as www.google.com) just write the 'live' bit and hold down **Ctrl and Enter** for the 'www.' and '.com' to be filled in for you.

Cycle through windows
If you've got Windows Vista Home Premium or Ultimate, holding the **Windows** key and pressing **Tab** repeatedly will cycle through all open windows in Flip 3D. Taking your finger off the **Windows** key will open the window highlighted.

New window
If you're in Internet Explorer or a program like Microsoft Office Word, you can create a new window by using this shortcut.

Show desktop
To get to the desktop quickly, you don't have to click on the show desktop icon. Just hold the **Windows** Key and press **M**.

Page refresh
Press this every time you want to refresh a page – ideal if you're waiting for an eBay auction to end.

Select all
When you've opened a folder brimming with all sorts of files, but want to quickly delete them all, or move them somewhere else, hold **Ctrl** and press **A** to select all the files in the folder.

CTRL   P

Quick print
Whenever you need to print – be it an internet site or an open email – just hold **Ctrl** and press **P** to quickly open the print box.

And don't forget...
Start Menu
Just press the **Windows** key to open the Start Menu, and if you want to search for something, type it into the Start Menu search box.

Advanced folder tips

Once you're comfortable with using the new interface it's time to start delving deeper into its features

 Over the last few pages you've seen how the new Windows Vista interface can help you store and track down all of your files far more easily and faster than ever before, and discovered helpful ways to work more efficiently with your files, using the basic tools and features provided by the interface. So, with the basics covered, it's time to start delving a little deeper and take a look at ways to get more from Windows Explorer and the useful features within it.

A couple of the more obvious options are available through the Organize menu. The Layout option enables you to pick and choose which areas of the standard windows are displayed. By removing different panes, you can maximize the amount of visible space available; by adding panes you can make

sure useful features are to hand. If you've used previous versions of Windows you might be wondering where the standard menu bars have gone. They are still there – they're just hidden away. As many menu bar options only need to be accessed infrequently, it's a bit of a waste of desktop space to have them permanently on show. It is possible to temporarily display the menu by pressing **Alt**, or it can be permanently displayed by choosing **Organize**, selecting **Layout** and then **Menu Bar**.

The Folder Options dialog is still available with many useful advanced options, such as being able to fix the window style and position or resetting the current window style.

Compress it

While today's hard drives have increased vastly in size, and worries about space

are no longer of so much concern, Windows Vista supports a variety of easy ways to compress files and folders so that they take up less drive space; perfect for emailing or storing files on small capacity USB flash drives. One way to do this is to right-click on a selection of files or folders and select **Send To →** **Compressed Folder**. This creates a single compressed file of the selected files or folders, which can easily be emailed or copied to another drive.

Alternatively, there is a more permanent method, by taking an existing folder and transforming it into a compressed folder, in which everything is compressed, but still looks and acts as a normal folder. You can do this by right-clicking a folder, selecting **Properties**, clicking the **Advanced** button and ticking the **Compress contents to save disk space** tick box. ⊞

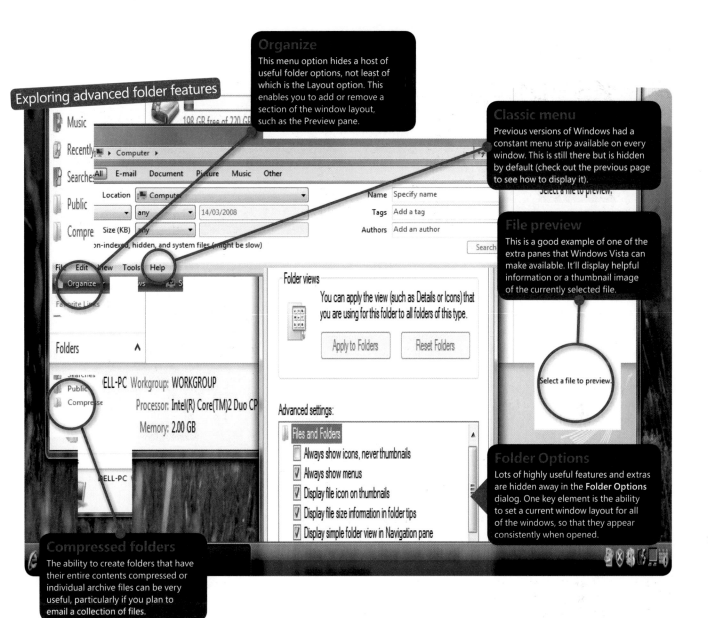

Exploring advanced folder features

Organize
This menu option hides a host of useful folder options, not least of which is the Layout option. This enables you to add or remove a section of the window layout, such as the Preview pane.

Classic menu
Previous versions of Windows had a constant menu strip available on every window. This is still there but is hidden by default (check out the previous page to see how to display it).

File preview
This is a good example of one of the extra panes that Windows Vista can make available. It'll display helpful information or a thumbnail image of the currently selected file.

Folder Options
Lots of highly useful features and extras are hidden away in the **Folder Options** dialog. One key element is the ability to set a current window layout for all of the windows, so that they appear consistently when opened.

Compressed folders
The ability to create folders that have their entire contents compressed or individual archive files can be very useful, particularly if you plan to email a collection of files.

File type management

Get a grip of your applications and the files they handle

A file is usually associated with the program that created it or the program that should open it. For example, in the case of a text document that was created in Notepad, the file will have the Notepad file type, and therefore display the corresponding Notepad icon; obviously, when you double-click it, it will open in Notepad.

Sometimes this isn't desirable as you want to edit the file within another program. In these cases, you can either run the application and locate the document that way. Or, you can right-click the file and select **Open With**; if you can see the program listed in the menu, select it to have the file open from that program. If you select the **Choose Default Program** this opens a new dialog box. Using this you can permanently change the

FILE TYPE Choose the program that opens specific file types to save you time and effort

program that opens that type of document, so in this example it's possible to have text documents open with WordPad.

Never lose a file or photo again

Windows Vista makes backing up easier than ever, so now there's no excuse not to protect your files from corruption or deletion

Data recovery is an expensive business – assuming it's actually possible to find anything to recover. Despite this cost, people forget how priceless their personal files are – you can reinstall any program from the disc that came with it, but you can't magically restore a photo, important document or vital email. The consequences of data loss are often ignored until people directly experience them for themselves.

In the past, data backup was a difficult and costly process, but that's all changed with Windows Vista. It features a built-in back-up tool that's simple to set up, supports a wide range of back-up media (including CD and DVD) and can be scheduled to run automatically in the background at set intervals. In other words, it's a perfect 'set it and forget it' solution that removes any excuses for never backing up important documents, emails and other files.

Windows Vista features a built-in backup tool that's simple to set up

When it comes to backing up, you have a number of choices. You can back up to CD or DVD, although you're restricted by capacities – 650MB for individual CDs, 4.7GB (or 8.4GB if you have a dual-layer drive and compatible discs) for DVDs. The Windows Vista Backup and Restore tool will split your backup so it can be spanned across many discs, but this isn't practical if you're updating your backup regularly.

You can also back up to another location on your network, like a shared folder or a Network Attached Storage device. It's simple to set up, but that device does need to be switched on when your backup runs, and performance will depend on the speed of your network connection, particularly if it's wireless.

The easiest option is to use an external hard drive. These can be attached via a USB or Firewire port, which are much quicker than a network connection. ➲

Backing up and restoring your files

Six steps to help safeguard precious documents, photos and videos

1 SCHEDULE BACKUP Type 'backup' into the Start Menu Search box and select **Backup and Restore Center**. Now click **Back up Files button**. Select whether to save to CD, DVD or external hard drive.

2 FILE TYPES Decide which types of files you want to include in the backup, such as TV shows, emails, etc. Hovering over each category reveals more details about what is included.

3 SELECT A FREQUENCY Choose how frequently you want to perform the backup. Obviously, the frequency will depend on how often you add to or change files on your hard drive.

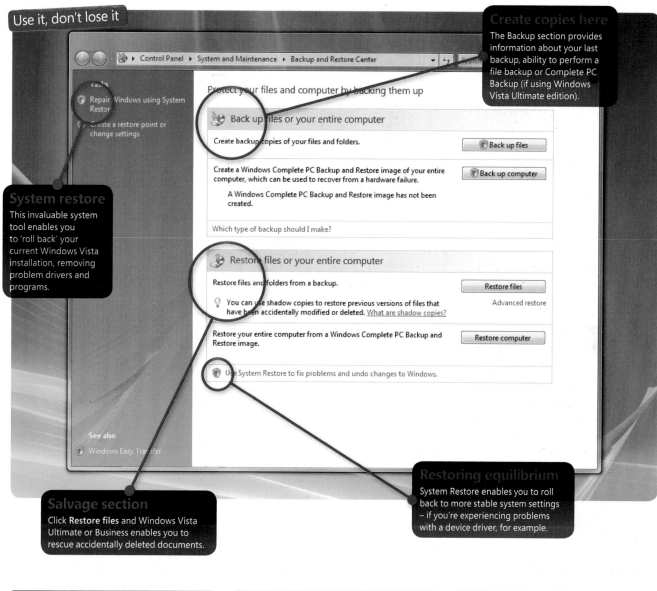

Create copies here
The Backup section provides information about your last backup, ability to perform a file backup or Complete PC Backup (if using Windows Vista Ultimate edition).

Control Panel ▸ System and Maintenance ▸ Backup and Restore Center

Tasks
Repair Windows using System Restore
Create a restore point or change settings

Protect your files and computer by backing them up

System restore
This invaluable system tool enables you to 'roll back' your current Windows Vista installation, removing problem drivers and programs.

Back up files or your entire computer

Create backup copies of your files and folders.   [Back up files]

Create a Windows Complete PC Backup and Restore image of your entire computer, which can be used to recover from a hardware failure.   [Back up computer]

A Windows Complete PC Backup and Restore image has not been created.

Which type of backup should I make?

Restore files or your entire computer

Restore files and folders from a backup.   [Restore files]

You can use shadow copies to restore previous versions of files that have been accidentally modified or deleted. What are shadow copies?   Advanced restore

Restore your entire computer from a Windows Complete PC Backup and Restore image.   [Restore computer]

Use System Restore to fix problems and undo changes to Windows.

See also
Windows Easy Transfer

Salvage section
Click **Restore files** and Windows Vista Ultimate or Business enables you to rescue accidentally deleted documents.

Restoring equilibrium
System Restore enables you to roll back to more stable system settings – if you're experiencing problems with a device driver, for example.

4 READY, SET, GO Click **Save settings and start backup** and Windows Vista will scan your files and copy them to your backup device. If backing up to CD/DVD, you'll be prompted to insert a blank disc.

5 RESTORE FILES If you need to restore files later, plug the back-up drive into your PC or put the back-up DVD into the drive. Go to **Backup and Restore Center**, click **Restore Files**, and choose to restore.

6 ADD FILES Click **Add files...** to browse files on your back-up drive. Select the files to restore and click **Next**. Choose whether to restore to original locations or a new one, then click **Start restore**.

Some PCs also come with eSATA ports – external ports that work with a limited number of drives, but which offer superior performance to even USB or Firewire. Capacities vary widely; choose one with plenty of space.

A fourth option – not supported by Backup and Restore in Windows Vista –

BACK UP BUDDY Restoring backed-up files is even easier and can be a real life saver

is to backup online. Various service providers offer space, as do some security programs.

What can I back up?

The Windows Vista Backup and Restore tool backs up important files but it doesn't record system and program preferences, like desktop or Microsoft Office settings... If you're running Windows Vista Business, Enterprise or Ultimate edition, you'll notice another option in the Backup and Restore Center – Back up computer. This launches the Windows Complete Backup tool, which enables you to back up key files and settings that will enable you to get Windows Vista back up and running should your PC fail – your programs and preferences will be preserved, making it a more convenient option than reinstalling Windows Vista from scratch.

For many other back-up programs you're able to pick and choose which folders get backed up, but these may not store program or Windows settings, either. If you don't have access to the Windows Complete Backup Tool, you'll need to install a third-party solution that will enable you to create an entire image of your hard drive. ⊞

Quick questions

With easy answers!

Q How do I restore my computer from a previous Complete PC Backup?
A You should boot from your Windows Vista installation disc, choose **Repair my computer** when prompted and click **Windows Complete PC Restore**.

Q I heavily edited an Excel file and saved over it. I now want the old version back – am I completely stuck?
A If you've been doing backups, you can simply restore the file. Windows Vista Ultimate and Business editions have another trick, though, called Shadow Copy – these are copies of files and folders that Windows automatically saves as part of a restore point. To revert to a shadow copy, right-click the file you want to restore, choose **Restore previous versions**, and then choose the one that you want to revert to. See the next page for further details.

Q Do Shadow Copy versions take up a lot of disk space?
A Shadow copying only stores changes made between versions – this means the file size isn't very different.

Q Why can't I see my documents in Search results?
A If you save files on a different hard drive to Windows Vista, you need to change the default Search settings to include this drive in the Search Index. Simply search for 'index' in **Control Panel** and select **Change how Windows searches**. From here you can add and remove locations.

Complete PC Backup and Restore

Ultimate Edition owners can back up their entire computer the easy way

Windows Vista doesn't just deal with backing up files, it can also make a perfect copy of your hard disk – which means if your computer runs into problems, you can get your system up and running on another PC in under 60 minutes.

Creating a Complete PC Backup works in much the same way as a normal backup, but as you might imagine it's a lot bigger; if you're using DVDs, you'll need between six and 10 blank discs for a typical system backup. You can't pick and choose what to back up, either –

Complete PC Backup makes a complete copy of your hard disk, with no exceptions or omissions.

To create a Complete PC Backup, go to **Control Panel → System and Maintenance → Backup and Restore Center**, then click on **Back Up Computer**. If disaster strikes and you need to recover your system from a Complete PC Backup, you'll need to restart your PC and hold down the **F8** key. This brings up the Windows Recovery Environment, from which you can then select **Windows Complete PC Restore**.

Shadow Copy in action

Accidentally overwritten or erased a file? Windows Vista can retrieve it

If you're running Windows Vista Business, Enterprise or Ultimate edition, you can take advantage of Shadow Copy; a regular back-up copy of files that you can open, copy to another folder or restore over current versions.

Shadow Copies work in conjunction with System Protection (**Control Panel ➜ System and Maintenance ➜ System** and clicking on **System Protection**). Incremental changes to files are stored along with backups taken by the Backup

and Restore tool as you work. To restore a previous version of a file, right-click it and choose **Restore previous versions**. You can open a file to check the version, make a copy of it in another folder or drive, or restore it to the desired version.

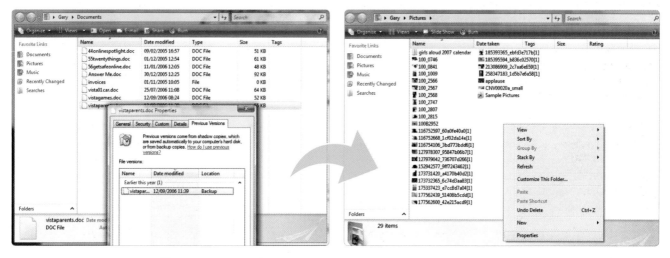

1 TIME TRAVEL Restoring a file is easy, right-click on the file to recover, choose **Properties** and go to the Previous Versions tab. A list of previous versions will appear in the list. Click on the version you want and click on **Restore**.

2 UNDO DELETE You can also use Shadow Copy to restore deleted files. Simply find the folder that originally contained the file, right-click (making sure you're not right-clicking on a file), and choose **Properties ➜ Previous Versions**.

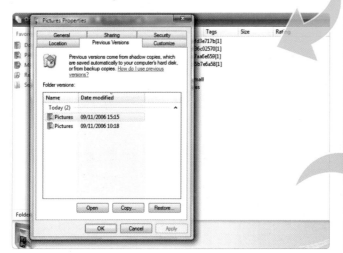

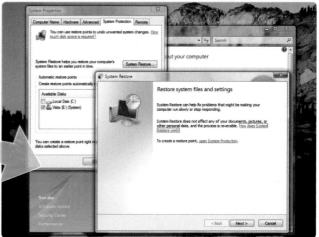

3 BACK AGAIN Choose the version that you want to restore and then click on the **Restore** button. This will replace the entire folder with an earlier version – restoring deleted files, but also removing any files added afterwards.

4 SORT IT In contrast, System Restore can take your entire system back in time, but documents and other files will remain unaffected as System Restore only covers the Windows system files, not personal ones.

Set up your network at home in just 10 minutes

The new networking features in Windows Vista make setting up a PC connection child's play

One of the most important changes in Windows Vista is its approach to networking. Whether you're connecting to other computers or to the internet, you'll find the process of connecting, using and troubleshooting network connections much easier than in Windows XP. Some of the changes are not immediately obvious, but some of the most important changes are very visible indeed.

Over the next few pages you'll discover more about the Networking and Sharing Center, the power of Windows Meeting Space, and how you can share not just documents but also entire programs with others on your network. If you've ever spent an unhappy day digging through the networking settings of an older Windows PC, you'll be delighted with the way Windows Vista does things.

Networking shouldn't be difficult – after all, a network is just a couple of computers talking to one another. However, there are lots of issues to consider. Security is a big one – you don't want just anybody wandering around your PC – but there are practicalities, too. Are you connecting via a cable or over a wireless network? Do you want to share your media files, your folders or your printer? In older versions of Windows, setting up even the simplest network or internet connection could be a time-consuming operation, but in Windows Vista it couldn't be easier.

Connecting to the internet
Windows Vista provides the quickest route to the information highway

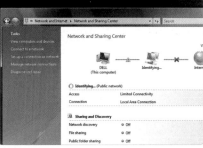

1 NO NET For Windows Vista PC to find a connection, click on **Start → Control Panel → Network and Internet → Network and Sharing Center**. A red cross indicates no connection is found.

2 GET CONNECTED When you run an Ethernet cable from your router to your PC, a grayed-out computer with the caption 'Identifying' appears as Windows Vista auto-detects the network settings.

3 EASY ACCESS After a short delay, the map of your network changes again. This time it shows that you're connected to the internet via your network. Click on **View Full Map** for a better look.

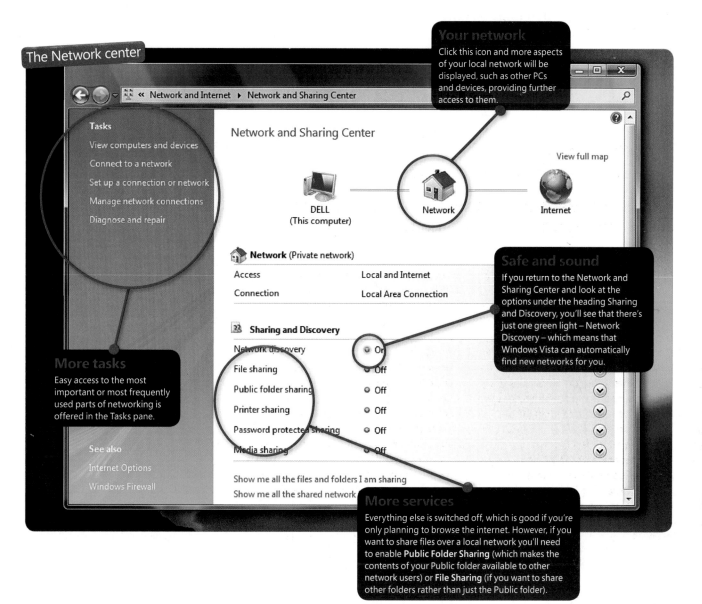

Your network
Click this icon and more aspects of your local network will be displayed, such as other PCs and devices, providing further access to them.

Tasks
View computers and devices
Connect to a network
Set up a connection or network
Manage network connections
Diagnose and repair

Network and Sharing Center

View full map

DELL
(This computer)

Network

Internet

Network (Private network)

Access   Local and Internet
Connection   Local Area Connection

Sharing and Discovery

Network discovery   On
File sharing   Off
Public folder sharing   Off
Printer sharing   Off
Password protected sharing   Off
Media sharing   Off

Show me all the files and folders I am sharing
Show me all the shared network

More tasks
Easy access to the most important or most frequently used parts of networking is offered in the Tasks pane.

See also
Internet Options
Windows Firewall

Safe and sound
If you return to the Network and Sharing Center and look at the options under the heading Sharing and Discovery, you'll see that there's just one green light – Network Discovery – which means that Windows Vista can automatically find new networks for you.

More services
Everything else is switched off, which is good if you're only planning to browse the internet. However, if you want to share files over a local network you'll need to enable **Public Folder Sharing** (which makes the contents of your Public folder available to other network users) or **File Sharing** (if you want to share other folders rather than just the Public folder).

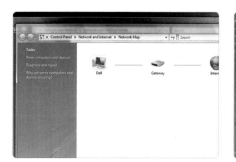

4 **YOU ARE HERE** At this point, you will be able to see the Network Map view, which shows that you're now connected to the internet via a gateway – in other words, your router.

5 **MORE DETAIL** If you click on the Network icon, Windows Vista will show more details about the network. To change your router's settings, right-click on it and select **View Device Webpage**.

6 **IDENTIFY YOURSELF** Like most routers this Netgear is password-protected. You'll need to enter your username and password here. By default, Netgear uses 'admin' and 'password'.

Share files and more with a home network

Connect your PCs together and share internet access, files, printers, music, video files and more

Buying your second family PC seemed such a great idea... No more queuing to use the computer. No need to wait for the kids to finish playing games before checking your email. And no "are you done yet?" when you're creating spreadsheets and they want to download MP3s.

Unfortunately, it doesn't always work out like that. Maybe the old Windows XP machine is upstairs, and only your Windows Vista PC is connected to the internet. You'll be pestered almost as much as you were before, unless you go one step further and link the two systems together in a home network.

Once your systems are connected, you'll be able to share internet access and other hardware, too. If the kids are doing homework upstairs and want to print it out on the printer downstairs, they'll be able to do so in a few clicks.

You'll also be able to quickly back up data from one system to the other – handy if you're infected by a virus or have some other kind of data disaster. And if you have young kids and want to protect them from the worst of the internet, then there are significant advantages in doing things this way. With the right combination of software and hardware you'll be able to monitor what they're doing online, block certain types of sites, even limit their access.

It pays to consider your networking options before making any expensive purchases. There are three common technologies you can use to connect your home PCs...

SECURITY MEASURES Most routers come packed with powerful security features such as hardware firewalls and intrusion detection

The first option is a conventional network crossover cable. Your PCs almost certainly have network ports already (check the manual to be sure), so all you need buy is the cable to run between them. These are widely available and inexpensive, but you will have the hassle of trailing the cable under carpet and maybe drilling through walls. The second option is to use wireless adapters, which means no need for cables at all. Much less set-up work but speeds will be reduced, perhaps considerably if the two PCs are a long way from each other. And you'll have to pay for the wireless network adapters, which vary in price depending on performance.

If those options don't appeal, then maybe you'll prefer the third: powerline networking. Here you buy an adapter for each PC, plug it into a nearby power socket and the system then shuttles data

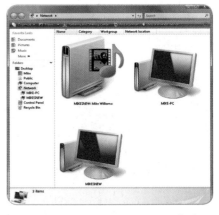

SHARE AND SHARE ALIKE Your networked PCs appear in the Windows Vista Network window, and are only ever a double-click away

around your home's electrical wiring. While more costly, this option delivers the no-hassle convenience of wireless. With better speeds and such ease of use, it may be a justified expense.

It's all a balance between price, convenience and performance. But there's another important issue you need to consider...

Network layout

Shared internet access is a key feature of any network, but there are two very different ways of setting it up. One answer comes with Windows, and it's called Internet Connection Sharing (ICS). If your Windows Vista PC is connected to the internet, then you can enable ICS and, after setting up a home network, your Windows XP PC would be able to get online, too.

This may sound good enough, especially as ICS comes with both

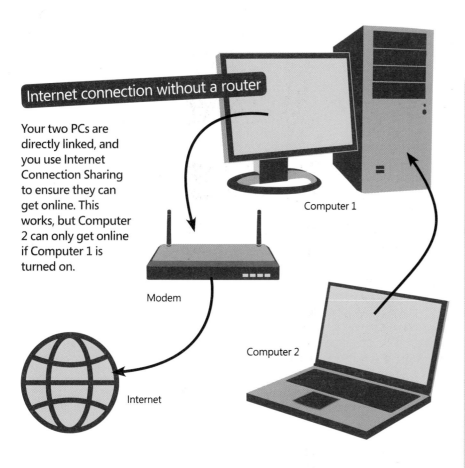

Internet connection without a router

Your two PCs are directly linked, and you use Internet Connection Sharing to ensure they can get online. This works, but Computer 2 can only get online if Computer 1 is turned on.

Computer 1

Modem

Computer 2

Internet

Keep it safe

Limit access to your network

■ **If you have a wireless network**, find out how to turn on security. The best method is an encryption system called WPA. This will help keep neighbors or passers-by from accessing your connection.

■ **Powerline networks** can also be accessed by neighbors; be sure to turn on security features.

■ **Routers** often come with a default password, or no password. Once set up, change this to something that's impossible for anyone else to guess.

■ **Sharing folders:** if you share the entire C drive, say, any hacker who breaks in may be able to place files in your Windows or Program Files folders, leaving you at risk of a software infection. Create a special folder like C:\MyShared and share that. Not as convenient, but safer.

Windows XP and Windows Vista for free, but there are some problems. ICS isn't always easy to configure, for instance; it doesn't support all applications (instant messaging probably won't work), and

using a software solution means your Windows Vista PC must be switched on all the time if your Windows XP system is to get online. A better solution is to buy a combined router and modem ○➔

Set up the Windows Vista PC
Follow the three simple steps to get networking

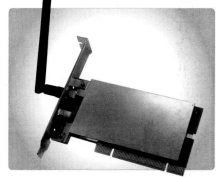

1 HARDWARE Get the network adapter working in the Windows Vista PC first (if you're using the built-in network port, skip this). Every adapter is different; read the instructions provided.

2 NAME IT Click **Control Panel → System → Change Settings**, and change the Workgroup name. Don't use your name or identifiable info, pick something general, like a famous city.

3 SHARE No router? Click **Control Panel → Network & Sharing Center → Manage Network Connections**, right-click the connection. In Sharing, check both boxes, click **OK**, then restart.

HIGH-SECURITY Buying a router for your network improves security and makes it much easier to share internet access

to manage the network for you. Connect your PCs to the router, instead of to each other, and they'll both be able to get online, even if the other's switched off.

Routers can help improve your PC security, too. They typically include powerful hardware firewalls and intrusion detection systems, perfect for keeping hackers out of your system.

Surprisingly, routers shouldn't add much to the cost of your network. Two basic wireless adapters will cost around $60; a basic wireless router and single wireless adapter lifts this to $100. The easier set-up means it's a price well worth paying for many.

What to buy?

That's quite enough network theory, then – it's time to get practical. Which networking technology is right for you?

If you're looking for a fast, very cheap solution; your PCs are less than 100 feet apart, and you don't mind doing a little preparatory DIY, then opt for the Ethernet cabling solution. Search on the internet to see what crossover cable you need, and establish the length required.

If you hate the idea of messing around with cables, and just want something cheap and easy, then a couple of 54Mbps USB wireless adapters will do ($60). A PCI wireless adapter card will be more reliable still, and an even better choice if you don't mind opening up your PC to install it.

Budget wireless solutions might be slow, especially if your PCs are a considerable distance apart (more than 100 feet, say). If you need good performance, then a 'pre-802.11n' wireless adapter could help ($100).

You might get improved long-distance results from powerline networking, though, which uses your home electrical wiring to transmit data. These vary quite a bit in capacity and price, so search

"Wow" Faster sharing

Good news for Service Pack 1 users – sharing files over your network can be up to 50% faster, while the performance of browsing network shares has been greatly improved

for a good deal.

If you're willing to spend a little more to get the best system, though, the ideal option would be to buy a router with built-in modem. It doesn't work out too expensive as you don't need a network adapter for your main PC. Again, a price comparison site can lead you to the bargains, or you can search regular online stores.

Don't choose solely on price, though. This can lead you to older kit that may not be compatible with Windows Vista, so read the small print carefully before parting with your cash.

First steps

You've found the technology that suits, and set it up with the instructions provided. So what now?

A good place to start is by sharing a folder. On the Windows XP system, create a new folder called something like C:\Shared. Right-click that, select **Properties → Sharing**, check **Share this folder on the network** and click **OK**. Finally, make a note of your PC's name,

Setting up the Windows XP PC

Just tell it where to look and you'll be surfing in no time

1 INSTALL Connect your chosen network adapter to the Windows XP computer. If you've gone for a wireless adapter, give it the same wireless network ID that you entered on the Windows Vista system.

2 NAME Click **Control Panel → System → Computer Name → Change**; set the Workgroup name (same as the Windows Vista PC) then close and restart the PCs. Connect to the internet and open a browser on the XP system.

3 CONNECT If IE wants to dial your old connection, click **Tools → Internet Options → Connections** and select **Never dial a connection**. If you still can't connect, check out the Troubleshooting advice opposite.

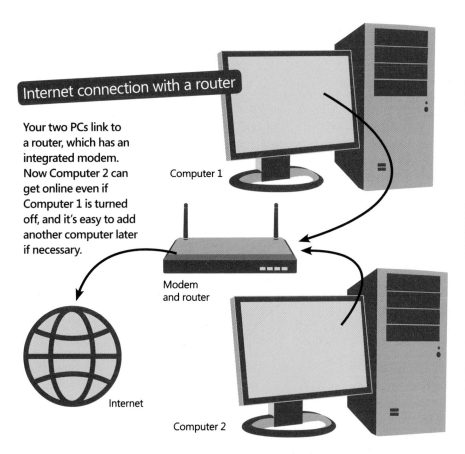

Internet connection with a router

Your two PCs link to a router, which has an integrated modem. Now Computer 2 can get online even if Computer 1 is turned off, and it's easy to add another computer later if necessary.

Computer 1

Modem and router

Internet

Computer 2

if you don't know it already (**Control Panel → System → Computer Name**).

Now go to the Windows Vista PC, click **Start → Computer**, then press **Alt** and click **Tools → Map Network Drive**. Enter the computer name, followed by the folder name (\\XP_PC_NAME\Shared), and a new Explorer window should appear. That is the C:\Shared folder on the XP system, and you can drag and drop files to and from it just as though it was on your own hard drive.

You can share folders and printers on the Windows Vista PC, too, so they're available from the XP system. Access the Windows Vista Network and Sharing Center (**Control Panel → Network**) and turn on whatever you need in the Sharing and Discovery section (printers will probably need to be reinstalled before they can be shared).

It's not all about working, though. If you're running Windows Media Player 11 or later on the XP system, then launch it, click **Tools → Options → Library → Configure Sharing,** select the icon for your Windows Vista PC and click **Allow**

NET AID The Network and Sharing Center has tools to get your network up and running

→ OK. Select **Computer → Network on the Vista PC** and you'll now see a Media icon; double-click on that, and you'll be able to use the network to access any music, pictures or video you have stored on your XP system's Media Player library.

It's an impressive feature list, especially as the technology is getting more and more reasonably priced – so what are you waiting for? Buy an adapter or two, set up your home network, and start getting the most out of your PCs. ⊞

Got a problem?
Try one of these fixes

■ **Networks are fussy**. If yours isn't working, turn both systems off and on. Go to the Windows Vista PC, click **Start → Network**; you should see at least one icon for each PC.

■ **No luck?** Is everything plugged in correctly? Right-click or double-click on the network system tray icon; wireless drivers will often tell you if they've detected a system.

■ **Check settings**. The Windows workgroup name must be the same on both PCs. Wireless adapters must have the same network ID (SSID).

■ **Disable firewalls**. Disconnect from the internet, then disable any firewalls. Make sure your firewall monitors the internet connection, but leaves your network alone.

■ **Computer Browser service**: Make sure this is running on Windows XP (**Start → Run → services.msc**) and that TCP/IP is set up correctly. Click **Control Panel → Network Connections**, right-click your **Local Area Connection** icon and select **Properties**; choose **TCP/IP, click Properties** and choose **Obtain an IP address automatically**. Close both PCs and restart.

■ **Still no good?** Windows Vista has a network setup wizard. Click **Start → Connect to → Set up a connection or network → Set up an ad hoc (computer to computer) network**. Set the Network Location Type as Private, not Public, so the Windows XP PC can access your files. Go to http://windowshelp.microsoft.com.

Connect, share and update

If you've more than one PC it's time to get connected; Windows Vista makes it easier than ever

 Networking multiple computers has many advantages. It enables different users to share files and applications, as well as share a single internet account. Setting up a network can be as simple as

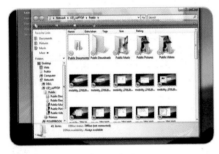

RESTRICT ENTRY If you don't want users on your network to edit your files, limit access

plugging in a few cables and, once done, you're soon able to gain the benefits of sharing files and resources.

There is, quite rightly, a certain level of paranoia associated with networks and the internet in general. The trick with networking is to take a less-is-more approach and limit access to the bare minimum. For example, if people only need to view the files in your Public folder but don't need the ability to edit them, it makes sense to limit their access accordingly, so you should use the Network and Sharing Center to give read-only access rather than full access.

Conversely, you're not limited to just sharing the Public folder and nothing else if you don't want to be. If **File Sharing** is switched on in the Network

and Sharing Center you can share any folder by right-clicking on it in Windows Explorer and clicking **Share**. Even with this level of access, it's still possible to add passwords to specific folders to limit availability.

Working together

Windows Vista also offers ways to make sharing files easier with its new Sync Center. This handy feature enables you to work on files while you're away from a network or while the shared PC is powered down; any changes made can then be synchronized once the shared files are available again. Follow the walkthrough opposite to see how this can be activated and how you can take full advantage of it. 🔳

"Wow" Media Extender

When it comes to sharing media Windows Vista is ready to rock. It can detect and share media with all manner of devices, including the Xbox 360, and other Window Vista PCs

---

That's Rally easy

New Windows technologies will make our networking lives easier

In addition to the networking technologies featured here, Windows Vista has another trick up its sleeve: Windows Rally. It's a group of technologies aimed at hardware firms and, while you're unlikely to use it directly, you'll still be able to reap its benefits.

With Windows Rally, installing any new device is as simple as switching it on; the device will automatically connect to your wired or wireless network, appear in the Windows Vista network

map and configure itself. If the devices are internet-enabled they'll also be able to get data from the internet via your network, and once again they'll set themselves up to do that!

The first Windows Rally devices will be networking kit, such as Wi-Fi access points and networked projectors, but over time Windows Rally should start popping up in everything from games consoles and set-top TV boxes to electronic photo frames and Pocket PCs.

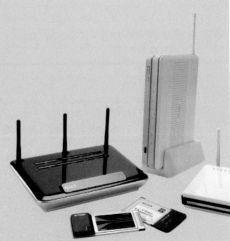

RALLY GOOD Once wireless kit starts to use Windows Rally our lives will be even easier

Connecting to another PC

Access other PCs and synchronize amended files

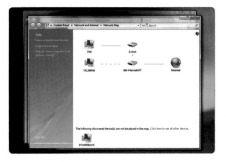

1 HELLO Click **View Full Map**, you should see something like this: in addition to the internet connection, the desktop PC can see the laptop. Right-click the other computer and click **Open**.

2 EASY EXPLORE Here, you're looking at the laptop, or at least the bits that the laptop's owner has given permission to look at. In this example, you can browse the Public and Printers folders.

3 SEE FILES Double-click **Public**. If you've got read-only access you'll be able to open and copy files; if you've got full access you can edit or delete files or copy files from your hard disk.

4 WAIT A BIT You can ensure these files are always available, even when you're not connected. To do this, go back one step, right-click on **Public** and click **Always available offline**.

5 SIMPLE SYNC Open Sync Center from **Control Panel → Network and Internet → Sync Center**. You'll see that there's an entry already in there – Offline Files. Double-click the icon to see more.

6 OFFLINE BROWSING You should now see the folder you wanted available at all times – in this case the Public folder on the laptop. Click on **Browse** to see the contents of that folder.

7 CHANGES The laptop is no longer connected but the files are available. By using the local copy of the laptop files, changes will be applied to the originals when the files are synchronized.

8 UPDATE Return to Sync Center. Above Offline Files you'll see Sync – which synchronizes files immediately, and Schedule – which enables you to sync files at specified times.

9 OPTIONS The Network and Sharing Center provides additional options. Under Public Folder Sharing you can limit access to your Public folders, or you can password-protect shared files.

Networking know-how

Windows Vista makes it easy to set up a home network, and also to troubleshoot any problems

There's nothing quite so effective as the topic of networking to make people's eyes glaze over at a party and have them mentally pacing the number of steps between you and the nearest escape route.

Thankfully, Windows Vista can free you from the complex, mundane tasks that make you feel like you're working as an unpaid system administrator for your household. It will let you get on with enjoying the benefits of having your own home network – like listening to the music stored on your desktop PC upstairs while you're relaxing in the lounge with your laptop to hand downstairs (see the guide below for what you need to do to achieve this).

The slick new Network and Sharing Center in Windows Vista makes it easy to see at a glance how your computer is connected to others, and makes it simple to highlight any problems that are stopping the data getting through.

Great leap forward

A key network area that Windows Vista now directly tackles is wireless networking, possibly one of the best technological advances ever made, meaning you can stay connected on your laptop no matter where you are in the house; the kitchen, the living room or even the bathroom should you wish – just watch out for water!

Provided your kit isn't more than a few years old, then getting set up is

remarkably simple. If your laptop has an Intel Centrino badge on it, then you've got everything that you need already built into the computer. Other laptops also have built-in wireless connectors – the easiest way to check is to open the Network and Sharing Center and then click **Manage network connections** from the list on the left-hand side. If you see an entry for a Wireless Network Connection, then you're good to go.

Finally, you'll need a wireless router, which enables your computers to connect to one another, but also helps them share a broadband connection. Once up and running, Windows Vista will spring into action. The main stages from connection to solving problems are covered in the following pages.

Set up media sharing in five minutes

Share your music and videos with other people on the network

1 GETTING STARTED You need to fire up the Network and Sharing Center. Locate Media sharing in the Sharing and Discovery section, click the down arrow and then click **Change**.

2 TURN IT ON Your home network should be private by default, meaning it's safe to turn on Media Sharing without worrying about strangers. Tick the box by **Share my media** then hit **OK**.

3 PICK USERS You can be selective about who you share with – browse available computers, pick which you want to give access to, then click **Allow**. If you change your mind, choose **Deny**.

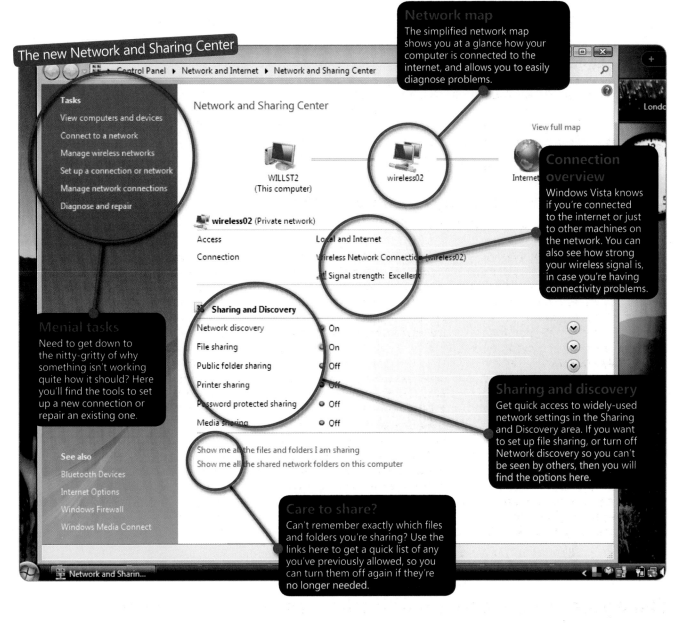

The new Network and Sharing Center

Control Panel ▶ Network and Internet ▶ Network and Sharing Center

Network and Sharing Center

Network map
The simplified network map shows you at a glance how your computer is connected to the internet, and allows you to easily diagnose problems.

View full map

WILLST2
(This computer)

wireless02

Internet

Connection overview
Windows Vista knows if you're connected to the internet or just to other machines on the network. You can also see how strong your wireless signal is, in case you're having connectivity problems.

Tasks
View computers and devices
Connect to a network
Manage wireless networks
Set up a connection or network
Manage network connections
Diagnose and repair

wireless02 (Private network)
Access   Local and Internet
Connection   Wireless Network Connection (wireless02)
                          Signal strength: Excellent

Menial tasks
Need to get down to the nitty-gritty of why something isn't working quite how it should? Here you'll find the tools to set up a new connection or repair an existing one.

Sharing and Discovery
Network discovery   On
File sharing   On
Public folder sharing   Off
Printer sharing   Off
Password protected sharing   Off
Media sharing   Off

Sharing and discovery
Get quick access to widely-used network settings in the Sharing and Discovery area. If you want to set up file sharing, or turn off Network discovery so you can't be seen by others, then you will find the options here.

See also
Bluetooth Devices
Internet Options
Windows Firewall
Windows Media Connect

Show me all the files and folders I am sharing
Show me all the shared network folders on this computer

Care to share?
Can't remember exactly which files and folders you're sharing? Use the links here to get a quick list of any you've previously allowed, so you can turn them off again if they're no longer needed.

Network and Sharin...

London

4 DECIDE SETTINGS By default you'll be sharing all unrated media files, and those you've given a rating of more than two stars. For more control, click **Customize** and fine tune the settings.

5 SWITCH OVER Move to the other computer you want to listen to music from. Open up the Network window. Look for the music and film icon next to a machine name and double-click it.

6 PLAY AWAY In Media Player you'll now see the other computer listed below your Library. Click on it, and you can navigate through the media files as if they were stored on your own PC.

Hooking up to a wireless network

"Wow" Wireless-N

With Service Pack 1 Windows Vista has been updated ready for the very latest draft release of the 802.11n wireless standard – so you get the maximum possible speeds

Connecting to the internet via a wired cable couldn't be easier, but what about wireless?

Wireless networking promises a world of leisurely internet access, media beamed direct to your living room and instant communication with all of your friends, family and colleagues. The reality is something close to this, but it's not always as easy to connect to your wireless network as it should be.

Thankfully, Windows Vista has done a huge amount to make this job far easier than with previous versions of Windows, as it has been built with wireless interaction at its networking heart.

Improved dialogs make it easier and faster to find and connect to legitimate wireless networks, with warnings provided if you're going to connect to an insecure connection. The Network Map shows where and what wireless devices are part of your network, and the new diagnostic tools make it far clearer to source problems and fix them.

The hard stuff

The terminology involved with wireless networking can get a little confusing, but it's worthwhile demystifying the most common terms. The wireless system uses standard radio waves to send data, but as time's marched on faster versions have appeared. Each version is called '802.11' followed by the letter a, b, g or n; with latter letters being newer, faster and, of course, more expensive versions.

Thankfully, newer versions are compatible with those that have gone before. As it stands, 'a' and 'b' are outdated, while 'g' is being superseded by the latest 'n' standard, which offers far faster speeds and a much greater working distance.

Obviously, one of the main concerns with enabling people to connect to your network wirelessly is security. As it is, you should at least use a system called WEP but preferably use the more recent WPA security system that all recent routers will offer. This essentially involves setting the router with a password. Any computer trying to connect will have to supply this password as well, otherwise it will be denied access.

Using a wireless network

Get your PCs connected wirelessly in just six simple steps

1 AUTO DETECT If your wireless adaptor is switched on and you're within range of a wireless network, Windows Vista will find the network(s) for you and pop up this message.

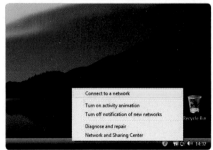

2 GET CONNECTED Right-click over the network icon (two PC screens with a globe) and you'll see a list of available options. Click on **Connect to a network** to see what networks are available.

3 WHAT'S AVAILABLE This computer is in range of its own network and next-door's. Check if they are protected and how strong their signals are by clicking one then clicking **Connect**.

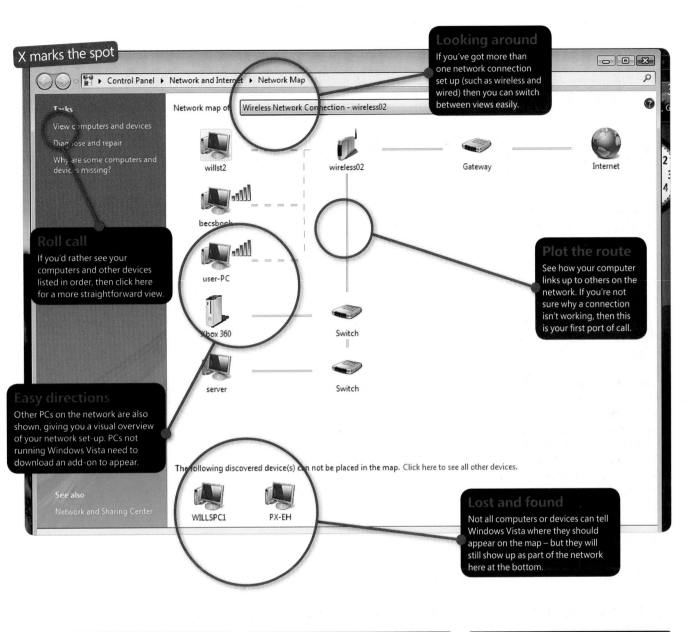

Control Panel ▶ Network and Internet ▶ Network Map

Looking around
If you've got more than one network connection set up (such as wireless and wired) then you can switch between views easily.

Tasks
View computers and devices
Diagnose and repair
Why are some computers and devices missing?

Network map of: Wireless Network Connection - wireless02

willst2

becsbook

user-PC

Xbox 360

server

wireless02

Gateway

Internet

Switch

Switch

Roll call
If you'd rather see your computers and other devices listed in order, then click here for a more straightforward view.

Plot the route
See how your computer links up to others on the network. If you're not sure why a connection isn't working, then this is your first port of call.

Easy directions
Other PCs on the network are also shown, giving you a visual overview of your network set-up. PCs not running Windows Vista need to download an add-on to appear.

See also
Network and Sharing Center

The following discovered device(s) can not be placed in the map. Click here to see all other devices.

WILLSPC1   PX-EH

Lost and found
Not all computers or devices can tell Windows Vista where they should appear on the map – but they will still show up as part of the network here at the bottom.

4 SAY HELLO Windows Vista will now attempt to connect to your chosen wireless network. If the network is password protected you'll be asked for the password at this stage.

5 READY TO ROLL This pop-up shows a successful connection to the chosen network, in this case there is both local access (to other machines on the network) and internet access.

6 WHERE IT'S AT Open the **Network and Sharing Center** and you'll see the name of the network you're connected to. Below the icons you'll see more information about that network.

Meet up with Windows Meeting Space

Share your desktop and invite others to meetings you can chair without leaving your PC

For many, especially those in business, the biggest networking feature of Windows Vista is Windows Meeting Space; a brand new replacement for the NetMeeting program in Windows XP, enabling you to share your screen with someone else on your network (either an individual or an entire group). You can share a single file, an application or your entire system, which means you can use Windows Meeting Space to deliver presentations or even training sessions.

Everything you do on screen is mirrored on the other person's screen in real time, and you can even give them remote control over your PC, so they can not only be shown how to do things, but try things out, too. If you combine it with internal phone calls or Windows Live Messenger's voice chat features, the potential is mind-boggling. Despite its power, it's easy to set up and use, and you can use Windows Meeting Space in any edition of Windows Vista (if you're running the Home Basic edition you'll be able to join other meetings, but won't be able to create meetings of your own).

You can leave the meeting at any time, but that doesn't mean the meeting will close as soon as the person who called it goes away; a meeting will continue until everyone leaves.

In real life...
Keep it secure

Neil Mohr, Technical Editor
If you're opening handouts created by other people they might contain a virus, so keep your security software running. There are low-tech risks, too... For example, you might share the wrong file as a handout, but you can avoid this by sharing a single file rather than an entire application.

Meeting and greeting
Invite your colleagues to a virtual conference

1 PEOPLE POWERED Enable a feature called People Near Me, which enables you to see whether there are any people near you on the network. Go to **Control Panel → Network and Internet** and click on **People Near Me**.

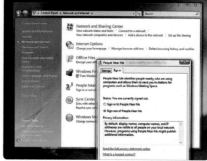

2 SIGN IN You will now have to go through the very simple signing in process, which begins with a new dialog box. Just select the **Sign In** tab and click on **Sign in to people near me**, then click **OK** to continue.

3 MEET AND GREET Before you can set up a meeting, you need to ensure that People Near Me is also set up on the PC(s) you want to communicate with. The process is identical to the one outlined in the previous steps.

4 START IT UP On your own PC, click on **Start a new meeting** and give it a password. Without this, people won't be able to join you – that's good, because it keeps out unwelcome attendees. Click the green arrow when you're done.

5 NO-ONE HOME The Meeting Space screen is divided into three; the big section on the left shares a program, the top-right section shows who's in the meeting, and the bottom-right section enables you to provide handouts.

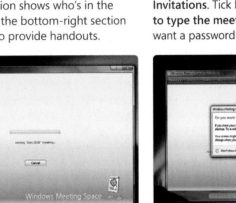

6 COME TOGETHER Invite People displays potential attendees. To invite a person, click their name then click **Send Invitations**. Tick **Require participants to type the meeting password** if you want a password-protected meeting.

7 JOIN THE PARTY In this example, the invite has appeared on the recipient's PC with a warning: you're not a trusted contact in their address book. However, the invitee knows you're trustworthy, so they click the **Accept** button.

8 MAKE AN ENTRANCE In this case the invitee does know the password, so they need to enter it and click on the green arrow. They'll see a progress bar for a few seconds as Windows Meeting Space joins the meeting.

9 SHOW OFF Back on your PC, it's time to show what Windows Meeting Space can do. Click on the **Share** icon and a security warning will pop up, saying that if you share your desktop other people will be able to see it.

10 PICK A PROGRAM You can select a program to share by clicking on it and clicking **Share**, or you can click on **Browse** to launch and share a file that isn't already open. For now, though, select **Desktop** and then click **Share**.

11 SCREEN SHARING This is what attendees will see – your desktop, in real time. You'll see that Windows Vista has changed the graphics slightly. Sharing uses Aero Basic instead of Aero Glass, as there's no need for fancy visuals.

12 TALK IS CHEAP In addition to sharing your desktop, you can also send notes to other people in the meeting. To do this, right-click over their name and choose **Send A Note**. Type your text and click **Send**.

Move files from your PC to your pocket device

Portable computers are getting smaller, as Pocket PCs and smartphones displace the laptop: Windows Vista is well prepared

With Windows Vista you can transfer files from your computer to your mobile device manually, but a far better option is to use the built-in Sync Center to automatically update your device whenever you connect it to your PC.

If you're using the 2007 Microsoft Office System, this can synchronize all manner of documents and data between the two devices, enabling you to take your emails, to-do list, notes, calendar, contacts and much more with you wherever you go. You can then make changes to them on your device and have the updates synchronized back with the originals, for when you're back at your desktop computer.

Pocket PCs have been around for some time and are a perfect way to take your documents, email and even media out and about with you, in a device that's a fraction of the size and weight of even the smallest laptop. With Windows XP it used to be necessary to install an additional application to synchronize data between your desktop PC and the pocket PC, but the good news is that this functionality is built right into Windows Vista, which makes working with your portable devices even easier.

Building upon the Pocket PC technology are smartphones. These are mobile phones that boast all the functionality of a fully blown pocket PC but happen to be mobile phones as well; making for incredibly useful devices. ⊞

CONNECT 4 Your mobile device can talk to your PC with Windows Mobile Device Center

Installing a Pocket PC

It's as easy as 1, 2, 3...

1 INSTALL THE DRIVERS Connect your pocket PC or Windows Mobile device with the supplied cable and switch it on. After a few seconds you'll see this message as your PC spots the device.

2 DECIDE THE DEFAULT AutoPlay asks if you know what you want Windows Vista to do when you connect – for example, you may want your PC to automatically transfer music..

3 SIMPLE SYNC Go to **Control Panel →
Network and Internet**. You can specify whether your device should connect via USB or Bluetooth, while Sync Center enables you to transfer files.

Using Sync Center

Moving files on to your mobile device is easy with Sync Center

1 **NO MOBILE** When you first open Sync Center it shows you a list of partnerships – because there aren't any set up yet, the list is blank. Click on **Set Up New Sync Partnerships** to introduce Sync Center to your mobile device.

2 **HELLO THERE** This example shows a Windows Mobile PDA/smartphone with a storage card. Sync Center spots it and confirms it can synchronize media files. Click on **Storage Card** and then **Set Up** to finish creating the partnership.

3 **SUFFICIENT SPACE** Sync Center opens Media Player and, if you've got a fairly small storage card, you'll see this warning saying you don't have enough space. Don't worry about it – you don't have to synchronize your entire media collection.

There are some types of file that Sync Center won't send; the good news is, manual transfers are easy

4 **MANUAL MOVING** There are some types of file, such as Word documents, that Sync Center won't send to your mobile device; the good news is, manual transfers are easy. Just click on **Start ➔ Computer** and you'll see your device at the bottom of the list of drives and devices.

Media on the move

As the power of mobile devices increases, you're able to do even more with them. Most are more than able to handle video playback, meaning that not only can you take your phone with you, but your media as well!

5 **TRADITIONAL TRANSFER** Double-click on your portable device to see the available storage options. In this case there are two: the pocket PC's internal storage and its storage card. Copying files to either location is simply a matter of dragging and dropping over the icons.

Simple ways to organize your photo collection

What's the point of having the world's best photograph if you can't find it and share it? Well, Windows Vista offers the perfect solution

The digital camera revolution has freed us from the tedium and expense of developing film. In doing so, it has given us the power to fire off as many shots as we like until we get that one great picture that perfectly captures a mood, reveals a person's character or creates an image just the way we saw it in our heads.

Taking great photos still isn't easy but with trial, effort and patience you can do it. Finding them on your hard drive, on the other hand, can be a lot tougher.

Even if you periodically clear out your hard drive by archiving all your images on to DVD, you'll soon find that you're

up to 25GB of disk space in your Pictures folder, and adding more each day. That's a lot of photos to sort through every time you want to find a particular shot.

There's a number of PC programs for categorizing photos on the market but, while several of them have their good points, they all have faults – the most common being that they leave little control over which folders they're monitoring. Because of this, the browsing convenience they offer hasn't been quite enough to justify using them over old-fashioned Windows Explorer.

With Windows Vista, however, all the tools you need for keeping track of shots and sorting them are at your fingertips. The difference is apparent as soon as you plug a camera, mobile phone or memory card into your PC. A dialog box pops up and asks if you want to transfer

the shots from your camera on to your PC. Once you've agreed to this, Windows Vista presents you with the option to add a 'tag' (or keyword) to the images you're transferring. So if, say, you've just got back from a trip to the beach and all your shots are of sand and surf, you might want to mention that.

By default, Windows Vista will then transfer all the files over to your Pictures folder, storing them in a subfolder named by the day of the transfer and the tag you've chosen – for example, the automatically generated folder might be called 'July 15 The Beach'. You'll also find that all the photos in the set have been renamed from the usual gibberish (such as 'DSC03415.jpg') to the rather more meaningful 'The Beach 1.jpg' and 'The Beach 2.jpg' and so on.

The heart of the new photography ●

In real life...
Use the Slide Show

Nick Odantzis, Writer, Windows Vista: The Official Magazine It's easy to overlook the Windows Sidebar Slide Show gadget as a way to view your pictures. Not only can you add your favorite pictures to it but it's a powerful tool, too – it will search subdirectories and work its way through thousands of images. If you click on a picture that takes your fancy you can also open the view page, from which you can then edit or print it. To find out more, select the gadget itself and then click on the spanner icon.

With Windows Vista, all the tools you need for keeping track of shots and sorting them are there at your fingertips

WATCH THE BIRDIE Now you can brighten slightly dull images in Preview mode

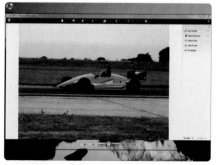

ONE TOUCH Auto Adjust is a good way to bring out the colors of your image

From snap to screen

Take, transfer, tag... then browse, share and enjoy

"Wow"
Change it back!

Made an edit that you regret? Don't worry. Click **File → Revert to Original** and your photo is magically returned to its original state – just as it was when you imported it

1 TAKE THE SHOT The most important thing about creating a good photo gallery is taking a good picture in the first place. There are lots of great photography web sites offering tips; visit one of them for instant inspiration.

2 TRANSFER ACROSS When you come to download your images, a card reader is the easiest way of moving them to your PC. Failing that, plug your camera in. Windows Vista will recognize the shots and ask if you want to transfer them.

3 RAW FILES Windows Photo Gallery and Windows Live Photo Gallery can open some kinds of RAW pictures, if the correct codec is available. If you edit a RAW file, Photo Gallery saves your modified photo as a JPEG file.

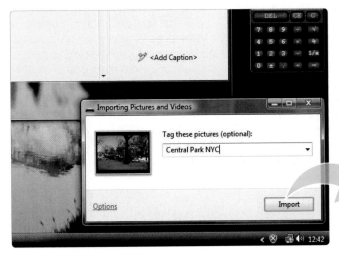

4 TAG LINES Adding a tag at this point will rename your images, and will file them in a folder using the same label. You can change how Windows Vista handles the transfer by clicking on the **Options** button. Check the **Erase after importing** box to keep your camera card clean.

The heart of the photography toolkit is the Photo Gallery application which monitors the contents of your pictures

Retrieve lost photographs

If you delete pictures from your camera's memory card by mistake, don't worry. There are many web-based applications that can not only retrieve the data from most sources, but also deal with most file types.

5 INTO THE GALLERY Now open up Windows Photo Gallery. Your pictures will be there, renamed and tagged. You can do an initial sort through by rating each image from one to five stars, and then pare down your collection ready for easy browsing or sharing with others.

I AM UNDONE You can revert to the original

toolkit, though, is the Windows Photo Gallery application. It monitors the contents of your pictures folder – and any other folders you ask it to, including those on external hard drives – and presents you with an Explorer-type thumbnail view of all the photos and videos stored there. You can alter the view to include bits of info attached to the image that are normally hidden, including the name, time taken and any tags or keywords assigned.

This is where you can really start to take control of your photo collection. The screen on the right shows a variety of sorting tools – you can sort images by name, date taken, location on the hard drive, tag, star rating, or by clicking on the **Recently Imported Items** to see only images taken from the camera in the last

30 days. On the far left-hand side is the 'metadata' (hidden info) for the selected image, and you can edit information such as name, time, date and caption.

If you select more than one shot and edit the information here, Windows Vista will apply the metadata to every file selected. Most importantly, if you rename a group of files it will add a consecutive number to each one – so you can quickly change your photo library from a random collection of files with arbitrary names to photos which are

for an enlarged preview, or double-click them to open in a viewing window. Shots can then be given a rating from 0 to 5, a great way to single out the best ones, without deleting anything. You can then find the best images quickly by clicking the rating you want to browse in the left-hand panel.

The suite is rounded off with some basic editing tools. What stands out about these is the ease with which you can use them. Simply click **Fix** and drag the Exposure slider to bring light to

You can really start to take control of your photo collection; sort images by name, date taken, location, tag, stars, etc

sorted meaningfully with usable tags.

One of the best features has to be the ability to select multiple photos and drag them over a tag in the left-hand pane – adding that tag to each shot.

Star quality

One of the most powerful sorting tools is the Star Rating. Once you've imported your images to your PC and edited the tags and names in Photo Gallery, you can scroll over them in the center panel

those photos that are just too dark, or hit **Auto Adjust** to have Photo Gallery run it through the system for you.

That one click can transform indistinct photos into stunning family shots – perfect for those whose photography skills aren't up to scratch. And no matter how long you've been using a digital camera, there are always times when you just can't get 'the shot' and have to resort to some fixing work. Well, with Windows Vista, it's never been easier. ⊞

Editing, printing and sharing...

You'll find all of the essential photo features in Windows Vista

1 SELECT A SHOT Once you've decided on your best shots, you can double-click on an image to go to the photo viewer, or click **Fix** from the top menu to take you straight to the editing screen.

2 PHOTO FIXES As well as a basic set of tools for altering brightness, contrast and color balance, there's a Red-eye Repair brush, and a Crop tool for cutting away unwanted background areas.

3 MAIL OUT There are several options for sharing your pictures. Click on the **E-mail** button if you want to mail the image directly to a friend. You'll be given the option of resizing it when attaching.

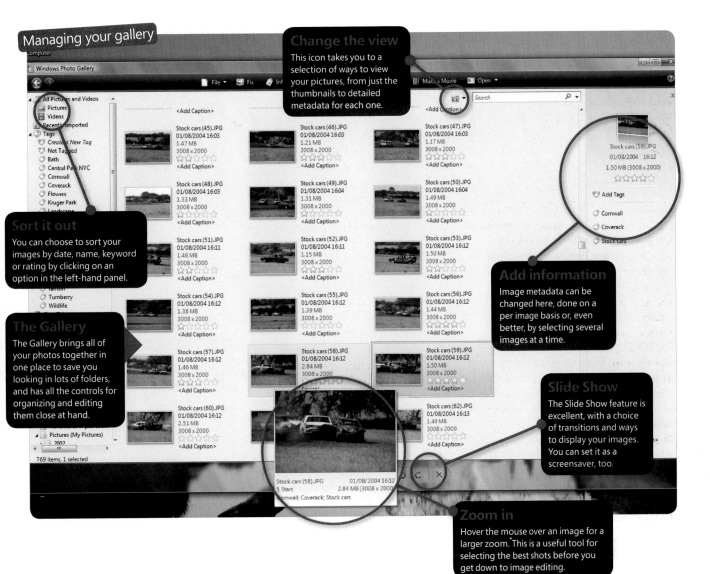

Managing your gallery

Change the view
This icon takes you to a selection of ways to view your pictures, from just the thumbnails to detailed metadata for each one.

Sort it out
You can choose to sort your images by date, name, keyword or rating by clicking on an option in the left-hand panel.

The Gallery
The Gallery brings all of your photos together in one place to save you looking in lots of folders, and has all the controls for organizing and editing them close at hand.

Add information
Image metadata can be changed here, done on a per image basis or, even better, by selecting several images at a time.

Slide Show
The Slide Show feature is excellent, with a choice of transitions and ways to display your images. You can set it as a screensaver, too.

Zoom in
Hover the mouse over an image for a larger zoom. This is a useful tool for selecting the best shots before you get down to image editing.

4 BURN TO DISC To create a video DVD with interactive menu that you can send to non-PC literate folk, select the images you want to include from the gallery and click the **Burn** button.

5 CHOOSE THE LOOK Windows DVD Maker offers you a choice of menu styles and backgrounds to add, as well as the option to create a slide show with backing track and customized fades.

6 TAKE CONTROL Windows Movie Maker enables you to select the order your pictures appear, add music, voice-overs and video clips, or write your own professional credit sequence.

Enjoying your music with Windows Vista

Why not try the best ever version of Windows Media Player?
Turn your PC into an all-singing, all-dancing multimedia monster!

Windows Media Player (**Start → All Programs → Windows Media Player**) has been transformed in Windows Vista. It's an excellent music player and organizer, and it can handle videos and DVDs, too. This section looks at how to create your own custom playlists, make CDs, copy your tunes to your PC and watch music videos without installing or using any additional software.

Share and share alike

Windows Vista can also share your music and movies with your Xbox 360 in two ways; using Windows Media Center, and through Windows Media Player. Within Media Center, click on the arrow immediately below the Library button and then click on **Media Sharing**. Tick the box next to **Share my media**. If your Xbox 360 is switched on and connected to the network, it should appear as an available device. By default, Media Player shares all your media but, if you wish, you can use the Customize screen to limit the list to specific kinds of file; files with certain star ratings or files with particular parental ratings. That's Windows Vista ready to share, so it's time to configure your Xbox 360. Choose the **Media blade** and then select **Music, Picture or Photos**. Choose **Computer**, then **Continue**, and your Windows Vista PC should appear in the list. Select it and you can now browse your computer's music, video and photo libraries.

NETWORK IT Sharing media with networked devices is easy with Windows Media Player 11

Playback, playlists and CD burning

Create customized lists of your favorite tracks then burn to CD

1 EASY DJ The links at the side enable you to sort your library by album, artist, etc, and Views enables you to change the way your tracks are displayed. Double-clicking on a track plays it.

2 CHOOSE THE TUNES Organize your music by creating playlists. You can put together a list of your favorite songs without having to hear the tracks you don't like. Click on **New Playlist** to start.

3 ADD TRACKS You'll see a panel that asks you to drag and drop tracks over it. Browse your music collection and when you find a song you want to add, drag it over the right-hand panel.

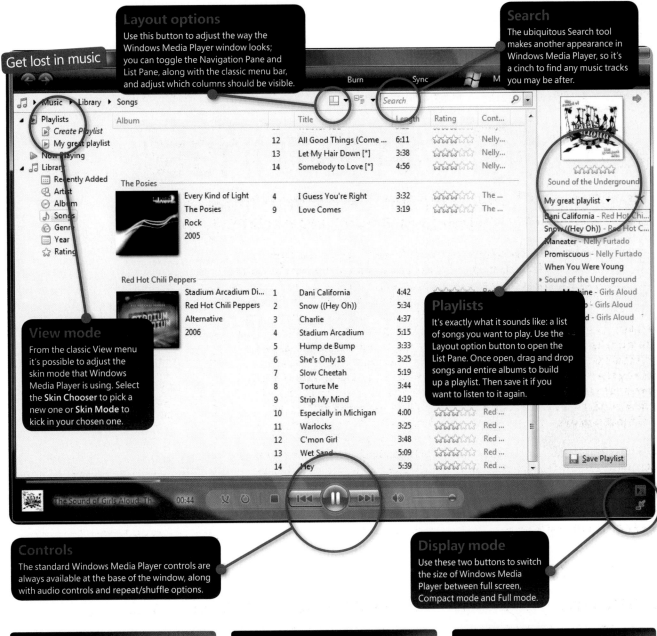

Get lost in music

Layout options
Use this button to adjust the way the Windows Media Player window looks; you can toggle the Navigation Pane and List Pane, along with the classic menu bar, and adjust which columns should be visible.

Search
The ubiquitous Search tool makes another appearance in Windows Media Player, so it's a cinch to find any music tracks you may be after.

View mode
From the classic View menu it's possible to adjust the skin mode that Windows Media Player is using. Select the **Skin Chooser** to pick a new one or **Skin Mode** to kick in your chosen one.

Playlists
It's exactly what it sounds like: a list of songs you want to play. Use the Layout option button to open the List Pane. Once open, drag and drop songs and entire albums to build up a playlist. Then save it if you want to listen to it again.

Controls
The standard Windows Media Player controls are always available at the base of the window, along with audio controls and repeat/shuffle options.

Display mode
Use these two buttons to switch the size of Windows Media Player between full screen, Compact mode and Full mode.

4 **NEW VIEW** Your new playlist will appear in the panel on the right, but you can change the view by clicking on the blue arrow. This will display your playlist in the main List view.

5 **SEE THE SOUNDS** The same arrow provides access to Windows Media Player's visualizations, which replace the display with swoopy visuals. It's particularly good in full screen mode.

6 **DO DVD TOO** Windows Media Player is as good with DVDs as it is with CDs. When you first go to play a DVD, you'll be asked whether to use Windows Media Player or Media Center.

Create playlists of your favorite tunes

Don't spend hours going through your music collection to organize an ensemble of your favorite tracks – let your PC do the hard work

Ever had one of those days when you just stare at all the music on your hard drive, uninspired by any of the albums and find it a struggle to choose something to listen to? Then The Filter is what you need. It's a new program that takes the effort out of the selection process by creating playlists that it thinks you will like.

No, it can't magically read your thoughts and choose something depending on your mood, but what it will do is look at all the music tracks on your computer and suggest a type of playlist according to your collection. For instance, if you've got some rock music on there, it will create a playlist with a selection of some of the rock songs in

your various rock albums; or if you like a particular singer, songwriter or band, The Filter will suggest songs by a similar genre of artist.

To do this, download and open The Filter, then click on **Suggest another** in the Create Playlist window and it will choose a playlist for you. Alternatively, you can go into Windows Media Player, right-click on a song and select **Send to → The Filter**, and The Filter will choose a playlist based around this one song.

By default, The Filter adds 15 songs per playlist, but you can set it to add a maximum of 99 songs in each playlist by simply clicking on **Playlist** under the Preferences heading in the menu, and altering the **Song count**. You can even put these playlists on to a portable

media player, so you can listen to them when out and about. Just click on one of your saved playlists under the **Recent Playlists** heading in the menu, and then in the main window choose the player you want to put your playlist on, and click on **Send to device**.

If you get bored of your current music collection and you're not sure which song or album to buy next, The Filter can even recommend some for you. Go to the menu in The Filter and click on either **Related Songs** or **Related Artists** under the **Discover Music** heading, and it will find similar songs or artists to your own. You can choose to find music from eMusic global or Amazon by choosing them from the **Preferred music store** drop-down menu. ⊞

Create a killer playlist in minutes
Let The Filter pick and choose tracks for you

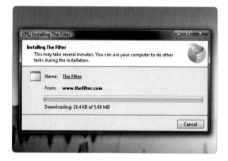

1 INCOMING Download and install The Filter from the front page of www.thefilter.com, and when prompted select Windows Media Player as the music player that you'd like to use.

2 PLUG-IN, BABY When you open The Filter for the first time, Windows Media Player will open. Go to Media Player, click on **Tools → Plug-ins** and make sure there's a tick next to **The Filter**.

3 PERFECT PLAYLIST Now open The Filter window and you'll see it has created a playlist based on your music collection. If you like it, just click on the **Save & Play** button to store it.

Library
In the Library section of Windows Media Player, click **Create Playlist** and then give it a name. Next, trawl your music, right-clicking on the ones you want and then selecting **Add to Playlist**.

Play now
When you have added tracks to your playlist, turn to the Now Playing tag. Your music will be displayed on the right pane, and the order can be manipulated by dragging them around.

Now Playing ▼

Right Thing - DJ Shadow	☆☆☆☆☆	3:15
Tears - Georgio Moroder	☆☆☆☆☆	2:25
Tickles - AC Lewis feat. Ndidi Cas...	☆☆☆☆☆	2:16
Nannou - Aphex Twin	☆☆☆☆☆	2:14
Underground (ambient mix)	☆☆☆☆☆	1:12
The Beach - New Order	☆☆☆☆☆	2:48
One of dem days (remix) - Part 2...	☆☆☆☆☆	2:05
Painkiller - Freestylers feat. Pend...	☆☆☆☆☆	1:45
Funky (a cappella) - 5 Deez	☆☆☆☆☆	1:27
Dans Le Club - TTC	☆☆☆☆☆	0:54
The Nice Up - Rodney P	☆☆☆☆☆	2:32
Reach Out - DJ Zinc	☆☆☆☆☆	2:35
Swords in the Dirt - Roots Man...	☆☆☆☆☆	3:56
Tarantula - Pendulum & Fresh fe...	☆☆☆☆☆	4:01
Witness - Roots Manuva	☆☆☆☆☆	2:00
It's no Secret - Jo Ann Garrett	☆☆☆☆☆	2:39
Are you being served? Theme	☆☆☆☆☆	1:56
Food for my soul - The Dragons	☆☆☆☆☆	4:48
Ernie - Fat Freddy's Drop	☆☆☆☆☆	7:17
Cay's Crays - Fat Freddy's Drop	☆☆☆☆☆	7:07
This Room - Fat Freddy's Drop	☆☆☆☆☆	5:00
Ray Ray - Fat Freddy's Drop	☆☆☆☆☆	7:38

Crossfading and Auto Volume Leveling
Turn on Auto Volume Leveling
Turn off Crossfading
0.0 seconds of overlap

More options
Click the tiny arrow under Now Playing to open a special menu which will enable you to unlock the host of options in Windows Media Player. Go to **Enhancements → Crossfading and Auto Volume Leveling** to bring up the best party menu (see 'Party time' left for details).

Party time
Make your party mix sound really professional by turning on Auto Volume Leveling, so louder tracks don't make people spill their drinks in surprise. Also, a second or two of overlap will eliminate gaps in the music – and you won't have to rely on conversation for entertainment!

Visualize this
There are loads of visualizations available to download from Microsoft that will make your music look as impressive as it sounds. Just click **Tools → Download → Visualizations** to see a list of free downloads.

4 GIVE ME MORE If you want to choose some more playlists, click on **Create playlist** in the left-hand menu, and click on save. If you're not happy with that selection click **Suggest another**.

5 STARTING POINT You can suggest a song to create a playlist from. Go into Windows Media Player, click on **Songs**, right-click a song you like, and go to **Send to → The Filter**.

6 AND AGAIN Click on the large **Create playlist** button. Once again, click on **Save & Play** to put it in your Recent playlists. If no song is selected it'll take the one playing as the basis.

Get the music you want to listen to

If your radio listening is always being spoiled by tracks you don't like, put together a tailor-made selection of your favorites

Tired of radio DJs and their dodgy playlists? Well, you could create your own... You've probably got enough CDs to provide a range of music. If you haven't already copied your CDs to your hard drive, simply open Windows Media Player, click **Rip**, put a CD in the drive, and it will copy your tracks over automatically.

Left to its own devices, Media Player will copy files using Microsoft's WMA file format. It's good for preserving audio quality, but there are a few players that don't support it. For something that's sure to work on every player, click the arrow under the **Rip** button and choose **Format → MP3**. In the same menu, choose **Bit Rate → 192Kbps** to raise the sound quality (this also increases the file size, so go for a lower bit rate if you have a small-capacity player).

Next, plug in your player. Click through the set-up questions (closing the **Autoplay** menu, if it appears) and the player will show up in your library – drag songs in here to create your line-up. Pick tracks by flipping through the options in the left-hand menu or using the search box. You can knock up an instant Greatest Hits by clicking under the Library button and choosing **Create Auto Playlist**. Choose the top **Click here** link and pick a **Play Count** entry to harvest the tunes you listen to the most.

The **My Rating** entry is a bit smarter, sorting by the star rating attached to each tune, but you've either got to set these yourself or use Media Player regularly so it can assign them automatically. Alternatively, click **Shuffle Music** for a random selection.

Make the most of your music

Creating your own selection from your favorite tracks

1 RIPPING GOOD FUN The first step is to get your music from shiny CD to capacious hard drive. Select **Rip** in the player's toolbar, stick your favorite album in the drive and it will automatically begin copying the music to your My Music folder.

2 PLAYING FOR KEEPS Now create yourself a playlist with your favorite tracks on it. Just click **Create Playlist**, enter an appropriate name and your empty list will appear in the right-hand pane. Drag and drop songs, then click **Save Playlist**.

JPN

$GB/BRX
£ 122.10 +0.00

+0.00

-46.78

11°
th, GBR

Reduce holiday stres...
Project kit: Make pe...
Project kit: Make chi...
Go ahead, break you...
▲ 57-60 ▶

Search and enjoy

This is one of the coolest, yet most innocuous, of the player's features. Whereas in previous versions of Media Player you'd type in a song, album, artist or genre and hit **Enter** to initiate a search, in Windows Vista the search process is instantaneous, with the results narrowing even as you type.

"Wow"
Create themed compilations

Type a term such as 'love' rather than an artist or title into the Search bar to create a nifty themed playlist

Swap shop

Right-click on **Library** to enable sharing for your entire collection across a private network – even, fittingly, a wireless one. This will ensure that, like real radio, your music can be enjoyed from any room in the house with a Windows Vista PC in it.

Plain pane

In Windows Media Player everything is laid out in a much clearer fashion than the usual list you see in many MP3 applications. You can see album covers and details, track listings, and even rate the songs directly from the main library screen. The options on the left enable you to sort your songs using various categories.

3 SYNCING FEELING Click the **Sync** tab and connect your MP3 player. Windows Media Player can sync with almost any USB storage device. You may get the option to name the device, then just drag songs, albums or playlists to the list and hit **Sync**.

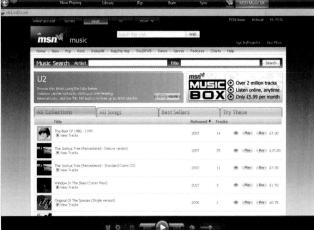

4 MISSING HITS Still pining for that vital U2 track that would complete your collection? You can buy it within the player. Click under the **Media Guide** button to choose an online music store, and have your credit card handy for registration.

Ripping yarns

Use Windows Media Player to get fast and flexible digital media playback with access to fantastic organization features

By default, Windows Media Player will turn your CDs into digital files using the Microsoft Windows Media format. This offers better compression (smaller file size) than MP3 – important if you've got a

player with limited capacity or if your hard drive is filling up. However, this format isn't supported by all players, so while they work fine on PCs you can't play the files on all devices. Unless you're certain you'll never want to use anything other than Windows Media-compatible

hardware and software, you might want to consider not ripping your CDs in Windows Media format. Windows Media is a perfectly good format, but MP3 is more widely supported, and you can easily change Media Player's settings to rip tracks in MP3 format. ⊞

Faster, quicker and better sounding

It's hip to rip, and Windows Media Player makes it easy too

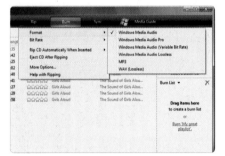

1 FIX THE FORMAT Before you put the CD in, ensure Windows Media Player will use the correct format. Click the arrow below Burn, then **Format**; it wants to use Windows Media. Click on MP3.

2 CHANGE THE RATE Music quality is measured in 'bit rates'. With MP3s, Windows Media Player defaults to a bit rate of 128Kbps, which delivers small files but doesn't sound great.

3 GET READY Now you can put the disc into the drive. Windows Vista may ask what program you want to use. If it does, you should select the **Rip Audio CD using Windows Media Player** option.

4 NO PROTECTION Do you want to add copy protection to your songs; if so, you might not be able to transfer them to a portable player or your next PC? Probably not... So click **No**.

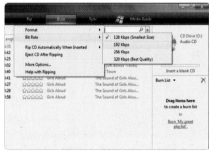

5 DOWNLOAD DJ Windows Media Player will go online, download the track listings and artwork and rip your CD. The time it takes depends on your drive, but should only be a few minutes.

6 FIX THE LIST Your ripped CD is automatically added to your library. You can edit the artist information; select the song and click on the artist name, then type the information in.

Using Windows DVD Maker

Now you can create professional-looking video DVDs of your home movies and photos

Creating your own playable DVD has never been easier. Using Windows Movie Maker you can send your footage to Windows DVD Maker by clicking on the **Publish to DVD** option, which asks you to save your work and then imports it directly into DVD Maker. You can send stills, to watch as a slide show, or recorded video.

You can use it as a stand-alone program too, by simply clicking on **Start → All Programs → Windows DVD Maker** and importing your videos manually. For the purposes of this tutorial, though, the export is done from Movie Maker.

1 PUBLISH Choose **Publish to DVD** when saving and your movie is transferred to Windows DVD Maker. The icon (bottom-left) shows how much space your movie will take up. Click **Next**.

2 CONTROL By default, the menu loads when the disc is played, but you can change it in Options. You can also specify the aspect ratio (4:3 standard TV or 16:9 widescreen). Click **OK → Next**.

3 MENU Windows DVD Maker enables you to add a commercial-looking menu – the main window shows what it will look like. (It's not required, but the example here shows what can be done.)

4 MENU OPTIONS Choose a menu design from the thumbnails in the right-hand panel. The main window updates automatically, so you can see exactly how your DVD menu will look.

5 SEE IT PROPERLY Click **Preview** to get a better idea of how your DVD menu will look. In this example, the footage is playing in the middle of the menu. Click **OK** to return to the editing options.

6 MENU MAKER Click on **Customize Menu** to import video or audio to personalize the menu or change button styles. Once you're happy, click **Change Style → Burn** to copy to a blank DVD.

Create the perfect home movie show

Home movies can take your friends on a tour of the world, or send them straight to sleep. Make the movies they'll actually want to see

Bad home movies? Shudder! They can be longer than many prison sentences, and home to multimedia's worst excesses. However, with Windows Vista you have no excuse for such nonsense. None. Go to war on bad home movies – right now!

With Windows Movie Maker, you immediately avoid the biggest pitfall... As it's a simple editor it focuses on the basic but fundamental things. You're not inundated with hundreds of transitions, effects and other flashy tools and, what's more, you're better off without them.

Editing in action

Let's think about a typical family vacation video. Don't worry about the PC yet – that's the easy part. Raw footage is where every project starts. The cardinal rule is: shoot everything you can, then throw out almost as much. A ruthless editor is a good editor.

Exactly what to keep will depend on your subject matter and intended audience, but you'll never go wrong by treating it as a professional project, rather than giving it a half-hearted approach. One thing to do whenever you start a new project is sit down and list anything that annoys you in other home movies you've seen and then avoid doing them, no matter what.

As an example, think of a classic rollercoaster shot. The number one 'gotcha' for this type of movie is the first-person shaky-cam as someone

desperately tries to keep the camcorder clamped to the side of their face. This never works. Ignoring the blurring of the world, and the nausea-enducing bounce of the camera on every twist and turn, the fact is you'll never be able to emulate the experience of being on that ride. So what do you do? Well, you do film it, but... the problem isn't the footage, it's the execution. You need to set the scene, then the action, then get the shears out at the editing stage.

First of all, the establishing shot. That should be easy enough – especially if the family is there, waving and looking nervously at the ride. Next, cut – a simple cut, nothing fancy – to the first-person camera, as a rollercoaster car pulls out of the station. ➡

The art of animation

Add both flash and substance to your movies

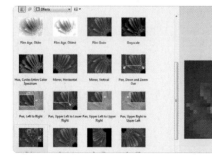

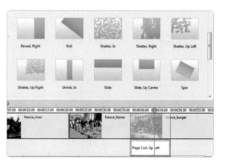

1 EFFECT/TRANSITION Effects work on individual clips, making them sepia-toned, blurred, or whatever you choose. Transitions link two clips – tearing, shattering and pushing the screen.

2 STAY CONTROLLED Do not overuse the transitions. One or two can add pace and look good, but any more and your film will be confusing, irritating or, worst of all, downright tacky.

3 WATCH THE SPEED Go to **Storyboard → Timeline** to switch editing modes, and drag the transition from the library. The maximum duration of the transition is the length of the second clip.

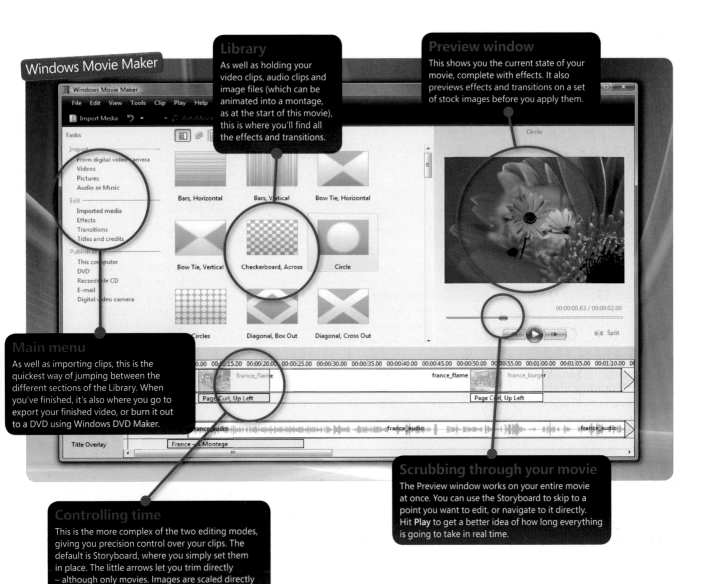

Windows Movie Maker

Library

As well as holding your video clips, audio clips and image files (which can be animated into a montage, as at the start of this movie), this is where you'll find all the effects and transitions.

Preview window

This shows you the current state of your movie, complete with effects. It also previews effects and transitions on a set of stock images before you apply them.

Main menu

As well as importing clips, this is the quickest way of jumping between the different sections of the Library. When you've finished, it's also where you go to export your finished video, or burn it out to a DVD using Windows DVD Maker.

Controlling time

This is the more complex of the two editing modes, giving you precision control over your clips. The default is Storyboard, where you simply set them in place. The little arrows let you trim directly – although only movies. Images are scaled directly by dragging the edges on the Timeline.

Scrubbing through your movie

The Preview window works on your entire movie at once. You can use the Storyboard to skip to a point you want to edit, or navigate to it directly. Hit **Play** to get a better idea of how long everything is going to take in real time.

4 **TITLES** These are handled separately, with presets available for one-line titles, two-line titles, and a longer list of credits. You can choose the font and color, but not a great deal more.

5 **TITLE ROLE** There are two title types; those that run before/after the movie, and text overlays. The former are like movie clips, and effects can be added, but you can't add effects to overlays.

6 **MIX AND MATCH** Overlays aren't locked to a clip, so you can stretch them out to caption a longer sequence. Any animation will only play at the start and end, rescaling as you move the clip.

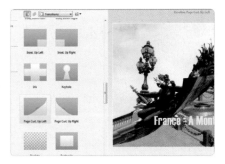

Obviously, don't stick with this for too long; cut to another external shot of the rollercoaster pulling away towards the big loop. When the rollercoaster plummets, cut to your go on the ride. Take a first-person camera shot, showing a family member's screams, then cut back to the external. If you've got a good bit of first-person camera footage of a drop, or a turn, or a particular bit of dramatic scenery, slip it in.

Finally, cut to the family waddling uncertainly out of the gates, and get some close-up shots of reactions – cries of "Again!" or "Never again!"

Now it's a simple editing job. One transition (Cut) and one editing tool (Trim). However, when you play the video, nobody will care about the technology behind it, just the result. And believe it or not, that's the big secret of editing. Simplicity always wins out over glitz, and less really is more.

Of course, there is scope to play around with the more complicated effects as well. If you're building a montage of photos, picking a transition to go between them can look good. Even then, though, the keep-it-simple mantra applies. A page-curl may look good, but a page-curl followed by a bar-wipe followed by a dissolve followed by a shatter is overkill.

Try to stick to one effect, one editing style and one (rough) length for each segment, and the whole thing will flow. It may seem like a lot of effort for a family video, but you'll end up with movie memories you really want to watch! ⊞

Quickfire questions

Q **What can I do to get better quality raw footage?**
A Getting a good camera is the obvious answer, but you can improve your movies a hundred times over with a few quick tips. For the best shots, you'll need a tripod to keep the unit steady – even the steadiest hand can only hold so still. When filming, avoid the temptation to constantly zoom in and out, and keep your movements as fluid as possible to avoid giving the audience a feeling of nausea. Give your camera time to focus properly before taking footage that you plan to use. And, of course, always film far more than you need to give yourself some breathing room at the editing stage.

Q **Why do I sometimes get poor-looking colors?**
A When you turn the camera on, make sure the white balance function is working. Put a piece of white paper in the middle of a shot and use it to color-balance the camera. Forgetting to do this will leave your footage looking off-color, and will ruin your masterpiece.

In real life... Movie Maker

Nick Odantzis, Writer, *Windows Vista: The Official Magazine*

Being relatively new to the video-editing world, I was a bit hesitant about how easy I was going to find using Windows Movie Maker but, as it turns out, I shouldn't have been. Windows Movie Maker supported my old Firewire-based DV camcorder, importing the video without a problem. If anything, the limited number of options makes it easy to navigate round the interface. The timeline option is very powerful, giving precise control over the footage you've imported. And then adding a soundtrack and creating a final DVD is simplicity itself!

Editing basic footage

Simple steps to make the most of your clips

"Wow"
Burn to DVD

With Windows Movie Maker, you can easily make a DVD of your film. Insert a blank disc, click **Publish → DVD** and you'll get all your action on disc

1 IMPORTING CLIPS You'll need your footage in digital format – either direct from your camera, or as a file on your hard drive. Windows Movie Maker supports most formats, including WMV and MPEG, although not QuickTime.

2 SPLITTING UP Cut longer clips into pieces so you can use them across your project. Click the video in the main Edit pane and play it in the viewer until you get to the break point. Click **Split** to carve it into two pieces, ready to place.

3 STORYBOARDING This is the simplest way to make your movie. Drag and drop clips from the library into the clip places at the bottom of the screen. This gets them into the correct order, ready to be trimmed and effects added.

Longer movie clips will need to be cut into smaller pieces so that you can use them throughout your project

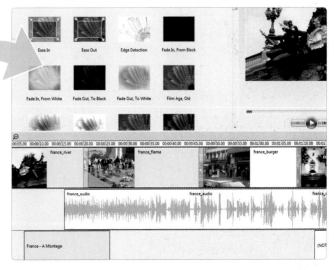

4 TRIMMING Select a clip on the Storyboard and it will jump to that point in the Preview window. Drag the scroller to the point that you want it to start on, and select **Trim Beginning** from the Clip menu. Repeat with **Trim End**. If you make a mistake, click **Clear Trim Points** and start over.

Using stock footage

Many videos use stock footage to add detail and tone, and so can you. While libraries are often expensive, the Internet Archive hosts videos at www.archive.org/ details/movies, many of which are in the public domain.

5 ADVANCED EDITING The Storyboard is a quick and simple way to lay out your movie, but you can get more control by switching to Timeline view. Click where it says **Storyboard** to bring up the option. The Timeline view shows all audio, video and overlays, with split-second timing options.

Windows Media Center

As we're putting all of our digital media on to our computers these days, it makes sense to enjoy it on them as well

Windows Media Center has been around for a while, but only for a select few; Windows XP Media Center Edition was only available to PC manufacturers, and if you wanted to get your hands on it you'd have to buy a fully-fledged Media Center PC.

With Windows Vista, you no longer need to shell out on shiny new hardware as long as you go for the Home Premium or Ultimate editions of Windows Vista. That's good news – Windows Media Center is well worth having.

The 10-foot interface

With a typical PC, you're sat a few inches in front of the screen with a keyboard and a mouse in front of you. That's not much cop if you want to kick back and watch a DVD.

Windows Media Center gives you the best of both worlds: the power of your PC with the convenience of your TV.

Instead of peering at tiny text, the Windows Media Center interface is designed for distance, so you view it on your TV screen or on a big PC monitor. You don't need to mess around with a keyboard either – dedicated Media Center PCs come with a remote control, instead of the bog-standard PC keyboard and mouse controls. In addition to the obvious stuff – playing your music and DVDs, showing off your photos and displaying your video clips – you can use the Windows Vista Media Center as a digital TV recorder.

You'll find Media Center under **Start ➔ All Programs ➔ Windows Media Center**. You'll then be taken through the set-up screens; as you'll see over the next few pages, set-up is straightforward and doesn't take long, although you'll need to be connected to the internet throughout the process if you want to use some of the advanced features, such as the electronic program guide.

In real life...
Parental controls

Paul Douglas, Editor, Windows Vista: The Official Magazine
It's easy to lock Windows Media Center so the kids can't access inappropriate content: go to **Tasks ➔ Settings ➔ General ➔ Parental Controls** and choose a four-digit PIN code. You can now block unrated DVDs or set age limits by DVD ratings. And, of course, you can also use the Parental Controls to block access to Media Center altogether – see page 48. All of which means you'll be able to leave your children in peace using Windows Media Center without worrying about what they are watching.

Getting a perfect set-up

Follow the step by step guide and get all your media in one place

1 START SETUP Running Windows Media Center for the first time starts the set-up. Re-run it by launching Media Center, then **Tasks ➔ Setup ➔ General ➔ Windows Media Center Setup**.

2 CHANNEL PHWOAR Here, Media Center has detected 62 different channels, including digital radio stations. If you think you're in range of more, click **Scan For More** to try to find them.

3 EASY INTERFACE Accessing each category is a matter of using the remote control or your computer's mouse and keyboard. Cycle through **Pictures**, **Music**, **TV** and **Tasks**.

And relax...

Don't forget the comfy chairs. The whole point of Windows Media Center is that you can enjoy all of your digital stuff in comfort and without the need for a computer room.

High-def TV

If you have one of the latest high-definition displays then these are even more versatile and can easily hook up to a living room PC, offering a pin-sharp digital display.

Quiet but good looking

An advanced Media Center system is what you need for the living room. You want something that runs quietly, doesn't look like a PC and is styled to hide among your TV and DVD player.

Remote controls

Windows Media Center can be controlled via a traditional remote control; using this you have full control over your selection of movies, music, photos and more.

Surround sound

To get the best cinematic experience, a surround sound system is really required. Windows Vista supports up to seven surround speakers with additional subwoofer for explosive bass.

Xbox 360

An Xbox 360 not only provides pulse-racing high-def gaming, it can also double as a Media Extender, providing an easy way to stream audio and video to your living room.

4 WHAT'S ON To view the guide, go to the menu and click on **TV+Movies →
Guide**. You'll see listings for the available channels for the next two weeks; you can view a program by clicking on it.

5 PIC PERFECT This is the Picture Library (first option under **Pictures + Videos**). View pictures by folder, tags or date, or turn them into an on-screen slideshow by clicking **Play Slide Show**.

6 MUSIC MAESTRO The music selection works in much the same way as the Picture Library; view tunes by album, artists, genres and so on. Clicking on an image opens the album.

Improving the Windows Media Center experience

By tweaking and adjusting Windows Media Center you can improve both image and audio quality

Any PC that's capable of running Windows Vista should happily run Windows Media Center, although if you're going to store a lot of music or record a lot of TV then a big hard disk is essential. Even a relatively modest music collection takes up more than 30GB of disk space, and a short TV show can be more than 100MB in size for a single episode; entire movies can vary from 700MB all the way to 4GB for full DVDs or high-definition films.

However, to get the best from Windows Media Center you'll also need a tuner card so your PC can tune in to TV broadcasts. These come in a range of flavours: PCI or USB, single tuner or twin tuner. So what should you choose?

If you've got a standard desktop PC, a PCI card – which installs in a spare slot at the back of your PC – is a better bet than a USB one. That's because PCI cards transfer data roughly five times faster than even a USB 2.0 connection, so there's no risk of bottlenecks affecting your recordings and you won't lose a valuable USB socket either.

If you're going to be using your PC in your living room, a twin tuner card is a sensible investment. Twin tuners enable you to watch one program while recording another. There are some other tweaks you can make to get the

"Wow" HD support

Service Pack 1 enhances support for the latest HD optical drives by adding new icons and labels that will identify HD DVD and Blu-ray drives and discs as high density ones

best possible entertainment experience, but you might not want to make any more changes if you just want to see it in action. If that's the case, simply click on **I am finished** and then on **Next**.

Getting the best possible results

Fine-tune your Media Center set-up for viewing perfection

1 DEJA VIEW Here you are at the Media Center set-up menu again and, as you can see, the first option is already ticked and grayed-out. Now, it's time to adjust the display settings. Click on that option and then on **Next**.

2 QUICK CLIP As the set-up screen explains, Media Center will now make the necessary adjustments to suit your display. There's also a video you can watch that explains how to adjust your screen for the best picture.

3 PRISTINE SCREEN If you click on the **Watch Video** link then **Yes**, you get to watch a video. It explains how to adjust your screen brightness and contrast, and it features people in beige pants and brightly-colored tops!

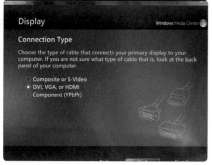

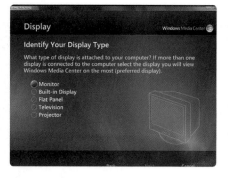

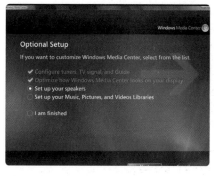

4 PIN-SHARP WIZARD Make sure your computer is connected to the display you'll be using – there's no point configuring the display so it looks good on your PC's screen if you'll actually be watching on a 50-inch plasma display.

5 SELECT YOUR SCREEN Windows Media Center uses different settings for different displays – what looks great on a computer screen may look less impressive on a digital projector. Click on the type of display and then on **Next**.

6 CHOOSE CABLE Next, you need to tell Windows Media Center what kind of display to computer connection you're using. For example, if you have a standard computer monitor (or a high-def TV), it'll be DVI, VGA or HDMI.

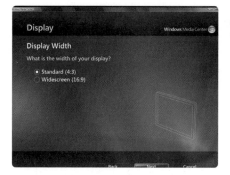

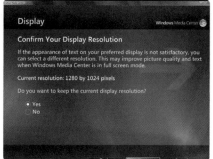

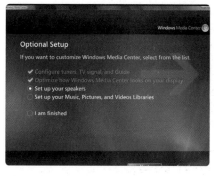

7 BORN TO BE WIDE Now, do you have a standard screen (traditional 4:3 ratio, which most TV shows were made in until recently) or a widescreen (16:9 ratio, like a cinema screen)? Choose the appropriate option and click **Next**.

8 WHERE IT'S AT Windows Media Center will give you the option to keep the current display resolution or change it. Run Media Center in full screen view – if you run it in a window the text may be less clear.

9 MR SPEAKER Back at the menu, Media Center's ready to configure the speakers. Whether listening to music or enjoying TV and movies, setting up the digital audio output properly will make a difference. Click **Next**.

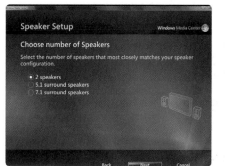

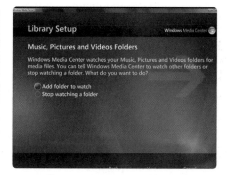

10 MAGIC NUMBERS Before adjusting audio settings, Media Center needs to know the number of speakers. If you've got a 2.1 system – that is, two speakers with a subwoofer – go for the '2 speakers' option.

11 EAR WE GO Media Center will now play a tone through each speaker in turn. If you don't hear the sound from each speaker, Media Center will help identify and fix the problem. If it's fine, just click on **Next**.

12 ADD A FOLDER Media Center looks in your Music, Pictures and Videos folders for your files. If you've stored your media files elsewhere, use the **Add Folder** option to make sure Media Center keeps an eye on it.

Get more from Windows Media Center

There's more to Windows Media Center than just watching movies and TV, check out how to find shows, enjoy slide shows and burn DVDs

It's all too easy to focus on the recorded playback side of Windows Media Center. While it's primarily thought of as a way to enjoy TV and movies there is far more to Media Center than this. Besides the newly-designed interface, its graphically-rich, remote-control driven interface enables you to navigate easily through media such as photos and movies, and it's easy to create slide shows, record entire seasons of programs and even browse the web.

One of the coolest features is that a PC with a TV tuner installed can function as a personal video recorder (PVR) to automatically record your favorite television shows. Not only does this enable you to pause and rewind live TV,

it also offers built-in support for archiving TV shows directly to DVDs.

Many of the previous technical hurdles associated with media use have been removed in Windows Vista. For example, everything required to play and burn DVDs is now included as standard, removing compatibility problems of the past. Provided the minimum system requirements are met, Windows Media Center can really enhance your PC use.

Extra abilities

When you're not watching movies, Media Center can act as a perfect music station and, with its funky visualizations, it's great for providing a bit of background entertainment during parties, while the remote offers simple

mouse-free control. The same goes for the slide show feature, – this is great for showing off family pictures when the relatives come round.

The fact that Windows Media Center can be enhanced with plug-ins shouldn't be overlooked, adding all manner of features to your media enjoyment.

You can either operate your standard PC as your home media system, or you can connect it to a TV or projector for a more dedicated entertainment set-up. Alternatively, you can leave the PC in your study and use a Media Extender – such as the Microsoft Xbox 360; with this kind of device, it's possible to extend the experience – and interface – from the PC to the TV using a home network. See pages 68 and 105 for details.

Finding your favorite programs

How to record shows currently on TV – and those yet to be shown

1 ADD RECORDING There isn't an option to create a new recording within **TV + Movies** of the main menu; this facility is contained as a sub-item called **Add Recording**, in **Recorded TV**.

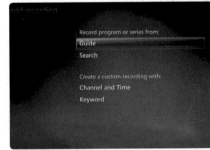

2 SELECT SHOW Windows Media Center gives you options when searching; selecting **Search** will prompt you to enter a title or keyword to create a one-time or series recording.

3 PICK TIMES From the matches, look up the screen times. After selecting the one to record, you will be given information to help decide whether to record the show or the series.

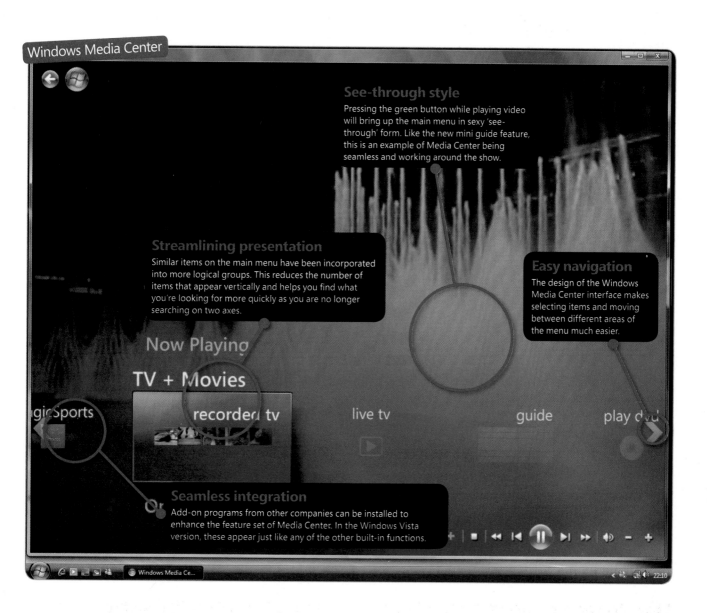

Windows Media Center

See-through style
Pressing the green button while playing video will bring up the main menu in sexy 'see-through' form. Like the new mini guide feature, this is an example of Media Center being seamless and working around the show.

Streamlining presentation
Similar items on the main menu have been incorporated into more logical groups. This reduces the number of items that appear vertically and helps you find what you're looking for more quickly as you are no longer searching on two axes.

Easy navigation
The design of the Windows Media Center interface makes selecting items and moving between different areas of the menu much easier.

Now Playing

TV + Movies

icSports   recorded tv   live tv   guide   play dvd

Seamless integration
Add-on programs from other companies can be installed to enhance the feature set of Media Center. In the Windows Vista version, these appear just like any of the other built-in functions.

4 SEARCH GUIDE A useful feature under Search is Categories. This can act as your personalized TV guide; use this facility to get a list of all the films to be screened in a two-week period.

5 ADVANCED RECORDING Select Keyword on the Add Recording screen to automatically record everything which contains specific matches to the key words.

6 YOUR OWN TIME Your program will appear in the View Scheduled List under Recorded TV; watch it when you want and, if you have a Media Center Extender, where you want.

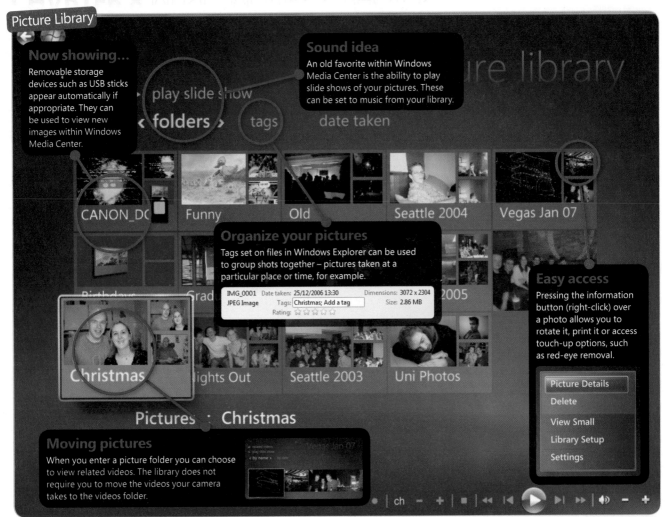

Picture Library

Now showing...
Removable storage devices such as USB sticks appear automatically if appropriate. They can be used to view new images within Windows Media Center.

Sound idea
An old favorite within Windows Media Center is the ability to play slide shows of your pictures. These can be set to music from your library.

play slide show

< folders > tags date taken

CANON_DC   Funny   Old   Seattle 2004   Vegas Jan 07

Organize your pictures
Tags set on files in Windows Explorer can be used to group shots together – pictures taken at a particular place or time, for example.

IMG_0001	Date taken: 25/12/2006 13:30	Dimensions: 3072 x 2304
JPEG Image	Tags: Christmas; Add a tag	Size: 2.86 MB
	Rating: ☆☆☆☆☆	

Easy access
Pressing the information button (right-click) over a photo allows you to rotate it, print it or access touch-up options, such as red-eye removal.

Birthdays   Grad   2005

Christmas   ights Out   Seattle 2003   Uni Photos

Picture Details
Delete
View Small
Library Setup
Settings

Pictures : Christmas

Moving pictures
When you enter a picture folder you can choose to view related videos. The library does not require you to move the videos your camera takes to the videos folder.

Windows Media Center: TV basics

Tune in for the right signal

Windows Media Center supports a range of TV signals from analog and digital transmissions, to cable and satellite using a set-top box (STB). When setting up an STB, the PC sends infrared commands to change channel. In the US, you can buy TV tuners for digital cable without an STB. Elsewhere support varies but, in most countries, two tuners can be used at once.

If you upgraded or purchased a Windows Vista machine without TV hardware, it is easy to add on. TV Cards marked with a 'Designed for Windows Vista Premium' sticker are suitable for Media Center use.

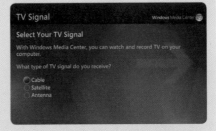

TV Signal   Windows Media Center

Select Your TV Signal
With Windows Media Center, you can watch and record TV on your computer.

What type of TV signal do you receive?
○ Cable
○ Satellite
○ Antenna

SIGNAL BOX Use this panel to tell Media Center how you receive your transmissions

UNIQUE WOW Create your own view in the new Windows Media Center music layout

Streaming from your PC to an Xbox 360

If you're lucky enough to own an Xbox 360, why not use Windows Vista to stream your movies to it?

So then, Windows Media Center is pretty nifty, but what about accessing it from elsewhere in the house? Microsoft has devised a technology called Media Center Extender that enables you to stream media from your PC to any room in the house, and there's an extender inside every Xbox 360. Provided your Xbox and PC are networked, either using a wired or wireless network, you can use your Xbox to access your PC's music, photo and video library. And getting your Xbox to communicate with your Windows Vista PC couldn't be easier.

"Wow" Media Extender

With Service Pack 1 there is now increased support for the latest types of Windows Media Center Extenders, such as new digital televisions and networked DVD players

1 EXTEND IT To stream things from PC to Xbox you'll need to configure the console's Media Center Extender. Launch Media Center, then select **Tasks → Settings**. Click on **Extender**.

2 GET READY Before you start the set-up, switch on your Xbox 360. From the main Xbox dashboard select the **Media** blade and then **Media Center**. Take note of the authorisation code.

3 FIREWALL FIDDLE To connect to your Xbox 360, the Windows Firewall needs to be configured to allow it. Click on **Next** and the set-up program will make the necessary changes for you.

4 SHARE YOUR STUFF Media Center Setup will now ask whether you want to share your various media folders with your Xbox 360. Click on **Yes** and then on the **Next** button.

5 FINISH THE JOB Windows Vista will now configure for Xbox streaming by looking for your console, adjusting the appropriate settings, and telling it where to find your music, movies and photos.

6 THERE IT IS You'll see a picture of an Xbox 360 in Media Center's Extenders menu. To add another, repeat the process by clicking **Add Extender**, or use the **Back** button to return to the main menu.

Play great games

DirectX is getting ever better, and if you thought PC games were eye-popping before, you ain't seen nothing yet

Windows Vista represents a great leap forward in PC gaming, and it's all because of DirectX. Version 10 has been rewritten from scratch to take advantage of today's ultra-powerful PCs and graphics cards, and the specification has become much tighter than before – so if a graphics card is DirectX 10 compatible, it's seriously powerful. And it's a Windows Vista-only technology.

So what does all of this actually mean? DirectX 10 offers better graphics and makes more efficient use of your PC's CPU and your graphics card's GPU, and that has very visible benefits.

The DirectX team reckons that games run up to eight times quicker than previous versions, which means that developers will be able to deliver higher-resolution graphics without affecting the all-important frame rate. If you'd like to see it in action, check out the in-game footage or download the demo for Crysis from www.crysis-online.com, but of course you'll will only see the benefits of the new graphics with Windows Vista and a compatible graphics card.

Because DirectX 10 is Windows Vista-only, as the system becomes increasingly popular you can expect the best new games releases to be Windows Vista-only. If you've ever tried to run Doom 3 or Half-Life 2 on an ageing computer, you'll know exactly what we mean; developers tend to write for the latest, greatest systems so older kit struggles.

DirectX 10 is the biggie, but Microsoft hasn't neglected the details. The new Games Explorer puts all your games in one place, and you can use the Parental Controls in Windows Vista to enforce age ratings for individual users, so if you'd rather not let the kids loose on something like Prey, it's easy to restrict access. The Games Explorer will also display the box art of new games. 🗗

"Wow" DirectX 10.1

With Service Pack 1 you also get the latest generation of DirectX, this adds support for the latest graphics hardware features that increase image quality to an even greater level

EYE CANDY Crysis was one of the first games to use DirectX 10 and its visuals are stunning

Get gaming in Windows Vista

Windows Vista is all set for gaming – you just need to know where to look

1 USEFUL INFO In Games Explorer you'll see your system's performance rating, plus the game's minimum/recommended requirements. The **Tools** button provides access to your hardware.

2 ART WORKS When you install new games, Games Explorer will download the artwork and available ratings information. You can disable this by clicking **Options** in the toolbar.

3 GAME ON Good news – Solitaire's still here! You also get a bevy of other games with Windows Vista, including kids' favorite Purble Place – incomprehensible to any post teen.

The future of PC gaming
Coming soon to a monitor near you

It's in the palm fronds that sweep back as you push through; it's in the spiralling smoke clouds, the remainder of a tasty bomb dropped on an enemy base... The strive for graphical excellence defines PC gaming, and DirectX 10 – exclusive to Windows Vista – really delivers.

DirectX is the code that games use to display graphics. Each version allows new effects; previous releases have allowed games to display realistic fur, water or fire. It's a big leap for game developers because it allows them to 'unify' the memory of PCs, allowing them to produce more 'open' worlds.

The first games to take advantage of looked astonishing. Here's a look at the stunning visuals in the DirectX 10-powered Age of Conan.

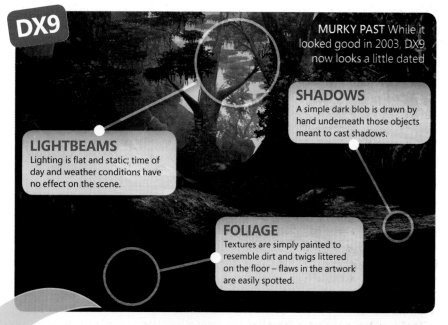

DX9

MURKY PAST While it looked good in 2003, DX9 now looks a little dated

LIGHTBEAMS
Lighting is flat and static; time of day and weather conditions have no effect on the scene.

SHADOWS
A simple dark blob is drawn by hand underneath those objects meant to cast shadows.

FOLIAGE
Textures are simply painted to resemble dirt and twigs littered on the floor – flaws in the artwork are easily spotted.

DX10

FOLIAGE
The flat surface is replaced with a realistic woodland; the trees are far more detailed. Suddenly, the forest feels more alive.

LIGHTBEAMS
The dappled light breaking through the canopy highlights areas of interest; breaking the light casts far more defined shadows on the forest floor.

SOFT SHADOWS
DirectX 10 lets all items cast realistic, sharply-defined shade. As the trees move in response to a slight breeze, the shadows slip left and right.

Check it
Test your PC's performance

1 **THE SCORE** Open the Control Panel from the Start menu; click **System and Maintenance**, then **Performance Information**. The highest score is 5.9.

2 **IN DETAIL** Click on the **Windows Experience Index** link; you'll see the score is set by the weakest link. So, if your memory only scores 2, that's what your overall score will be.

3 **CHECK AGAIN** If you want to recheck your score, close all other running programs; click **Update My Score**. Windows Vista will run a series of checks and report the result.

Get ready to play
It's easy to get your games running smoothly

Some PCs don't have the ability to run the incredible light shows of DirectX capable games. But, for the first time, there is an easy way to see through the boggle of acronyms, numbers and specifications listed on the back of the game box. Built into Windows Vista is the Windows Experience Index: this scores your PC according to its capabilities, with fast, game-ready PCs scoring highly. Follow the steps (left) to check your PC's score.

Now, on games that are certified for Windows Vista, you will see this number printed on the game box, so you can see at a glance if your PC will run it. Broadly speaking, if your PC scores over 4, it should run all currently available games OK. If the computer scores between 2 and 4, however, it will have trouble playing new releases; if it scores below 2, it may not run games at all.

All is not lost, however. Most new games automatically adjust themselves so they are less demanding on weaker PCs, and you can make further adjustments yourself. Just go into the graphics settings for each game and reduce the resolution and advanced lighting effects like anti-aliasing and shadows.

LESS PRETTY Lowering the graphics' settings means basic looks but a faster-running game

STAY FRESH Run Windows Update regularly; new drivers can make a big difference

Get an easy upgrade
Boost your gaming performance in just a few minutes

Improving your PC's score can be easy. Memory can be upgraded in only a few minutes – find out what you need and how to fit it at a dedicated PC memory web site. Gaming graphics are a little trickier, but not much; you can find a guide at the *Windows Vista: The Official Magazine* web site – www.windowsvistamagazine.com/graphics. If all your scores are low, it may be worth buying a new PC.

Some manufacturers specialize in cutting-edge gaming PCs, so think about the main use for your PC when making your purchase.

Fill a slot to make your PC hot

How to fit a graphics card in five easy steps

1 OPEN UP Obviously, for safety's sake, and to avoid damage, turn off the computer and unplug it from the mains before you remove the case door. You should also be aware this could invalidate any warranty, so proceed at your own risk.

2 TAKE IT OUT It's also advisable to take anti-static precautions – an anti-static wrist strap offers the best protection. Unclip the old graphics card from its slot – it's usually held in place by a screw but in newer PC cases, like this one, it's held by quick-release clips.

3 SLOT IN PLACE Fit the new graphics card by pushing it firmly into the now vacant slot and securing it in position. This can be a little tricky as you need to make sure the backplate is lined correctly. If the card needs an additional power supply, plug it in.

4 CLOSED CASE Make sure you screw the graphics card securely in place. At this point, you should easily be able to fasten your computer's case door back in place. Attach the monitor lead to the graphics card – it may require an adaptor – and now reattach the mains lead and power it up again.

5 INSTALL IT Once Windows Vista loads, the new graphics card is detected and the appropriate drivers are automatically installed, so you're now ready to play. Graphics drivers are regularly updated for improved performance, so it's worth checking the manufacturer's web site for any updates.

Set up your Windows Mail account today

It's time to get organized, and Windows Vista is just the operating system to help you do that with its powerful mail package

For years, every copy of Windows came with the email program Outlook Express. It wasn't a bad program when it first came out but, over time, it became a major headache as spammers, scammers, virus writers and other net nasties tried to con people out of cash and infect systems with all kinds of unpleasantness – which is why many abandoned Outlook Express altogether. Thankfully, with Windows Vista, Microsoft has dumped Outlook Express and replaced it with something considerably more useful and more secure: Windows Mail.

For most people, email has become a day-to-day tool and a very important one. Because of the significance email

communication now holds for all of us, Microsoft has increased the security in Windows Mail to protect the vital areas.

Of course, these security improvements run alongside functional upgrades, too – there's now a greatly-improved search facility that fully integrates with Windows Vista itself making it easy to track down that vital email, no matter where you may be. The reliability of Windows Mail is a great asset; it is capable of handling vast amounts of stored emails without any problems, meaning even the most deluged of inboxes will stay responsive.

Over the next few pages, you'll see some of the fabulous features that Windows Mail has to offer – and how to get the most out of it.

In real life...
It's the little things

Neil Mohr
Technical Editor
The biggest revelation for day-to-day Windows Mail use is the new integrated search feature. This not only makes it child's play to track down emails but, no matter where you are in Windows Vista, it's easy to see relevant emails when you're searching for certain terms. It also doesn't hurt that the whole application has been given the new Windows Vista look!

Adding an email account
The latest generation of email is easier than ever

1 ALL ACCOUNTS There's already an account: Microsoft Communities. Set up a new account by clicking **Add**. Make sure you've got your email account details from your ISP before proceeding.

2 CHOOSE A KIND Make sure **E-mail Account** is highlighted; click **Next**. The name you enter will appear on all emails you send from this account. Enter your name and click **Next**.

3 PLANET POP Enter the details of your incoming email server (usually a POP server) and your outgoing one (usually SMTP). Your ISP should have given you the information you need for this bit.

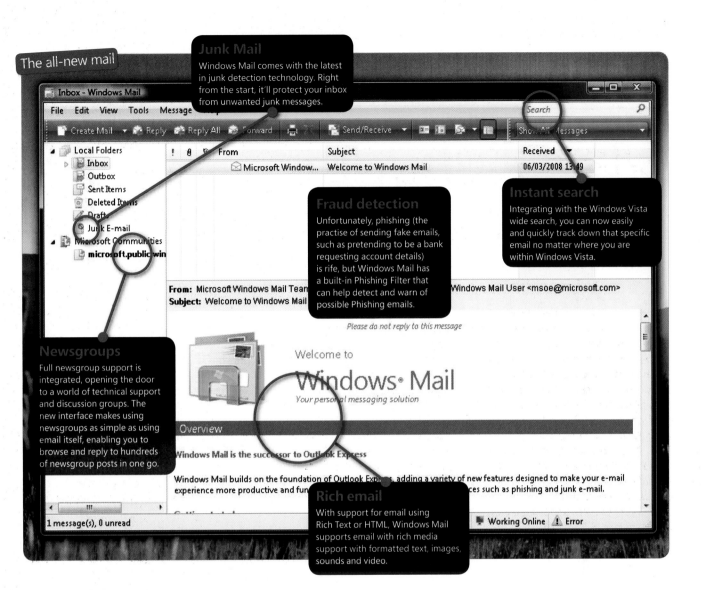

Junk Mail
Windows Mail comes with the latest in junk detection technology. Right from the start, it'll protect your inbox from unwanted junk messages.

Fraud detection
Unfortunately, phishing (the practise of sending fake emails, such as pretending to be a bank requesting account details) is rife, but Windows Mail has a built-in Phishing Filter that can help detect and warn of possible Phishing emails.

Instant search
Integrating with the Windows Vista wide search, you can now easily and quickly track down that specific email no matter where you are within Windows Vista.

Newsgroups
Full newsgroup support is integrated, opening the door to a world of technical support and discussion groups. The new interface makes using newsgroups as simple as using email itself, enabling you to browse and reply to hundreds of newsgroup posts in one go.

Rich email
With support for email using Rich Text or HTML, Windows Mail supports email with rich media support with formatted text, images, sounds and video.

4 TWEAK TIME You're up and running, but you still need to alter security settings before accessing mails. Select an account in the main part of the dialog box and then click on **Properties**.

5 ESSENTIAL INFO The first screen enables you to change the name that appears on outgoing emails but, if you want to alter a setting in the Servers tab, click on that tab to continue.

6 MAIL ORDER Once you've changed your account details, close the Accounts dialog box and then on the **Send & Receive** button. If everything's OK you should see a screen like this one.

Make sending emails a pleasure, not a chore

As good as Windows Mail is, you can make it even quicker and easier to use by changing its looks and its filters

Once you start using Windows Mail on a day-to-day basis, you may find you want to alter certain aspects to suit your needs. Fortunately, it's easy to customize.

Many changes are possible, ranging from simple things such as how emails are sorted to more radical elements, such as changing the layout of the entire application. You can also configure and alter the Windows Mail interface to make it look how you want it to look.

You might not think it, but something as simple as choosing the order in which columns are displayed can make all the difference to usability. Removing some columns or making others smaller can really help if you're having to work on a space-constricted display, such as a laptop computer.

Follow the rules

You can even tailor the filtering rules that enable you to alter how Windows Mail processes emails as they arrive. These rules make it easy to automatically file emails as they arrive or, if you're working on a special project, to create rules to automatically look at each email based on subject or mailing list and move them to a corresponding folder.

The Windows Mail Message Rules is a powerful system that makes dealing with large amounts of email far easier. It's a similar feature to that found in the full-blown Microsoft Outlook application, which goes to show how flexible it is. You're able to set rules that determine how Windows Mail processes emails based on content, recipient, sender and subject – either exactly or just by matching a single keyword. Then, depending on if it's a match or not, the rule can send the email to a specified folder (including the trash) forward it or send it on in another form. It all adds up to a faster, more user-friendly email experience. The easiest way to learn about Message Rules is to try creating one, so follow the walkthrough... ⊞

Changing the email sort options

Filter your messages on receipt to stay on top of your mail

1 CHANGE THE VIEW If you don't like the default layout in Windows Mail, change it by clicking **View → Layout**. You can hide elements such as the folder list or search bar, or change the location of the Message Preview pane.

2 SENSIBLE SORTING The Group By Conversation feature condenses related messages and puts a plus sign next to them. To see all messages in a conversation click on the plus sign and the conversation will expand.

3 CHOOSE THE COLUMNS By default the list of messages shows you whether an item is flagged high priority, whether it's got an attachment, whether you've flagged it, who it came from, its subject line and when you received it.

4 **A CLEANER LOOK** Here, the attachment and priority columns have been moved to the right to make things a bit cleaner. You can adjust the width of individual columns by dragging the gray lines between the columns.

5 **THE RULES** It's a big help if your email program can sort messages. The Rules feature enables you to create simple or sophisticated sorting options for incoming messages, and you'll find it under **Tools → Message Rules → Mail**.

6 **NEW RULES** To create a rule, click on the **New...** button. You can specify what Windows Mail should look for and then do. For example, to filter mailing list messages by subject, tick the **Where the subject line contains specific words** box.

7 **CHOOSE CRITERIA** Specific Words is now a blue link. Click on it to choose the words Windows Mail should look for. The example here is looking for messages that have [rsi-uk] in the subject line. Click **Add** and then **OK**.

8 **PROCESS IT** Choose what to do with your messages. If you want them filed in a specific folder, tick **Move it to the specified folder** in box 2. You'll see a new link, saying **Specified**. Click on it to tell Windows Mail which folder to use.

9 **FIND THE FOLDER** To use a folder, click on the '+' sign next to Local Folders to expand the list, select the folder and click **OK**. If you want to create a new folder, make sure Local Folders is selected then click on **New Folder**.

10 **AND ANOTHER** You can create another rule to process mailing list messages. This time, these are from a freelance mailing list so it's scanning the subject for 'freelance' and moving mail to a new folder called Freelance.

11 **RUN THE RULES** Once you've created your rules, click on **OK**. Check to see if the rules are doing what you want them to do. Click on **Apply Now** and a new dialog box will open with a list of all the rules you've created.

12 **MORE OPTIONS** Click on **Tools → Options → Read** to change the way Windows Mail treats your messages. You can read all messages in plain text and you can use the **Fonts** button to change the typeface Windows Mail uses.

Getting news and files with newsgroups

Newsgroups provide a wealth of knowledge and a way of sharing ideas and information; here's how to get the best out of them

Like Outlook Express, Windows Mail can also handle newsgroups – essentially online bulletin boards dedicated to particular subjects. Most internet service providers provide newsgroup access, and you can add your ISP's server details by clicking **Tools ➔ Accounts ➔ Add** then selecting **Newsgroup Account**. You'll be asked for the server details, which will be something like news.myisp.com. Windows Mail will then download a list of all the groups provided by your ISP.

Third-party newsgroup services also offer a wider number of groups, if you really get the bug. Microsoft supports a newsgroup server of its own that's available from within Windows Mail. This will give you an idea of how newsgroups work and how to use them; of course the topics on offer are of a Microsoft nature.

Funk the junk

Junk email blows online via the internet, gathering in annoying piles in your inbox. While it seems like an unavoidable modern plague, you can – at least to some extent – enforce some controlling measures. Part of the trick is to use the power of Windows Mail junk filters.

The junk filters offer a number of protection tiers (see the opposite page). The most obvious is the defacto junk filter, which uses advanced algorithms to separate the wheat from the chaff. It has a number of levels of severity, up to the point where *everyone* is suspected. ⊞

THE VIEW Groups you subscribe to appear under Microsoft Communities in Folder List

Accessing newsgroups

Keep up to date with selected bulletin boards

1 THE LIST Windows Mail comes with connection details for Microsoft Communities, a collection of themed newsgroups. When you first click on the link in the folder list you're asked if you want to see a list of all groups. Click **Yes**.

2 SPOILT FOR CHOICE You'll see a list of available groups; there are plenty to choose from. Scroll through the list or use the Display newsgroups that contain... field at the top of the dialog box to look for specific words.

3 CLICK TO CHOOSE When you find a group you're interested in, click on it and then click **Subscribe**. This means Windows Mail will automatically check this group for new messages in future. Click on **OK** when you're happy.

No more junk mail

The junk filters in Windows Mail keep unwanted riff-raff out of your inbox

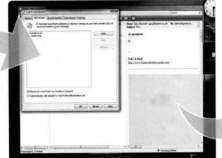

1 EASY OPTIONS Click on **Tools → Junk E-mail Options** to get the tabbed dialog box, which enables you to choose how strict the filters should be. You can get Windows Mail to delete suspected junk emails rather than store them.

2 SAFE SENDERS To make sure certain emails don't get labeled as junk, click on **Safe Senders** and **Add**. Enter individual emails or entire domains, eg '@microsoft.com' so that they will be classed as from a safe sender.

3 BUILD BORDERS You can go to the **International** tab and click **Blocked top-level domain list** to block emails from a particular country. You can also use **Blocked Encoding** to banish messages in non-English characters.

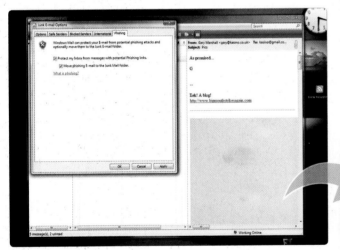

The final tab in the dialog is devoted to phishing – the official-looking emails that pretend to be from your bank

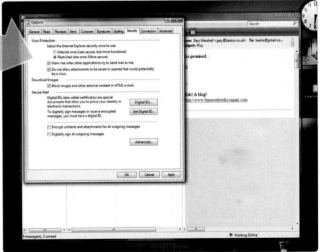

4 PREVENT PHISHING The final tab in the Junk Email Options dialog is devoted to phishing – the official-looking emails that pretend to be from your bank or from eBay but which are sent by identity thieves who want your username and password. It's advisable to tick both boxes.

Don't give it away

Don't give your main email address to anyone, as you'll just end up getting tons of junk. For example, use a second Windows Live Hotmail address for signing up for less important online services.

5 MAKE IT SAFER Click on **Tools → Options → Security** and you'll see you can block potentially unsafe file attachments, images and other content from HTML emails. When a legitimate email comes in you can unblock the images by clicking **View → Blocked Images**.

Organize your life with Windows Calendar

With Windows Vista you can ensure you never miss another appointment. And you can organize the entire family, too

Windows Vista has been designed to sit at the center of your life and help you run it more smoothly, and what better way to do this than to include the most powerful calendar ever to grace a Windows operating system?

The Windows Calendar not only has everything required to organize your own life, it also enables you to share and update calendars with your friends, family or co-workers. To launch the Windows Calendar, click **Start → All Programs → Windows Calendar.**

At its heart – as you'd expect – is a flexible calendar. It enables you to view dates on a daily, weekly and monthly basis. The whole point being that you can add appointments and tasks with attached reminders. These help you organize your life; making sure you don't miss appointments, forget birthdays or generally get overwhelmed by life.

The program also supports multiple calendars so, if you want separate work and personal itineraries but want to access them from the same application, it's easy to create separate calendars and then choose whether to have them all visible or filter ones out.

It's also possible to have your calendars published for others to see, and to subscribe to online calendars. This could be as simple as a list of national

WE ARE LEGION Organize a busy household: the calendar supports multiple schedules

holidays, or it could be a friend's calendar detailing when they're on holiday or hosting a barbecue.

This feature can be really useful ➔

Make a date with Windows Calendar

Start to organize your life the easy Windows Vista way

1 FIRST STEPS The first time you run Windows Calendar you get a blank day. The left-hand panel shows the month view, available calendars – there should just be one, called Yourname's Calendar – and a blank task list.

2 MAKE A DATE To add an event, use the month view (top-left) to find the date you want, then double-click on the time in the main view. The right-hand panel provides additional options, such as reminders, recurring events and so on.

3 NAME THE DAYS It's a good idea to have different calendars for different things – work, personal, and so on. To change the name of a calendar; double-click on the calendar name in the left-hand panel and type in its new name.

4 ADD MORE Click **File → New Calendar** if you'd like to add another calendar to your set-up. Windows Calendar automatically color-codes it to differentiate it from your first calendar and save any potential confusion.

5 ADD ATTACK There's no limit to how many calendars you can add, so create as many as you like. The tick box next to each calendar on the list in the left-hand pane means that it's visible; unticking the box hides that calendar.

6 GROUP THEM If you have lots of calendars, it's a good idea to create a group. You can untick the group to hide all the calendars within that group. Click on **File → New Group** to create a group and then give it a sensible name.

7 DRAG DATES To put your calendars inside a group, drag them over the group name in the left-hand panel. In this example all work-related calendars – including podcasts, radio and books – have been put inside the Work group.

8 SEE IT ALL You don't have to stick with the Day view; if you want to see what you're supposed to be doing over a longer period, click on the **View** button to toggle between Day, Week, Work Week and Month views.

9 TACKLE TASKS Windows Calendar also enables you to create to-do lists. Click on **New Task** in the toolbar, give your task a name and use the right-hand panel to specify what calendar it relates to or add additional details.

10 SEND IT Not everyone is online all of the time, so you can email your calendar to friends and family as an ICS file, which they can import when they next download their mail, by clicking the **Share → Send via E-mail** menu.

11 ONLINE CALENDARS You can also subscribe to other calendars that have been published online – these could be from your friends and family, or general public calendars that list public holidays, for example.

12 MORE OPTIONS If you'd like to tweak and personalize Windows Calendar even further, you can click on **File → Options** to change the way the program handles reminders, tasks and appointments.

for future planning. If you have a large family it's possible to have everyone's calendars running. And, if you're planning a holiday with a group of friends or family members, you can see when everyone is free, because everyone's schedule is accessible to you.

Unlike normal calendars, Windows Calendar enables you to do much more than simply add appointments, dates and reminders. You can manage your tasks so that important jobs are completed to deadline. And you can share calendars with friends, relatives or colleagues, so that organizing every area of your life is easier. And using the program to its full potential couldn't be easier.

Once you've loaded your calendar you can make two types of entry: an

appointment or a task. Appointments are written in the traditional way; the tasks option enables you to create entries which are displayed in a list. To make a new task, just click the shortcut on the toolbar, and a form is displayed for you to enter the relevant information. You can change the priority, deadlines, which calendar it should appear on, and add notes. When the task is completed, just tick it off the list.

To add an appointment, navigate to the correct date, as if you were using a diary, and click **New Appointment**. You can then drag your appointment block to the correct start time, and expand it if necessary. Any other appointments that coincide appear on the right-hand side of the window, so spotting clashes is easy.

Compatible calendars

While Windows Calendar makes it easy to organize yourself, it's also very simple to bring others into the equation. You can share your calendars with friends, family and co-workers, making it easier to synchronize what you're doing.

The beauty of Windows Calendar is that it also provides support for other iCalendar programs (the standard for calendar information exchange), enabling you to use your operating system as your calendar, instead of using different types

of software. You can do this by exporting your previous calendar into a file, or by subscribing if you're currently using a web-based service. To import a file, go to **File → Import** and browse to the location of the .ics file. If your current calendar provider only posts from a web address, click **Subscribe** on the toolbar, and copy and paste the address from your other calendar service.

Windows Calendar enables you to have multiple calendars running, giving you ultimate control over your busy life. Once you have imported your social and work calendars, you can keep them on show or dismiss them by checking the boxes in the left-hand pane.

GO ONLINE If you're on the move a lot, export your calendar to Windows Live Calendar

Share your schedule with others

Publish your calendar for others to view in a number of ways...

1 SAVE To save your calendar as a file, select it from the list, click on **File → Export**. You can then email it, blog it or share it using Windows Live SkyDrive; it won't automatically update though.

2 PUBLISH To share calendars online, publish to a network folder or web location. To use the web, you need an address from your ISP. Once you have it, right-click the calendar, select **Publish**.

3 AUTO UPDATE If you're publishing to the web, copy the address here (or use the browse function to find it). Check **Automatically publish changes made to this calendar** to keep it up to date.

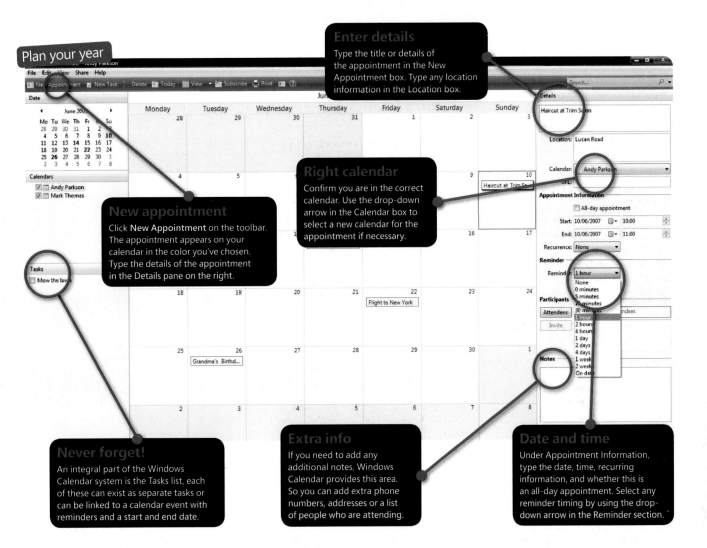

Plan your year

Enter details
Type the title or details of the appointment in the New Appointment box. Type any location information in the Location box.

Right calendar
Confirm you are in the correct calendar. Use the drop-down arrow in the Calendar box to select a new calendar for the appointment if necessary.

New appointment
Click **New Appointment** on the toolbar. The appointment appears on your calendar in the color you've chosen. Type the details of the appointment in the Details pane on the right.

Never forget!
An integral part of the Windows Calendar system is the Tasks list, each of these can exist as separate tasks or can be linked to a calendar event with reminders and a start and end date.

Extra info
If you need to add any additional notes, Windows Calendar provides this area. So you can add extra phone numbers, addresses or a list of people who are attending.

Date and time
Under Appointment Information, type the date, time, recurring information, and whether this is an all-day appointment. Select any reminder timing by using the drop-down arrow in the Reminder section.

Compare dates with friends or colleagues
Subscribe to a calendar to make arrangements easy

1 SUBSCRIBE If you want someone else's calendar to appear with yours, click the **Subscribe** button. If they've uploaded theirs to a web address, paste the address in to add their life to yours.

2 ICS FILE Alternatively, your friends or colleagues can export their calendar to an ICS file (the standard for most on/offline calendar programs); they can then email this or post it on the network.

3 UPDATES In Windows Calendar go to **File → Import** and find the .ics file. When located, the information is automatically updated to your calendars and you can compare dates.

Getting the most from Windows Contacts

Keep all your important numbers and email addresses stored in this easy-to-access folder

Contact management is an increasingly important element of modern life. With email messages and mobile phone calls as primary forms of communication, it's essential to keep up to date with all your work and social contacts.

Windows Vista takes a huge departure from Windows XP in terms of how to use and access contact information. The Windows Address book is no more; instead, Windows Contacts is a folder on your PC that makes storing details easy.

You access Windows Contacts from within Windows Mail by clicking **Tools → Windows Contacts**, or you can launch it

from the Start Menu by going to **Start → All Programs → Windows Contacts**.

The new look and way of accessing Windows Contacts makes for a far more logical experience and one that, thanks to the new Internet Explorer design, can be accessed at any point.

Even though the facility is firmly integrated into Windows Vista, that doesn't mean functions have been lost. It's still more than possible to import and export contacts using a variety of programs, in a variety of different formats; particularly useful if you need to hold contact data in various different places – it's no fun having to re-enter information you already have logged.

Of course, when it comes to finding contacts, you simply tap in the name of the person you're after and let Windows Vista Search do the work for you.

EASY EXPORT You can share contact details, even if your friends don't have Windows Vista

Manage your contacts with ease

Import, organize and communicate with those all-important people

1 NO ONE HOME If you've upgraded from Windows XP then Windows Contacts will automatically import your old address book. However, if you did a clean install you'll find a blank slate like the one shown here.

2 EASY IMPORT If you've got contact data stored in another program, Windows Contact enables you to import it easily and quickly. Just click on the **Import** button in the toolbar and choose the appropriate option.

3 QUICK ADD There are no contacts to import in this example, so they'll need to be entered manually instead. To add a new contact, just click on **New Contact** in the toolbar and you'll see the tabbed dialog box shown here.

4 ENTER THE INFO If you've got a picture of the contact, you can add it to their entry by clicking on the arrow underneath their picture. There are a number of fields here, but if you don't know all the details it's not a problem.

5 ALTERNATIVE EMAIL More than one email address? No problem, just add the email addresses to your contact's details and then click the **Set Preferred** button (bottom right of the dialog box) to choose the one you'll use most often.

6 MORE DETAILS Use the tabs to add any additional information, such as your contact's home or work address, notes, birthdays and so on, then click **OK** to return to Windows Contacts. Your new contact should appear in the list.

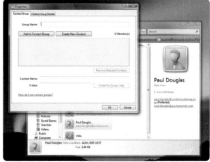

7 EASY ACCESS When you've added a contact, clicking on it displays the details in the right-hand panel. The email addresses are links; clicking on an address will launch Windows Mail with a new blank message to that address.

8 ORGANIZE YOUR INFO Windows Contacts can also manage groups. This comes in handy if you need to send the same information to several people. It's also useful for reminding you who certain people are!

9 COME TOGETHER Click on **Create Contact Group**, then **Add to Contact Group**. Highlight the contacts you want to add to your group by holding down the [Ctrl] key and clicking on the contacts. Click **Add t**o continue.

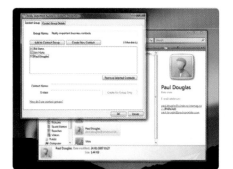

10 EVERYONE'S ADDED The names of your chosen contacts should now appear in the middle of the dialog box. Give your group a meaningful name (for example, a work-based name or a sports club name), then click on **OK**.

11 SEE THE RESULTS Your new group should appear in your contacts list, and as you can see it has a different icon for easy identification. If you want to email everyone in a group, just right-click and select **Action ➜ Send Email**.

12 CHANGE THE LOOK As with other folders in Windows Vista you can use the **Views** button to change the way contacts are displayed. This screen shows large icons, but you can see contacts as a list, a details view or as small tiles.

Enjoy better browsing with Windows Vista

Equipped with Internet Explorer 7 and its suite of applications, Windows Vista provides a fast and safe online experience

When Windows 95 first appeared, nobody knew how important the internet would become. It had been around for a few years but expensive call charges, slow modem access and complicated software meant it was hardly a 'readily available' service. The 2001 launch of Windows XP improved the software side of things with easier networking and a better web browser, but the internet itself was still slow and expensive. Then broadband came along, absolutely slashing the cost of getting online and boosting connection speeds.

Broadband changed everything. While downloading songs had taken the best part of an hour, broadband could download entire albums in a

matter of minutes. Before, online video had struggled to offer anything bigger than a postage stamp; with broadband we could suddenly enjoy crystal-clear, decent-sized movie clips. And while previously we'd only stayed connected for a few minutes at a time, we could stay constantly connected – which unfortunately meant that virus writers, malware creators and malicious hackers could attack our PCs 24 hours a day...

The internet became a dangerous place and, by 2006, if you connected your PC to the internet without first stuffing it with security software you could expect it to become infected within minutes. It's no longer enough

for your web browser to be useful – it needs to be as secure as Fort Knox, too. Luckily, with Windows Vista, it is.

Feel secure

Windows Vista comes with a brand-new browser, Windows Internet Explorer 7. In addition to its characteristic bright, fresh look and excellent features, it's also the safest version of Internet Explorer that Microsoft has ever created. That's partly because of Windows Vista itself, which is considerably more secure than any Windows platform in the past, but it's also because Internet Explorer 7 has been built with security as its priority. Now you can browse with confidence.

In real life...
Better browsing

James Stables, Reviews Editor
The new Internet Explorer can take some getting used to – the radical new interface is quite a departure. However, it is well worth persisting with as the new tabbed browsing is a revelation to use. It's rare that you browse just a single site; using online applications, conducting research or reading the news is made far easier as different pages can be contained within one window.

MOVE IT In Internet Explorer 7 the menu bar is now on the right-hand side

Explore the web with Internet Explorer 7

Windows Vista packs the latest in browser technology

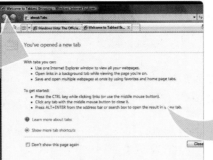

1 HIT THE BAR If you know the address of a site, enter it in the address bar. Alternatively, carry out a Windows Live search. But what's that gray box by the *Windows Vista: The Official Magazine* logo on the toolbar? Click it and see...

2 TAB-TASTIC Welcome to the best thing about Internet Explorer 7: tabbed browsing. If you want to open several sites simultaneously you don't need a separate window for each one; you can run tabs in a single window.

3 TONS OF TABS Here's how things look when you've opened multiple sites in tabs. To see another tab, just click on it. Alternatively, use keyboard commands (check out www.microsoft.com/windows/products/winfamily/ie/quickref.mspx).

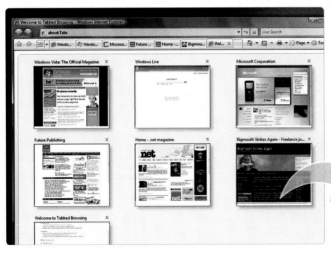

If you want to open several sites at once you no longer need to have a separate window for each one

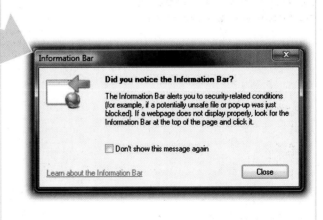

4 QUICK TABS On the left you'll see a button with four squares on it: the Quick Tabs button. Click on the arrow to the right of it to get a list of currently opened tabs. Click on the button itself and you'll see each open tab shown as a thumbnail; this makes it easy to see what's open.

Internet Explorer 8

The web is constantly evolving and so Microsoft is constantly striving to improve and enhance your browsing experience. A beta version of Internet Explorer 8 is now available from www.microsoft.com.

5 BLOCKED POP-UP At the top of the screen the Information Bar tells you Internet Explorer 7 has blocked a pop-up. It also displays a dialog box drawing your attention to the Information Bar. If you click **Don't show this message again** you'll still get the bar but not the dialog box.

CHAPTER 10 WINDOWS APPLICATIONS

Tailor your internet connection

There are further options available in Internet Explorer's tab system

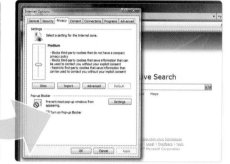

1 GENERAL KNOWLEDGE In the General tab, you can set not just one home page but multiple ones by adding several addresses in the Home Page box. When you launch Windows Internet Explorer these sites will open in tabs.

2 SOLID SECURITY The Security settings are stricter than previous versions of Internet Explorer, and there's a tick box for Protected Mode. Add trusted sites to the Trusted Sites list, which reduces the security level only for those sites.

3 PROTECTING PRIVACY By default, the Privacy tab blocks cookies from sites other than the one you're visiting. As with the security tab you can go for a higher security level and use the Sites button to add the addresses of sites you trust.

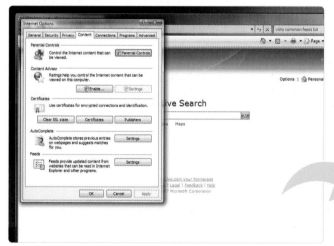

By default, the Privacy tab blocks cookies from sites other than the one you're currently visiting

4 CONTROL CONTENT The Content tab enables you to set Parental Controls to stop your children from seeing unsuitable sites, and you can also enable the Content Advisor to block sites that don't have specific age ratings or which contain particular kinds of content.

Getting tooled up

Enhance your browsing experience even further by downloading the Microsoft Live Toolbar from get.live.com/toolbar/overview, providing shortcuts to your favorite search, news and much more!

5 ADVANCED OPTIONS In the Advanced tab you can disable or enable pretty much any element, from text size to the way Internet Explorer deals with secure web sites. This section is very much for power users; for most of us the general, security, privacy and content tabs suffice.

Get internet feeds delivered

Don't waste time trawling internet news sites, you can get all the top stories to come to you

When the internet first came to mainstream attention, it was quickly monickered the 'information superhighway'. Well, now that superhighway can deliver its cargo of information to your door in handy streamlined form.

If you want to keep on top of news stories and new products, but don't have the time to trawl the internet for every latest bit of information published, web feeds are the answer. Originally named (and still often referred to as) RSS feeds, these news services are now more often called web feeds or news feeds. Web feeds enable you to take headlines from hundreds of sites and collect them in one handy place, so you can browse

through your favorite news or information sources in a matter of minutes. Instead of wasting time trawling through a number of news web sites at different times of the day, you simply choose the providers you want, set them up, and then receive an alert whenever a new story is posted.

Your feeds can be integrated into Internet Explorer 7, Microsoft Office Outlook 2007 and Live.com, collating your news in one place. A huge number of sites are offering feed options, such as www.cnn.com, YouTube and, of course, www.windowsvistamagazine.com.

The explosion of user-based blog content has revolutionized the way we get our news, and has triggered an abundance of community sites, such as

Digg.com. Initially, this explosion actually made things more difficult for people to keep abreast of breaking news, as even the major news organizations played second fiddle to the blogs. But now more people are using feeds to their advantage, by taking news straight from blogs and niche sites rather than traditional sources. This is great for 'news addicts' who love to be the first to know any juicy gossip or kept informed of the latest headlines.

Feed me now

There are hundreds of web-based feed readers on the internet, but Internet Explorer 7 enables you to integrate your favorite feeds with your day-to-day activity, so there's no time wasting. ➡

"Wow" Windows Media Center RSS feeds

Read news items from any RSS feed on your Windows Media Center TV. See the three-step tutorial on page 127 to find out how

Set up your web feeds in five minutes
Get your news in Office Outlook 2007 and Internet Explorer 7

1 GETTING STARTED Check that your chosen site (eg, www.windowsvista magazine.com) publishes a feed. If it does there will be an orange icon on the toolbar. Click this to add it to your feeds.

2 SUBSCRIBE When you click the icon a screen will appear with the stories listed, so you can check it's the right feed. Click **Subscribe to this feed** and it will be added to the Favorites list.

3 VIEW Click the **Favorites** icon, represented by a star. A submenu called Feeds will show a list of services you've subscribed to. Each set of headlines can be viewed easily.

In real life...
The RSS advantage

Alun Rogers, Technical Director at Risual, specialist in security, management and infrastructure solutions

While RSS means new ways of subscribing to content, it may become a new way for viruses and spyware to spread. Windows Vista and Internet Explorer 7 defend against this on two counts:

■ Malicious code embedded in a RSS news item is disabled by sanitizing all scripts in the feed, and all feeds are handled in the restricted internet zone – the most secure setting for Internet Explorer. So anything dangerous doesn't get a chance to install itself.

■ Potentially dangerous attachment types, such as programs or scripts, are blocked. The only way to install is if you allow it – make sure you know what it is before clicking **Allow**.

Adding feeds is simplicity itself. When you visit a site, check that the feed symbol in the toolbar of Internet Explorer is orange (if it's gray there is no feed option). If it is orange, click on the icon to add that particular feed to your Favorites list, which now includes a dedicated web feed section. The feeds will also be automatically updated in Outlook 2007.

top stories and headlines are then beamed straight to your desktop.

You can also download gadgets for specific news sites. These enable you to get all the news that is really important to you. You will also find that all the major news services offer gadgets that will deliver breaking news direct to your sidebar, meaning you'll never miss an important story.

The benefit of using your email program to view feeds is that it gives you the unique ability to treat stories like emails

The benefit of using your email program to view feeds is that it gives you the unique ability to treat individual stories like emails. You can sort feeds day by day, so you can see how old a story is. There are many options; you can also group reports together, save them to your inbox and send them on to other people.

Windows Vista has Sidebar gadgets that enable you to find feeds that you've subscribed to in Internet Explorer or Outlook. Go to the Options menu for the gadget and choose from the list of feeds; the

Finally, if you use Live.com, you can integrate feeds directly on to the page. This means when you log on to your home page – usually the first venture of the day – all your feeds will be listed in front of you. How's that for convenience?

Feeds are often centered on news, but loads of other organizations are successfully using feeds as an effortless way of reaching and informing people, such as parcel delivery services or real estate agents. Set up a few different feeds today and see how much time you could save. ⊞

Get the news you want to read
Stay up-to-date by getting feeds from your favorite sites

1 ADD STUFF If you use Live.com as your home page, you can add different feeds, so when you first log on, the top five stories are listed. Click **Add Stuff** to make changes to your page.

2 SEARCH On the Add Stuff page you can scroll through news pages and add main provider feeds. If a feed is less mainstream, click **Advanced options** to use the Feeds search in Live search.

3 TIME SAVER Click on a link to add it to your Windows Live home page. The top five headlines will now appear every time you load up your home page, saving you stacks of valuable time.

1 Digg it!

The Digg gadget feeds all the hottest topics straight to your desktop. The benefit of Digg is that it will provide a vastly different set of stories to traditional news sources, and your feed is guaranteed to inform and entertain you all day.

46 diggs	Tumor V. Pot... Governmen
52 diggs	Girl finds missing dog's
53 diggs	The Office - Dwight's Spe
551 diggs	Turn google into your own
78 diggs	Family: Brad Delp, Lead S

Reload
Thu Mar 15 18:21:04 UTC 2007

Reading...
Reload
Got Bad Data From Dig
Got Bad Data From Dig
Got Bad Data From D
Got Bad Data From D
Got Bad Data From Digg
Got Bad Data From Digg
Got Bad Data From Digg
Got Bad Data From Digg
Got Bad Data From Digg

2 Local news

A host of different types of news stories and general information are available through different Sidebar gadgets, this MSN one provides local gas prices direct to your desktop. If you wanted an example of the way the internet is revolutionizing news, this is it.

msn.
Lowest: $2.96⁹
Average: $3.16⁹
Highest: $3.49⁹

Station/Brand	Address	Unleaded	Plus	Premium	Diesel
GETTY MOBIL FRIENDLY SERVI	3205 HUDSON AVE UNION CITY, NJ 07087	$2.989 03/11/08	N/A	N/A	N/A
HESS HENDERSON 30503	590 LUIS MUNOZ MARIN BLVD JERSEY CITY, NJ 07310	$2.979 03/11/08	$3.119 03/10/08	$3.239 03/11/08	N/A
Hess HOBOKEN 30504	1400 WILLOW AVE Hoboken, NJ 07030	$2.979 03/11/08	N/A	$3.179 03/11/08	N/A
SUNOCO SUNOCO SRVC STATION	1301 WILLOW AVE HOBOKEN, NJ 07030	$2.979 03/10/08	N/A	N/A	N/A
Hess WEEHAWKEN	612 BOULEVARD E Weehawken, NJ 07086	$2.979 03/11/08	$3.079 03/11/08	$3.179 03/10/08	$3.799 03/11/08
GULF KEVORK KILEDJIAN	2715 KENNEDY BLVD NORTH BERGEN, NJ 07047	$2.989 03/11/08	N/A	N/A	N/A
Hess UNION CITY	3900 KENNEDY BLVD Union City, NJ 07087	$2.989 03/11/08	N/A	N/A	N/A
BP BP ACA 00644	1400 PARK AVE HOBOKEN, NJ 07030	$2.989 03/11/08	N/A	N/A 03/11/08	N/A
BP	815 8TH ST UNION CITY, NJ	$2.9	N/A	$3.239	N/A

msn.
Lowest: $2.96⁹
Average: $3.16⁹
Highest: $3.49⁹

Black puns face dogg...

Tourists hijacked in C...

Restore an old ver...

Top tips for worki...

▲ 49-52 ▼

3 Windows Vista

The feed viewer that comes with Windows Vista can be adapted to include any feed received by Internet Explorer. Simply add feeds in the usual way, then in the Options menu of the gadget, choose the feed from the list. You also can decide how many stories are fed at a time.

Networking know-...
Windows ...   Wed Mar
The art of animation
Windows ... Tue Mar 13
Windows Live One...
Windows ... Tue Mar 13
Keep all your files ...
Windows ...   Mon Mar
▲ 5-8 ▼

View feeds in Windows Media Center
Get news alongside your music, video, picture and television content

1 INSTALL Visit http://vistamcrssreader.oabsoftware.nl and install Windows Vista RSS Reader; this will be added to **Accessories** in Media Center. Sign up for the activation code, and enter it.

2 FEED ME NEWS All the feeds you've added in Internet Explorer will be listed in Media Center. Choose a feed and, from the headlines, choose a story. The synopsis will show in your viewer.

3 READ IN FULL To view a story's full text, click **Show page**. Media Center will say the content is not suitable for viewing, but click **Show anyway** and you can view the page in all its glory.

Protect your ID with Windows CardSpace

With identity theft and credit card fraud increasingly common, Microsoft has come up with a safe way to work online

It's a pain in the neck entering the same data again and again in web sites, but these days it's a necessary evil. If you've stored your personal details on your computer, it's possible that someone else could intercept it and abuse it.

However, Windows CardSpace may have the answer. That's because it stores the sort of information you'll use again and again in a way that combines ease of use with rock-solid security.

In some ways Windows CardSpace works in a similar way to Internet Explorer's AutoFill, which you can use to automatically add your details to online forms, but the big difference between AutoFill and Windows

CardSpace is that the former doesn't do anything to protect your details while the latter wraps your personal profile in secure devices. As you'll see, creating cards in Windows CardSpace is easy, and the cards themselves are well protected. But how do you actually go about using them?

When you visit a CardSpace-enabled site you'll see the option to log in via Windows CardSpace, and if you choose that option, CardSpace will launch in a safe environment – the rest of your Windows Vista desktop will be faded out – and tell you about the site you're visiting. You'll then be able to choose which card you want to use to log into the site, and you can be confident that the whole process is safe and secure.

With the financial world being such a cautious place of late, CardSpace is currently only being used in a widespread way at one place – at the Microsoft Live Login. If you visit https://

ID PROTECTION Click on **Start → Control Panel → User Accounts and Family Safety → Windows CardSpace**

Storing details in Windows CardSpace

Join today and beat identity criminals by protecting yourself while online

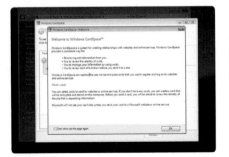

1 SAFE AND SOUND Windows CardSpace essentially halts the rest of your PC. The rest of Windows Vista fades into the background, so there's no risk of your activities being intercepted.

2 ADD A CARD Click **OK** on the welcome and you'll see the main screen, as shown here. To create a new card, click on **Add a Card** then click **Add** at the bottom of the dialog box.

3 PICK A CARD You have a choice: create a personal card with basic info, or install a Managed Card you've been given. This example is for the personal option; click **Create a Personal Card**.

login.live.com/beta/managecards.srf, you will be able to create and manage an Information Card to log in to your MSN Live account. This is a great way to draft up your first real Information Card – while test sites are useful, they're no substitute for a real-world application.

While CardSpace may not be in widespread use just yet, you'll find that most big firms are holding on until everyone's upgraded to Windows Vista, at which point supporting CardSpace software will make sound financial sense. So will CardSpace become common? It should do; it's a clever system that makes filling out online forms much easier while keeping your personal details safe.

In real life...
Validation technology

Simon Arblaster, Disc Editor, *Windows Vista: The Official Magazine*

Much like the real world, the internet is full of good and bad people. Most are law-abiding 'netizens' who are happy enough discovering the wonders of the online world. However, some less well minded folks aren't. And, just as you wouldn't go waving your credit card details around for all and sundry to see, the same goes while you're online.

The problem with the internet is that it's this huge collection of computers all working together to pass information around the world. Very clever, but it means at any stage one of those computers could decide to take a look at the information passing by and that could be your debit or credit card details.

Thankfully, some very clever people have solved the problem. It's called Extended Validation SSL and it's a technology embedded inside Windows Vista. This advanced technology guarantees that information being passed between your computer and the legitimate destination computer can only be read by that destination computer. If a system somewhere in-between tries to read the data all it will get is a bundle of garbled rubbish.

If you're planning on sending information to a web site, look for the padlock symbol at the end of the address bar. This means the site is using encryption to protect your data. If the symbol is not there then don't send the information.

PADLOCK If you're about to hand over your details online, make sure this icon is visible

---

4 ENTER THE INFO Enter the data you want stored. You can add as much or as little information to your card as you like, and you can replace the default image with a picture from your hard disk.

5 MULTI CARDS Once the info's in, you return to the main screen. You can create multiple cards, and when available you'll be able to get Managed Cards from firms such as credit card companies.

6 EXTRA To see the contents of your card, click **Preview**; in the top right of the dialog box you'll see an option to lock your card. This adds extra protection by asking you to enter a PIN.

Taking your PC out and about

The whole world's going mobile – and Windows Vista is the way to get the best out of your laptop

There was a time when if you wanted sheer power you'd buy a desktop, and if you wanted portability – and had a great deal of money to spare – you'd buy a laptop. However, in recent years that has all changed. Laptop prices have plummeted while at the same time their power has increased so, as a result, many people are now buying laptops as desktop replacements. In fact, by late 2006, laptops were outselling desktops by a significant margin.

Performance v portability

These days, there are two main kinds of laptop buyer. Those who want a laptop solely for home or office use don't need to worry about battery life as their machines will generally be plugged into a wall socket. To these guys, it's performance that matters. Mobile users, on the other hand, need to squeeze as much life out of their batteries as they possibly can – a tough challenge when they too need their PCs to perform at a high standard, often while using power-draining wireless networking.

Versatile Windows Vista

With Windows Vista, Microsoft needed to provide features for both kinds of laptop user. But that's not all. Home and office users occasionally take their laptops out and about, while mobile users often use their laptops at home or in the office, so Windows Vista needs to

be flexible enough to deliver maximum performance when a laptop's plugged in and still provide maximum portability when it's on the move. As if that wasn't challenging enough, tablet PCs complicate things even further. Twist a tablet's screen this way and it's a standard laptop; twist it that way and it's a touch-sensitive screen that uses handwriting recognition instead of a keyboard, and a stylus instead of a mouse. Then there's the Pocket PC, which ditches the keyboard altogether, shrinks a tablet PC to the size of a hardback book and is as likely to be used on a sofa as in a roadside café.

Windows Vista has to satisfy all of these demands – and here you'll discover that it does so very well indeed. ⊞

"Wow" On in an instant

Windows Vista takes advantage of new hardware-based low-power modes. This means that when you 'shut down' a PC it's actually in a low-power state, so it can spring back to life in seconds

Introducing the Windows Mobility Center

Memorize this shortcut, because it's your new best friend...

1 INSTANT INFO Press the **Windows** key and **X** and the Windows Mobility Center pops up. It's a dashboard for various mobile system settings. Here, the battery's charging and Wi-Fi is on.

2 QUICK CHANGE The Battery section enables you to switch between power management schemes – handy if you've been running in power-saving mode but need a quick burst of power.

3 MISSION CONTROL Click specific icons to go the appropriate Control Panel section. Here the battery icon has been selected, going to **Control Panel ➜ Hardware and Sound ➜ Power Options**.

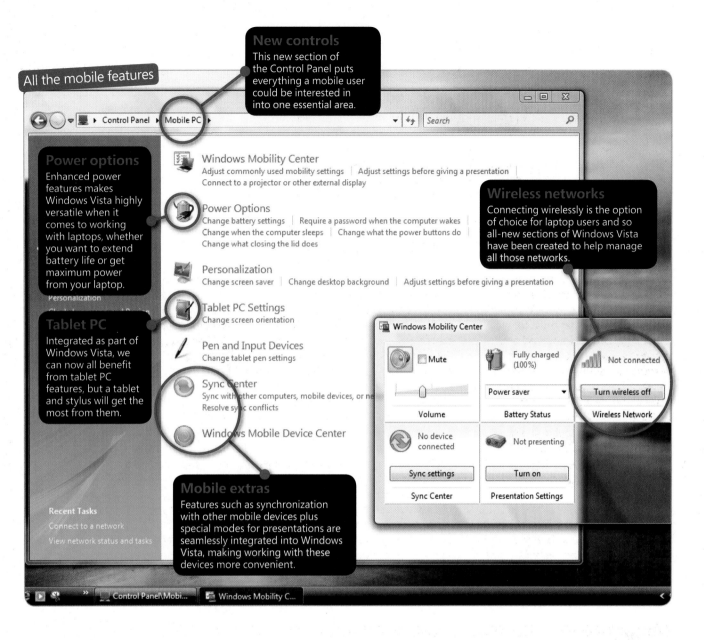

All the mobile features

New controls
This new section of the Control Panel puts everything a mobile user could be interested in into one essential area.

Control Panel ▸ Mobile PC ▸ | Search

Power options
Enhanced power features makes Windows Vista highly versatile when it comes to working with laptops, whether you want to extend battery life or get maximum power from your laptop.

Windows Mobility Center
Adjust commonly used mobility settings | Adjust settings before giving a presentation
Connect to a projector or other external display

Power Options
Change battery settings | Require a password when the computer wakes
Change when the computer sleeps | Change what the power buttons do
Change what closing the lid does

Wireless networks
Connecting wirelessly is the option of choice for laptop users and so all-new sections of Windows Vista have been created to help manage all those networks.

Personalization
Change screen saver | Change desktop background | Adjust settings before giving a presentation

Tablet PC
Integrated as part of Windows Vista, we can now all benefit from tablet PC features, but a tablet and stylus will get the most from them.

Tablet PC Settings
Change screen orientation

Pen and Input Devices
Change tablet pen settings

Sync Center
Sync with other computers, mobile devices, or ne
Resolve sync conflicts

Windows Mobile Device Center

Recent Tasks
Connect to a network
View network status and tasks

Mobile extras
Features such as synchronization with other mobile devices plus special modes for presentations are seamlessly integrated into Windows Vista, making working with these devices more convenient.

Windows Mobility Center panel: Mute — Volume; Fully charged (100%), Power saver — Battery Status; Not connected, Turn wireless off — Wireless Network; No device connected, Sync settings — Sync Center; Not presenting, Turn on — Presentation Settings

Control Panel\Mobi... | Windows Mobility C...

4 WHICH WIRELESS? Clicking on the wireless network icon opens the Connect to a Network dialog box, which displays any wireless networks nearby that you could connect to.

5 MONITOR MONITORS The display icon launches the Display Settings dialog box, which enables you to control any external displays that you have connected to your computer.

6 PERFECT PRESENTATION Presentation Settings gives you options such as turning off the screen saver so it won't cut in mid-slide, and turning the volume down or off.

Battery power to the people

Improving your battery life so you can work for longer on the move isn't as hard as you might think

Windows Vista has three pre-set power management modes: High Performance, Power Saver and Balanced. The first option delivers speed but eats battery power. The second squeezes out every drop of juice but can slow down your system. And the third tries to strike a balance between power and battery life. Here you can discover how to tweak these modes and take advantage of some clever power management features. While some are laptop and tablet PC-specific, many of the power management features are available on desktop PCs, too.

The biggest factor in battery life is the way you use your PC. As well as optimizing Windows Vista for battery power, if you want to prolong battery life you'll need to use your laptop slightly differently than when it's plugged into the wall. With mobile PCs, less is more: the less you expect your PC to do, the more life you'll get from its battery.

Power savers

So what do you need to think about? Accessing CDs or DVDs drains your battery more quickly than accessing your hard drive; processor-intensive tasks such as gaming drain your battery more quickly than word processing, and wireless communications such as Wi-Fi or Bluetooth have a bigger impact on battery life than wired connections.

Turn down the brightness of your screen – the brighter your display, the more power it's using – and unplug any external devices such as USB mice, keyboards or lava lamps.

What you do in Windows Vista makes a difference, too. If you want to get the longest possible battery life, it's a good idea to make sure you're not running any programs or eye candy that you don't need. For example, while animated backgrounds in the Ultimate edition look great, they're using processing power. Similarly, if you're not connected to the internet or to a network, temporarily disable security software such as anti-virus scanners (remembering to switch them back on again before you connect to anything) as they tend to churn away in the background, increasing the demands on your PC's processor.

"Wow" Power modes

Within the new Mobility Center there are power options that enable you to tailor how much 'juice' a laptop will use. This makes it easy to run at full speed or make that battery last and last

---

In real life...
Look after your battery and it'll look after you

Neil Mohr, Technical Editor
It may surprise you to know that the battery inside your laptop makes up a significant chunk of the computer's total cost. Look up replacement ones online and you'll see they can easily cost the best part of $200. So doesn't it make sense to look after them?

Almost all laptops come with a type of battery called Lithium Ion (Li-ion). This is a very high-capacity rechargeable battery. As with all rechargeable batteries it has a limited lifespan, typically lasting for around 1,000 charge cycles. However, certain conditions can reduce its lifespan, so they're worth knowing about – and avoiding. Firstly, Li-ion batteries do not like being stored fully charged. If you plan on not using your laptop for a long while then the general advice is to discharge the battery to around 40 per cent of its full charge. Secondly, if you're using a laptop that stays plugged into the mains for a long time it could be an idea to remove the battery from it completely – it won't need it while it's plugged in. Finally,

LIFESAVER Treat your battery well and it will reward you by lasting a lot longer

laptop batteries don't like high temperatures; if you're storing your laptop, make sure it's in a cool place away from direct sunlight.

Energy management in Windows Vista
How to get maximum performance for minimum power

1 POWER UP You can access the power management features in two ways – by clicking on the battery in Mobility Center, or by clicking **Start → Control Panel → Mobile PC → Power Options**.

2 PICK A PLAN There are three standard power management modes, or 'power plans'. At the left of the window is the option to **Choose what the power buttons do**: click on it.

3 BUTTON IT Here you can change the behavior of the power buttons and what happens when you close the lid. You can use different settings for either battery or plug-in power supply.

4 MORE SETTINGS Underneath each power plan you'll see a link that says **Change plan settings**. Here you can adjust the plans, and again have different settings for battery and mains power.

5 MORE POWER If you click on **Change advanced power settings** you can tweak all kinds of things. Next to each device you'll see a plus sign; click on it to see the available options for that device.

6 WHACK THE WI-FI Here are the settings for our wireless. It makes sense to go for Maximum Performance on mains power but Power Saving with batteries: Wi-Fi can be a power hog.

7 STOP SEARCHING Indexing your PC can have an effect on battery life, so use the Search and Indexing option to emphasize battery over performance and eke out more power from the battery.

8 DISPLAY DECISIONS Adaptive Display means Windows Vista can tell when you're reading rather than just away from your PC. In the Display section you can enable or disable this feature.

9 SAFE SHARING The Multimedia Settings enable you to change the way Windows Vista handles media sharing. Away mode enables your PC to share files while appearing to be off.

Discover the secrets of the tablet PC

Designed to make interacting without a mouse or keyboard a reality, now its features are available to all

If you twist a tablet PC's screen one way it's a normal laptop – but twist it the other way to use its touch-sensitive screen and you can enter text via handwriting recognition. The Control Panel's Mobile PC options have a dedicated section for tablet PC users, which should please everyone that likes to make use of their stylus and expensive touchscreen.

Introduced back in 2002, Windows XP Tablet PC Edition brought the ease of use of tablet PCs to all users. With the introduction of Windows Vista, people using the Home Premium and Ultimate editions can also take advantage of its

useful features, which hinge around natural input based on both handwriting and voice recognition.

Strike the right note

Tablet PCs come into their own with note taking, as you can treat the folded-back screen as a giant pad of paper; make handwritten notes, doodle, scrawl diagrams and flip page after page. When you're back in the office after the meeting or note-taking exercise, you're able to review the notes, convert written words to text, save images as diagrams and generally reorganize your rampant scrawling into a useful form, fit for consumption by others.

FLEXIBLE FRIEND Most tablets are convertible, so they can be used as normal laptops, too

In the past, many people envisioned these would use a 'slate' style design. However, most tablet PCs today take the 'convertible' approach. This makes sense as you can either use it as a traditional laptop or rotate and fold back the screen on itself for tablet PC work. This increases their usefulness, as sometimes straightforward data entry via the keyboard is the fastest way of working while at other times an electronic notepad is the most convenient.

Tweaking your tablet

Make life with a tablet more fun with these handy tweaks

1 TWEAK YOUR TABLET If you're using a tablet PC, you'll already have spotted the **Tablet PC Settings** link in Control Panel's Mobile PC section. Click on the link now to find out all about the various options.

2 PICK A HAND The General tab enables you to choose whether you're left- or right-handed, and Windows Vista will display on-screen menus accordingly (to the left if you're right-handed, and vice versa).

3 GET IT WRITE Handwriting Recognition enables you to turn the automatic learning feature on or off (only available on genuine tablet PCs). This constantly analyzes your handwriting to improve recognition.

4 ORIENT EXPRESS The Display tab enables you to change your display's orientation – so you can make your tablet default to Landscape or Portrait. And use the Sequence button to change how your Rotate Screen button behaves.

5 ORDER ORDER Click **Sequence** to see the order in which the Rotate Screen button will change the display. By default it's primary landscape, secondary portrait, secondary landscape then primary portrait – rotating 90 degrees each time.

6 PEN AND TELL-ER Close the Tablet PC settings dialog box and you return to Mobile PC in the Control Panel. Click on **Pen and Input Devices** to configure the way Windows Vista handles your tablet PC's pen input.

7 FIX FEEDBACK Windows Vista gives visual feedback according to the way you tap the screen – a small circle for a single tap, a double circle for a double tap. You can disable any of these by unchecking the relevant box.

8 SEE A FLICK Flicks are gestures that make Windows Vista do something. By default, you can navigate by flicking the pen across the screen, but click on **Navigational Flicks and Editing Flicks** to make them even more useful.

9 CHANGE THE FLICKS Clicking the button changes the picture on the tab; in addition to standard navigation Flicks, you've got four editing Flicks. You can stick with the defaults if you like, but to change them click on **Customize**.

10 NEW TRICKS The Customize Flicks dialog box appears, with a drop-down list next to each available Flick showing the default options. You can change them by clicking on the arrow at the end of the appropriate drop-down.

11 EASY ADDITION Adding your own Flicks is easy as pie. For example, if you wanted the vertical upwards Flick to launch Windows Mobility Center you'd click on its drop-down, choose **Add**, give it a name and then click on the **Keys** field. Press the **Windows** key and **X** (the shortcut for Mobility Center), then click on **Save** and your new Flick will be available.

Save time on the move

Windows Mobile Device Center can help organise your life and save you valuable time. We show you how to make it happen

Today our lives are jam-packed with work, family and social commitments. Everyone's looking for ways to speed up mundane tasks, and a great way to do this is with a Windows Mobile device, keeping information and files to hand while away from your computer. However, so much time can be wasted trying to synchronize the information held on your PC with a mobile device, that the chore of doing it can often outweigh the benefits.

The whole point of Windows Vista is to make life easier, and a new feature called Windows Mobile Device Center has been included so you can update your mobile device in less time than it takes to make a cup of coffee.

To get started simply plug your Windows Mobile device into your PC's USB port – or if you've got a Bluetooth connection for your PC you can synchronize your devices wirelessly.

Once connected, Windows Mobile Device Center will automatically appear and show a picture of your device; you'll then be presented with two options.

If you're connecting to a computer that you want to be synchronizing files with on a daily basis, select **Set up your device** as this will make a permanent

The whole point of Windows Vista is to make life easier

pairing between your PC and that specific device. However, if this is a one-off pairing, click **Connect without setting up your device**.

You'll then be given a list of the types of data that can be automatically synchronized with your device. If you use Microsoft Office Outlook, you can set it to automatically synchronize your inbox,

contacts, appointments and calendar, so wherever you are, you'll never be without that vital information.

Tweak to fit

These synchronization settings can be changed at any time by plugging in your device as usual and going to **Mobile Device Settings → Change content sync setting**. Check or uncheck each type of information to control whether it will be updated when the sync is complete. Most options also have a **Sync Settings** menu where elements can be tweaked.

With Windows Vista your devices don't have to be about work. Windows Mobile Device Center seamlessly links into Windows Media Player where it's easy to add music, pictures and videos to devices. Just drag and drop files into the sync pane on the right, click **Start Sync** and let Windows Vista do the rest. All that's left now is to enjoy that coffee – and your extra bit of free time.

Introducing Windows SideShow

Check out these tiny screens that have some very big ideas

When your PC's powered up it's capable of almost anything, but sometimes you don't need all that power – and booting your laptop just so you can look up a phone number or play an MP3 file seems like overkill. Enter Windows SideShow, which combines Windows Vista and PC hardware to make your computer even more useful.

SideShow-enabled devices have a second, external screen that runs Gadgets – little applications that get information from Windows Vista. For

example, you could use SideShow to look up addresses from your laptop without switching it on, or to check your email for new messages, or just to listen to some of your music. It's very clever and it isn't limited to computers, either; SideShow has also been designed to work on mobile phones and other portable devices. There's not very many about at the moment, but we'll see a number of SideShow-friendly devices – and in particular, lots of laptops – appearing in the near future.

ON THE SIDE SideShow enables you to gain instant access to the data on your device

Setting up your mobile device
How to create the perfect partnership

1 CONNECT Plug in your device via USB (or use Bluetooth to connect wirelessly) and Windows Mobile Device Center should recognize it and start up automatically. If it doesn't load, search for it in **Start Search** and open it manually.

2 PAIR UP When you first plug in your device you can choose whether or not to start a permanent partnership. If this is your main PC, choose **Set up your device** to save effort next time. You can delete the partnership later if you wish.

3 START SYNCING You will see a list of media types to synchronize. The items you choose will be updated each time you sync. If you want to use email, contacts and calendar synchronization you'll need Office Outlook.

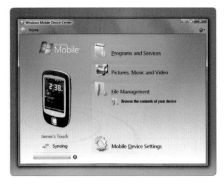

4 EXPLORE You can use Windows Mobile Device Center to peruse all the data on your phone. This allows you to add files manually to the device, or copy data from the phone to your hard drive using Windows Explorer.

5 MULTIMEDIA Setting up your mobile device doesn't have to be about emails and appointments. Mobile Device Center lets you set up pictures, music and video clips which you can easily export. Go to **Pictures, Music and Video → Add media from Windows Media Player.**

6 ON THE MOVE When you've got your work and media loaded you're ready to go out and start reaping the full rewards of Windows Mobile.

Ensure a smoother, faster PC system

Keeping your system in tip-top condition has never been so simple – with help from Windows Vista

A healthy system is a happy system, and a happy system is a fast system. Maintenance and performance go hand in hand, which is why you'll find tools for both in the System and Maintenance section of the Control Panel. In addition to the features you'd expect – cleaning up unnecessary files, tweaking your PC's display, getting rid of programs that start when Windows Vista does, adjusting the power management options and so on – you'll find some key new tools, too. There's the Windows Experience Index, which makes it easy to see how well your PC is performing, identify bottlenecks and decide whether your kit is powerful enough for particular programs; the Problem Reports and Solutions tool, which can identify and, where appropriate, fix software and drive problems; and the System Health Report, which gives your PC a check-up.

Two other key features are ReadyBoost and ReadyDrive. The former enables you to use cheap USB drives or memory cards to speed up your system, and the latter gets the best from next-generation hybrid hard drives.

Get experienced

There is a huge range of hardware on the market, such as memory, graphics cards, hard disks and processors... Obviously, the choice is great, but with so many different possible combinations you can never be entirely sure how a particular program will perform on your system – whether it'll have a positive effect on your PC's overall performance or a negative one. With previous versions of Windows the answer was 'Buy the program and hope for the best', but with Windows Vista you can see exactly what your PC is made of and where any bottlenecks might be.

The new Windows Experience Index can analyze your hardware to see what's speedy and what's slow. It calculates an overall score that tells you just how quick your PC is, and also calculates individual scores for components. This feature has two benefits –you can immediately see which components might be worth upgrading and, in future, when you're buying software, you can tell how it will perform on your PC. ⊞

Experience in action

Updating your Windows Experience Index score is easy

1 INDEXING Go to **Control Panel →** **System and Maintenance →** **Performance Information and Tools** to open the WEI. If anything has been changed recently, click **Update my score**.

2 BIG BASE You'll see a giant button with a number in it. This number is the overall score for your system. The bigger the number the faster your kit. The highest possible score is 5.9.

3 SUBSCORES Your base score is calculated from five crucial parts: processor, memory, graphics card, gaming graphics and hard disk. Click **View and Print details** for full details.

Memory
As you'd expect, Memory calculates a score based on the speed of your memory. The faster your RAM performs, the higher the score you'll get here.

Overall score
If you're mathematically minded you'll already have spotted that when the Windows Experience Index calculates your base score to reflect your overall system performance, it doesn't just add up the subscores and divide them by five. That's because your system's only as fast as the slowest component, so if you've got a cutting-edge graphics card and a blazingly fast processor but your RAM isn't up to the same standards, you'll get a lower base score than you might expect.

« Performance Information and Tools

Tasks
- Manage startup programs
- Adjust visual effects
- Adjust indexing options
- Adjust power settings
- Open Disk Cleanup
- Advanced tools

Rate and improve your computer's performance

Not sure where to start? Learn how you can improve your computer's performance.

Your computer has a Windows Experience Index base score of **3.2**

Component	What is rated	Subscore	Base score
Processor:	Calculations per second	4.7	
Memory (RAM):	Memory operations per second	4.5	
Graphics:	Desktop performance for Windows Aero	3.6	
Gaming graphics:	3D business and gaming graphics performance	3.2	**3.2** Determined by lowest subscore
Primary hard disk	Disk data transfer rate	5.7	

View and print details

Learn more about the scores online

View software for my base score online

Last rating: 30/01/2007 10:22:33

What do these numbers mean?

Update my score

Windows graphics
The graphics subscore shows how much horsepower your graphics card has for running Aero Glass. If your PC has an integrated graphics system you'll get a low score here – or Aero Glass may even be automatically disabled.

See also
- Security Center
- Problem Reports and Solutions

Hard drive
Last but not least, the WEI calculates a subscore based on your hard drive speed. The faster your hard disk can chuck data about, the faster you'll be able to access files, and slow hard disks are a common performance bottleneck, especially on laptops.

Gaming graphics
The gaming graphics entry is all about 3D, and the name's a bit misleading; while it does indeed check your system's 3D power, 3D isn't something that you only need for games. Some heavyweight business programs – particularly design ones – also use 3D.

In real life...
Pick your upgrades with the Windows Experience Index

James Stables,
Reviews Editor,
Windows Vista:
The Official Magazine

My cheap laptop was running slowly, so I used the Windows Experience Index to identify potential upgrades. The base score was 2.0, but the processor wasn't the problem as that got a subscore of 4.1. The hard disk was good, at 4.6, but things started to fall down with the integrated

graphics card, which scored 3.1 for gaming and just 2.4 for Aero Glass. I considered upgrading the graphics, but then noticed that the RAM was reporting a subscore of 2.0 – ah, so that's why the base score was so bad. A single upgrade would boost the Windows Experience Index score to 2.4, because then the graphics card would be the weakest link.

Basically, a subscore of around 2.0 means upgrading's a good idea.

If that's impractical, it's worth considering alternatives, such as disabling Aero Glass or, in the case of memory, using Windows ReadyBoost.

A subscore of 3.0 is OK, and an upgrade might not be worth the money. The exception is when the component in question is having an obvious effect on your system. For example, a graphics subscore of 3.0 is adequate for everyday PC use but might not be enough for gamers.

CHAPTER 12 SYSTEM TOOLS

Windows ReadyDrive and ReadyBoost

A new raft of flash-based technologies enables
Windows Vista to run faster and smoother than ever

The best thing about buying a new PC is booting into Windows for the first time. With no background applications to start you've barely time to put your hand on the keyboard after pressing the 'on' button before the desktop is there, ready and waiting to be used. A couple of months later, you can make a cup of coffee and a pancake and syrup breakfast in the time it takes to go from power-on to a usable desktop. It's frustrating, to say the least.

The key to faster boot times lies in improving hard drive speed, but even with a fast multi-core processor and lots of memory it can still take applications minutes rather than seconds to load.

The culprit is the magnetic hard drive. It's not all bad. This kind of drive is great for two reasons – first, it can store lots of information for not a lot of money;

secondly, hard drives can shift lots of bits of consecutive data around extremely quickly. Unfortunately, most of the time your hard drive is moving lots of small bits of information around, not giant consecutive chunks all in one go.

Mix and match

As well as having to electronically process a request for data, there's the time it takes the read head to move across the platter. This seek time is what slows hard drives down.

The next generation of hard drives will be hybrid drives. Instead of a small buffer of fast but volatile cache memory, they'll come with both magnetic platters and between 128MB and 1GB of non-volatile NAND-based flash memory. NAND memory has the opposite strengths and weaknesses of magnetic storage. Where magnetic disks struggle

with finding and transferring lots of small files simultaneously, solid-state memory copes with ease. On the other hand, due to relatively slow read/write speeds, flash memory isn't very good at burning large pieces of data in a hurry.

With only a small price premium planned, the advantages go far beyond the access speed of the flash memory. Because the magnetic part of the disk will only be used when writing large files or when the flash memory is full, a hybrid drive is in motion for less than a tenth of the time a normal hard drive is.

That's means it uses less power and should have a much longer lifespan. Because flash memory is non-volatile, though, boot files can be moved to this part of the disk during shutdown, ready for a lightning-fast boot. You can expect to shave 8-25 seconds off your start-up time with a hybrid drive.

The Windows Vista advantage

Windows Vista is hybrid hard drive friendly

There are two obvious downsides to hybrid drive technology. First, it's not actually here yet, because it's proved harder to implement than expected. Second, hybrid drives won't be compatible with older PCs. They'll need a revision to the current SATA interface, and they only work with Windows Vista. To take advantage of the flash part of the drive, Windows Vista has a new ReadyDrive feature

that works out how to obtain the best performance. The SuperFetch feature of Windows Vista, that pre-caches data, will be able to use the speed advantage of flash memory for an even bigger performance gain when task switching. Meanwhile, Windows Vista ReadyBoost, which can use USB drives as superfast page files, will be able to access hybrid drives with unused flash memory.

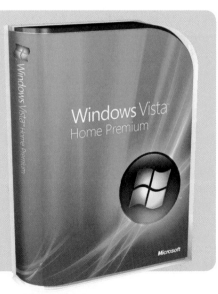

Speed up with Windows ReadyBoost

Use flash memory to give your PC instant zip

Lack of memory can be a big problem because hard disks are so much slower than memory chips. When you've filled your memory your PC starts using the hard drive instead, slowing things down. Adding RAM can be expensive, and there's only so much room. With ReadyBoost you can solve this problem by using flash memory, such as USB drives or memory cards, to add extra memory quickly, easily, and cheaply.

ReadyBoost is very clever, but before you start you need to make sure your USB drive or memory card is up to the job. You'll need a minimum of 256MB storage and a maximum of 4GB, and it needs to be capable of specific speeds: 2.5MB per second for random reads and 1.75MB per second for random writes. ReadyBoost will test your memory when you first plug it in and, if it's not up to scratch, ReadyBoost will refuse to use it.

The good news is that provided your memory card or USB drive meets the specs, ReadyBoost is simple to set up and makes a massive difference to your kit.

Q Isn't using flash memory slower than a hard disk?
A In terms of data transfer speeds, yes – but finding things on a flash memory device is much quicker than most hard disks, and it's the seek time rather than the data transfer speed that really matters here.

Q If I remove the memory card or USB drive, will it crash my PC?
A No. Everything ReadyBoost does is mirrored on your hard disk for that very eventuality, but as long as your memory is connected ReadyBoost will use it. If you unplug it, ReadyBoost just uses your hard disk instead. And you don't need to worry about privacy, either; ReadyBoost scrambles every bit of data that's stored on your memory card or USB drive.

Q How much memory do I need to have available my flash drives?
A Microsoft recommends a ratio of one to three times the amount of memory installed in your system. So,

for example, if you've got 512MB of installed RAM then you should consider a ReadyBoost drive of between 512MB and 1.5GB. There's little point in exceeding the recommended amount, as you'll get little noticeable benefit.

ReadyBoost really makes sense when your PC's suffering from inadequate memory – it's the perfect solution.

Q What's the difference between ReadyBoost and ReadyDrive?
A The same technology that powers ReadyBoost powers another performance feature in Windows Vista: ReadyDrive. Unlike ReadyBoost, though, chances are you can't take advantage of it yet. That's because ReadyDrive is designed for new hybrid drives, which combine traditional hard disks with flash memory and deliver faster performance, better reliability and, in laptops, longer battery life. However, while ReadyDrive means Windows Vista supports such devices, hybrid hard disks are only just beginning to appear.

Ready, steady, boost

Provided you have the right specs, ReadyBoost is simple to set up

1 NO GO Make sure to check the specs before buying; when you plug it in and choose ReadyBoost, Windows Vista checks it's up to scratch. If it's not, ReadyBoost will refuse to use it.

2 RIGHT SPECS Try again with a memory card at the required speed. When you plug it in you'll see the AutoPlay dialog shown here. Click **Speed Up My System** to enable ReadyBoost.

3 TURN IT ON Here's the ReadyBoost tab of the Removable Disk Properties dialog. Windows Vista works out the best amount of space for ReadyBoost, then click **Use This Device → OK**.

Top 10 speed boosts

Knowing what affects performance can help speed up an older system, or get more from the latest PC

An easy way to make your computer run more quickly is to remove unnecessary eye candy, and you can do this from the Performance Information and Tools dialog box. Make your PC feel quicker by disabling visual effects, so, for example, if you click the **Adjust for Best Performance** button Windows Vista will disable Aero Glass altogether. That's probably a bit dramatic, though, and you'll find that *disabling* the following display options will make your system seem speedier:

■ Animate controls and elements inside windows
■ Animate windows when minimizing and maximizing
■ Fade or slide menus into view
■ Fade or slide tooltips into view
■ Fade out menu items after clicking
■ Slide open combo boxes
■ Slide taskbar buttons

Search and destroy

The search system in Windows Vista is very handy, but the more files it's keeping an eye on, the more of an effect it's going to have on performance. If things are a little sluggish use the Adjust Indexing Options link. Use the Modify button to change the locations the Index keeps an eye on, and use the Advanced button to limit the list of files – for example, if you use your PC mainly for work, you could disable the indexing of non-work files such as images, media files, document templates, and so on.

The power management feature is another handy tool. Many desktops default to the Balanced power plan, and

LESS IS MORE It's easy to get more display performance by turning off fancy features

switching to High Performance results in a noticeable speed boost when running processor-intensive applications. But if even the High Performance mode isn't delivering as much speed as you'd like, click on **Change plan settings → Change advanced power settings**. You can now change settings such as maximum and minimum processor performance, whether indexing should favour energy efficiency or sheer speed, and so on.

The last link provides you with some additional performance tools; Task Manager, which shows you what programs and processes are running on your PC, and Disk Defragmenter, which automatically reorganizes the contents of your hard disk at scheduled times to speed up file access. There's also a range of information tools including System Information, Event Log (which tracks any problems with your hardware or software), the Reliability and Performance Monitor, which tracks your PC's robustness and shows the results in reports and graphs, and System Health Report, which provides a detailed

Manage your startup programs

Check your software and get rid of unnecessary programs

When you click on **Manage startup programs** you'll go to Software Explorer, the part of Windows Defender that enables you to see what programs are running. The menu at the top should already be set to Startup Programs, and the list below tells you what programs run when you boot your PC.

Many unwanted programs will install themselves for all users, so to remove or disable them, click the **Show for all users** button. Then just select the program you want to get rid of and choose **Disable** to stop the program running temporarily or **Remove** to stop it running for good.

Because it's easy in Windows Vista to have different settings for different users, it's worth having two accounts – especially if you use your PC for different things at different times.

IT TAKES TWO Consider having two accounts for different performance needs

insight into the state of your system. This takes 60 seconds to get data and reports on everything from whether your PC has anti-virus software to how active your network adaptor is.

Upgrade your memory

Memory is an essential part of your PC – programs including Windows Vista itself are loaded into random access memory (RAM) because it's the quickest way of accessing them. Windows Vista requires a minimum of 512MB of RAM to run, but if you want to enjoy its advanced features, you'll need at least 1GB (1,024MB). If your budget will run to it, a memory upgrade is one of the most effective ways of speeding up your PC.

If the idea of opening up your computer to fit more memory doesn't

LOCATION, LOCATION, LOCATION While very useful, the indexing system can actually slow down your computer, so it's a good idea to change the locations your PC keeps an eye on

appeal or you want even more performance, take advantage of Windows Vista ReadyBoost. If you have a USB flash drive that is compatible you can speed up your PC by inviting Windows Vista to use some or all of the drive to store information it needs to access. Just plug your flash drive into a spare USB port, and when the Autoplay menu pops up, select **Speed up my system using Window ReadyBoost** to enjoy a faster computer.

As you add, edit and delete files on your hard drive, they become all jumbled up – or fragmented – across the disk. As a result, your computer takes longer to access each file. Windows Vista has a tool called Disk Defragmenter that runs at set times to keep your files in order. You can alter this schedule to a more convenient time, or run the utility manually, by clicking **Start → All Programs → Accessories → System Tools → Disk Defragmenter**.

Give your PC a spring clean

Maintain a good level of hard drive space by clearing out clutter

A computer can accumulate a huge amount of unwanted files and it can be a real chore to track these down to reclaim hard drive space.

The good news is that Windows Vista comes with a handy program called Disk Cleanup, which can help get rid of unnecessary files. This scans your hard drive for anything you might not need – log files, downloaded programs, files created

when your system was hibernating, and so on – and it enables you to get rid of some or all of them.

When Disk Cleanup has finished, click on **More Options**. Here you'll find two options: the first enables you to get rid of programs or components you no longer need, the second enables you to get rid of old restore points (keep the most recent one), backups and other safeguards.

SPRING CLEAN Use Disk Cleanup to remove temporary or unnecessary files

Cut down on crashes and solve PC problems

Does your PC crash or hang up? Windows Vista contains tools that can help you discover why, and make your system more reliable

Anyone who uses a PC soon gets used to error messages; applications that hang up, and others that simply die. After a while, you see it all as an occupational hazard. But with Windows Vista, it doesn't have to be that way. The new system includes a rewritten crash-handling facility that does a far better job than previous versions of Windows in recording what errors have occurred. And it's packed with useful tools to help diagnose crashes, and hopefully prevent them from happening again. There's no need to live with an unstable PC – Windows Vista can help get your system working again.

Easy to use

The traditional path to fixing PC crashes involved trying to decipher cryptic error messages, or browsing incomprehensible log files. Fortunately, Windows Vista offers a different route. It maintains a database holding the details of all your program crashes (for up to a year), and can go online to look for possible fixes.

MEMORY PROBLEMS Use the new Memory Diagnostics Tool to check for faulty RAM

To give this a try, connect to the internet, then select **Control Panel → Problem Reports and Solutions**. Windows Vista will send information about your crashes to a Microsoft server, and will then display solutions. These aren't always helpful – sometimes it will just say your application isn't compatible. But usually they offer practical help, telling you that you need to download a new driver or Windows patch, and even providing a link to where you can find it. Sometimes, the program won't find any

Windows Vista includes a completely rewritten crash-handling system

solutions, but Microsoft is adding new fixes all the time, so you can always try again in a week. And there are tricks you can try for yourself, too.

Help yourself

Occasionally Windows Vista will record an error, but not report it, which means you won't see a solution even if one's available. To find out if that's happened, click **View problem history** in Problem Reports and Solutions. If you see a crash marked as Unreported, right-click it to report the error and, hopefully, get help. If you spot the status Solution Available, and you've not fixed that problem, right-click it and select **View Solution**.

Of course, you don't have to rely entirely on the Windows Vista reporting options. If you spot a common crash in the problem history, for instance, and there's no solution available, double-click

it for more information and make a note of the 'Problem Event Name' and 'Application Name'. Use these as keywords in a search engine – if anyone else has reported the same crashes, you might just find a solution.

The Problem Reports and Solutions applet is a welcome addition to Windows, but won't solve everything. But there are other tools around...

The new Reliability Monitor provides in-depth coverage of your crash history. It also details software you've added and removed, making it easy to tell if your problems began right after you installed a particular application. Device Manager now has its own Control Panel applet. Open this and you'll see faulty devices highlighted with a yellow exclamation mark. Double-click to read more advice, and click the **Check for solutions** button.

One of the most welcome additions to Windows Vista has to be the new Memory Diagnostics Tool. Faulty RAM can cause all kinds of problems, but now there's an easy way to detect it. Click **Start**, enter 'Memory' in the search box to launch the program, then allow your computer to be restarted. Press **F1** to choose Extended tests, select **0** as the Pass Count to keep them running, and let the tests repeat overnight. If faulty RAM is behind your problems, a few hours with the Memory Diagnostics Tool should be enough to reveal it. ⊞

Find out what's causing crashes

Use Windows Vista to chase down and fix problems

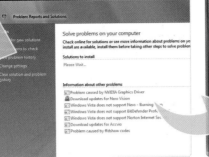

1 GET HELP It's frustrating when your applications keep crashing, but Windows Vista may be able to help. Go online, then click **Control Panel → System and Maintenance → Problem Reports and Solutions**.

2 CHECK ONLINE Windows Vista will check with Microsoft to find out if there are known solutions to your crashes. This might take a moment, particularly if there's a lot to report or you've a slow internet connection.

3 DETAILED ADVICE Follow the links on the solutions provided. Often you'll find these to be very helpful – for example, you may be advised to update a driver, and be given links to where you can download the update.

> Often you'll find solutions; for example, explaining that you need to update a driver, and providing links to download it

4 FIND OUT MORE If Windows Vista can't find any solutions then you can still search yourself. Click **View Problem History**, double-click an error and note its Problem Event Name. Enter that and the application name into Live Search, and see what results come up.

5 PRIVACY WORRIES Some people think sending error reports to Microsoft will compromise their privacy. In reality, they contain no personal information at all; if you're concerned click **Change Settings → Advanced Settings** to turn reporting off.

Making the most of System Restore

If your PC becomes unstable, Windows Vista boasts a number of features to help restore to its former status

Each time a critical change is made to Windows Vista, the System Restore software creates what it calls a Restore Point. This stores a back-up copy of all the system files that are about to change, so if it turns out the new software or hardware driver causes your PC to become unstable, for whatever reason, you're able to restore your PC to its previous status, before the changes were made, and – typically – remove any associated problems.

And, in true Windows Vista user-friendly style, System Restore works entirely invisibly in the background, creating restore points automatically as new software and drivers are installed.

It is possible to create these manually through the Backup and Restore Center but for the vast majority of people this is unnecessary. Take a look at the opposite page to get a better idea of how to access and use System Restore.

Roll back

A spin-off of the System Restore feature is that each driver on a PC can be Rolled Back. This means if you're having problems with a new driver it's possible to use the Device Manager – found within the System Control Panel – to revert Windows Vista back to an earlier, problem-free driver.

The easiest way to access this is to open the Start Menu, type 'Device Manager' and press **Enter**. If you open one of the device-type categories, double-click a specific device and click the **Driver** tab. Here you'll find information about the current device's driver and a selection of options. It's best not to make any changes here but, if you were having problems with the current device it is possible to disable it, remove it or, most helpfully, roll its driver to the previous version.

System Restore and the Roll Back option combine to offer powerful yet simple problem solving, enabling you to quickly and easily remove troublesome software, drivers or even problems of unknown origins with just a few clicks of the mouse button. ⊞

Discover hidden PC alerts

How to find the problems that don't cause a full-blown crash

The typical PC crash is almost impossible to miss. An application displays a big error message, locks up or disappears completely. But it's not the same with every problem. Some errors may be raised as events, and while Windows logs these, it doesn't display them. So if your PC seems unstable and you don't know why, it's a good idea to check recent events for clues.

Click **Start**, type 'eventvwr' in the Search box, and press **Enter** to see what the Event Viewer reports. Expand the Custom Views section in

EVENTFUL The Event Viewer is packed with information on your computer's problems that you won't find elsewhere on your system

the tree on the left-hand side of the screen, then click **Administrative Events** to see a list of issues that have cropped up on your system.

Not all these events are important. If you find one that looks trivial, just move on. You'll often find more serious registry issues, application errors, even reports of imminent hard drive failure, none of which may have been reported elsewhere. The contents of your Event Log could well point you to the application, device or Windows component that's behind most of your current crashes.

Troubleshoot computer drivers

How to pinpoint your PC's driver problems

Faulty drivers are one of the major causes of PC crashes, but could they be responsible for the issues on your system? There's one way you can try to find out, but be careful – this method of enquiry is not for beginners! If you're not familiar with, for instance, booting into Safe Mode to recover a faulty PC, you'll probably want to give this a miss.

Otherwise, if you do feel confident, confirm that you want to start in Safe Mode – reboot your PC and keep tapping the **F8** key until you see the

Startup Menu. Use the cursor keys to choose **Safe Mode** from the list and press the **Return** key. If that works, boot Windows Vista normally again, then launch Verifier.exe. Select **Create standard settings → Next**, choose **Automatically select all drivers installed on this computer** and **Finish**.

Reboot your PC and Verifier will begin testing your drivers. If it reports a problem, then make a note of the driver name – this is the one you'll need to replace. Unfortunately, that problem will also crash the PC, so reboot back into Safe Mode, launch Verifier and select **Delete Existing Settings**.

If Verifier doesn't spot a problem, you'll see no messages. Give it five minutes, then try the process again. If there's still no response listing problems, use the **Delete Existing Settings** option to remove Verifier, as it looks like your drivers may not be faulty, after all.

DRIVE-BY Detect driver problems with this useful, if technical, Windows Vista tool

Quick questions

Solving your crashes

Q My applications are crashing frequently. What can I do?
A Click Control Panel → System and Maintenance → Problem Reports and Solutions and let Windows Vista check for fixes.

Q That helped, but there are some problems left...
A Click View Problem History, make sure all your problems have been reported, and you've installed recommended solutions.

Q I'm still crashing occasionally. Any other ideas?
A Double-click on any unsolved errors. Use Live Search to search for the error name, and you may find some answers.

Q How can I fix my one or two remaining problems?
A Use tools like Device Manager, the Reliability Monitor and Memory Checker.

How System Restore works
Rolling back your Windows Vista installation is just a matter of 1, 2, 3!

1 START RESTORE System Restore can be accessed via Backup and Restore Control Panel, or open the Start Menu, type 'System Restore' and press **Enter**. This will open the basic starting window.

2 CHOOSE A POINT Click **Next** to view the restore points. These are listed with a time and date and an explanation of why it was created, usually listing a program or driver installation.

3 RESTORE AWAY If you spot a likely restore point select it by clicking on it with the mouse and clicking **Next**, and **Next** again. You're given a warning, click **Yes** to proceed.

CHAPTER 12 SYSTEM TOOLS

CHAPTER 12 SYSTEM TOOLS

Performance and Reliability Monitor

If you're still concerned about the status of your system, Windows Vista measures the performance of your PC

As part of the Windows Vista remit to provide a secure system, the Reliability and Performance Monitor is on hand to provide you with advanced performance analysis. If your system goes wrong, this is where you'll find details of what happened. Although the Task Manager gives you some of the same information and options, the Reliability and Performance Monitor gives you that little bit more.

You can use it to determine how the programs you run affect the overall performance of your system. There are a number of features built into it that you can use to create logs, measure the state of your system and monitor activity.

To launch the Reliability and Performance Monitor, click **Start**, type 'perfmon.exe' and press **Enter**. Click **Reliability Monitor** and in the right pane you'll see a detailed chart. Each column represents a particular day and you'll see the corresponding date beneath. The five rows indicate potential problem areas, including hardware, software and Windows itself. If you see a cross against anything that means an error's occurred. To see information about an error, click a date. Look at the System Stability Report that appears under the graph, and check for dates that carry a symbol. Either a cross, information or exclamation mark notes something worthy of inspection. As well as complete applications, this

category also covers updates for individual programs; updates for Windows Defender are also recorded here. System problems often result from the installation of a particular program, and you can follow a program's progress under Application Failures. The exact name of the application is listed here, along with a reason for the failure.

If your system does crash, the information provided here will help pinpoint the reason. Errors under Windows Failures are rare, but if one does occur, look under Failure Detail for specific error codes. Carry out a search on this code using either Windows Live Search or the Microsoft Knowledge base – you'll usually find a solution.

What is the Stability Index?

Understanding your stability rating in Windows Vista

Under the date drop-down box in the Reliability and Performance Monitor, you'll notice an Index score. This refers to the rating your system has been given for a particular date. The System Stability Index uses a number between 1 and 10. The lower your rating, the poorer your PC is performing. The rating that's given is based on data gathered since you first started using your system. The number of errors and failures you've encountered in the course of use affect the measurement. For example, uninstall a problem

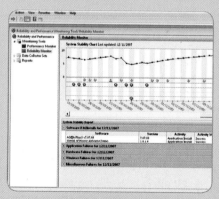

PC LIFELINE If you've been experiencing problems, check the System Stability Index to see how your PC is performing

application and keep an eye on the Reliability and Performance graphs – you should see your score improve. Your rating is calculated by taking into account a number of different factors. For example, greater significance is placed on the most recent errors. To avoid inaccurate readings, any days when your system is powered off aren't included. Don't confuse the System Stability Index with the Windows Experience Index. The latter measures the performance capability of your PC's hardware and software configuration.

How stable is your PC?

View the charts, graphs and stats to see just where all your problems are

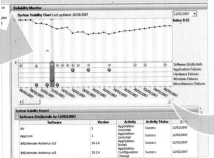

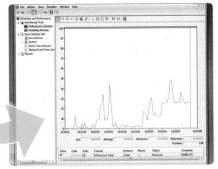

1 **RELIABILITY MONITOR** Your PC seems to be getting more unstable. But is that really true? Click **Start**, type 'perfmon' into the Search box and press **Enter** to launch the Reliability and Performance monitor.

2 **DETAILED GRAPH** The System Stability Chart shows just how reliable your computer has been. Scroll back, and you might even see where problems began. Did you install a program at that time? Maybe that's the cause of your issues.

3 **CHECKUP** Click **Performance Monitor** to see how things are running. Click the green '+' sign and choose something to watch (eg, **Memory → Available MBytes**). Now run programs as normal and watch as your free memory changes.

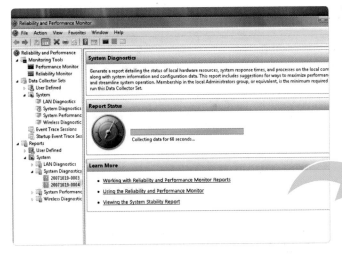

The System Stability Chart shows just how reliable your computer has been; you might see where problems began

4 **COLLECT DATA** The program can also run system diagnostics reports – a handy way to identify PC problems. Click **Data Collector Sets**, then double-click **System** to see everything it checks. Now click on **System Diagnostics** to see everything it tests, then **Action → Start** to begin the report.

Report feedback

Many people are cynical about reporting problems back to Microsoft; however, each report is useful to Microsoft for reporting back to hardware and software partners, along with tracking general errors.

5 **DIAGNOSTIC REPORTS** It can take a moment for the report to be generated, so be patient. When it's complete you'll find there's lots of information here, but anything particularly significant will appear in the first Warnings section so you don't actually have to read every word.

Do More

Use Windows Vista to get more from your everyday life with our fun, practical and downright useful projects

Watch recorded TV on your cellphone

Want to watch the latest episode of your favorite TV series on the subway? It's easy to play it on your phone...

"Wow"
Flash fantastic

New for Service Pack 1, Windows Vista supports the new ex-FAT file system. This enables larger overall capacities and file sizes, and is aimed at flash storage devices such as mobile phones

RECORD YOUR PROGRAMME
The easiest option is to use Media Center, although any TV tuner card and video-recording software should work fine.

With all the continuing enthusiasm for video-capable music players, it's easy to forget that you're probably already carrying around a multimedia device in the form of your cellphone. Most handsets boast headphone connections and color screens ideal for music, photos and even recorded TV – and Windows Vista makes it very easy to fill them with footage.

How you transfer material depends on the phone you've got. It's easiest with phones running Windows Mobile, as these come with pocket versions of assorted PC programs including

Windows Media Player – so you don't have to worry about different file types or having to master a new interface. If you've got a different sort of phone, then it's still fairly straightforward to copy files over but you'll need a decent-sized screen and a memory card slot; very few cellphones come with the hefty amounts of storage space required to store video. You may also need to install a separate bit of software – usually this comes on CD in the box your phone came in, but you can also download it from the manufacturer's web site.

The final crucial component is a way to copy the files over. The simplest option is

a good old-fashioned bit of cable – most Windows Mobile phones just use mini-USB connections, so you can usually pinch the cable from your digital camera if required. Other models might require a specific cable that you should be able to buy from a mobile phone shop or the manufacturer's web site.

Smaller phones might only have wireless connections, such as Bluetooth or infra-red (IR). Check your phone's details in the manual or on the manufacturer's web site. Infra-red connections aren't much good for copying anything bigger than text or photos; Bluetooth is faster and easier.

GET READY TO COPY First, find your video and open up the folder it's in. TV recorded in Windows Vista Media Center will be in C:\Users\Public\Recorded TV; other formats will be where you saved them.

CONVERT THE FILES If the clip you want to watch can't be converted by Media Player, use a conversion program such as MyTV ToGo. If you have an ATi graphics card, you can use Avivo.

CONNECT YOUR PHONE Hook up your phone using the supplied cable, and Windows Mobile Device Center starts automatically. Click the **Pictures, Music and Video** button and Windows Media Player opens.

Click **Sync** and Windows Media Player converts and copies your video over automatically

WINDOWS MEDIA PLAYER The Sync window is already open; all you have to do is drag your video file from its folder into the left-hand Sync pane. You can see how much space you've got using the graph at the top.

MEDIA FRIENDLY If you're using Media Center, then you don't even need to use Media Player. Just connect your phone, and go to **Tasks → Sync** to select what video or music you'd like to copy over.

KING OF QUALITY If your phone has a lot of memory and a big screen, you might want to use higher-quality video; increase it by going to **Sync → More Options → Properties → Quality**.

SYNC ACROSS Click **Sync** and Windows Media Player automatically converts your video (if required) and copies it over. This can be a long process, particularly with large video files, so be patient as it completes.

WATCH ON THE GO And that's it. Open Media Player on your phone, go to **Menu → Library** and select your footage from My Videos.

Use your PC to control your TV

With Windows Media Center you can record and watch your favorite TV shows whenever you want

There are just too many television channels out there today; while much content is of debatable quality, many shows are truly unmissable. Fortunately, viewers are no longer at the mercy of station controllers... Bring your PC into the picture, and you can ditch the TV listings. Record what you want and watch it when you want.

If you own Windows Vista Home Premium or Ultimate edition, you've got Windows Media Center, which offers quick, no-fuss access to the multimedia content stored on your PC, and the effortlessly navigable menu is designed to be easy to view on a TV.

You'll need a TV tuner or Cable card in your PC to use the television features in Windows Media Center, but if you haven't already got one, it's a simple business to add a USB TV tuner.

Making life easier

The first time you run Media Center, you'll need to go through a brief set-up (see opposite). Once you've got it working, press one of the cursor buttons on the keyboard or remote control (if you've got one) and a mini guide will pop up at the bottom of the screen. From here you can check what's on or, alternatively, hit **Pause** to freeze live TV as if it were a tape or DVD – the signal is recorded to the hard drive, so when you come back you can click **Play** and it will start where you left off.

That's the answer to those irritating phone calls that come through just as your main character is about to do

something heroic, but the really good stuff comes from planning ahead. Delve into the integrated Guide, take a look at what's coming up over the next couple of weeks and tag the shows you want to watch. When they roll around, Media Center will record them automatically.

You can even record a whole series with just one click, thanks to Record Series. However, it's worth noting that older stuff does get deleted to make room, so if you plan on building up an archive, go to **TV + Movies** on the main menu and choose **Recorded TV ➔ View Scheduled ➔ Series**, select the series and click **Series Settings ➔ Keep**. The

You can record a whole series with just one click – and then burn to DVD

number of episodes you can keep depends on the size of your hard drive. If you start running out of space, consider boosting it with an external hard drive. Plug it in and tell Media Center to record to it under **Tasks ➔ Settings ➔ TV ➔ Recorder ➔ Recorder Storage**. Not that you have to leave everything on the computer... You can easily burn to a DVD, or even sync to an external device such as a portable video player.

Again, both of these processes can be handled straight from the Media Center menu, under **Burn DVD** and **Sync to Portable Device** respectively.

On the subject of DVDs, Windows Media Center offers basic playback controls, and a handy extra: Parental Controls. Go into **Tasks ➔ Settings ➔ General Parental Controls**, set up a four-digit code and you'll be able to set limits based on a movie's rating.

The last great advantage of using your PC for your viewing pleasure is that you can junk the airwaves and download shows direct. Keep an eye on the Online Spotlight section of the main menu for the ability to get the latest shows whenever you want them.

In real life...
Time-saving series

Paul Douglas, Editor, *Windows Vista: The Official Magazine*
Having been around since 2002, Windows Media Center is well known by those who have used it, but many Windows users didn't know how to add it or even if they had it at all. As it's now part of Windows Vista Home Premium and Ultimate Editions it's far more available. It's worth persevering with the set-up as, once it's up and running, features such as TV guide and Record a Series make enjoying your favorite shows so much easier. For many, though, watching on a PC monitor isn't great and this is where Media Extenders, such as the Xbox 360, come into their own.

Windows Vista PC turns TV

Setting up the ultimate remote control is so easy

1 TUNING UP The first thing you need is a TV tuner or cable card – a device that can take a signal from an aerial or cable source. If your PC lacks one, you'll need to get one. Naturally, ensure that it's compatible with Windows Vista.

2 SETTING UP Setting up Windows Media Center requires a number of steps (see page 98); needless to say, you will need to select the correct type of TV tuner card that you have and allow it to detect available stations.

3 ANTENNA-SHUN! Now it's time to plug an aerial or cable connector into your tuner card. For the best analog signal, a rooftop antenna is the ideal option. For the best results, buy a wideband one with a signal booster.

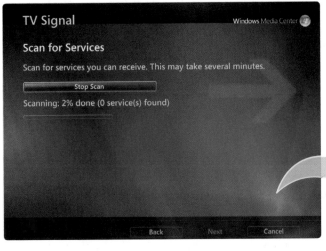

For maximum comfort, you'll need to connect the PC to your TV – using an Xbox 360 is the flashiest route

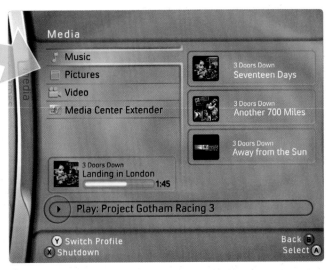

4 SETTING UP TIME Fire up Media Center and in the menu select **Tasks**, then **Settings**. Enter the TV sub-menu and choose **Set Up TV Signal**. The computer will take you step by step through the tuning process, seeking out and storing channels. Now you're ready to start watching.

Media extenders

These are handy devices that can connect to a Windows Vista PC via a wired or wireless network and make it easy to share your media, streaming movies, music and photos through to your TV.

5 VEG OUT For maximum comfort, you'll need to connect the PC to your TV. Using an Xbox 360 as a Media Center Extender is the flashiest route, but a cable will do. See which ports you have on your TV and PC and ask at an electronics store or check a web forum to see which one you need.

Go high-definition with Windows Vista

Your guide to getting hi-def video from your PC to your TV – with Windows Vista it couldn't be simpler

So, you've invested in a high-definition LCD TV? Then you're about to watch TV and movies with significantly sharper, clearer picture quality than anything you've goggled at in your own living room before. Congratulations!

And now you can use your PC as a gateway to a massive hi-def archive – either on Blu-ray or HD DVD disc or downloaded from a web site.

There are two ways to get movies and TV shows from the PC to the TV; through a Media Center Extender or by connecting your PC or laptop directly to the TV. Only video files on your hard disc that you've downloaded or created will work with an extender; if you're looking to use your PC to play HD movies from disc, directly connecting to your TV is the only way.

Xbox 360

The most popular Media Center Extender, of course, is the Xbox 360. When Windows Vista spots an Xbox 360 on the same network it will automatically configure the connection between the two for media sharing. It's as simple as turning on your console, switching to the video blade and selecting a file to play.

Except that it *isn't* quite as simple as that… There are two standards for hi-def video, described by the number of vertical lines in the picture – 720p and 1,080p. Even the basic 720p resolution requires between 15-20Mbps of continuous bandwidth for smooth playback. So trying to stream an HD feed over a Wi-Fi connection is almost impossible – especially as the Xbox 360 wireless adaptor uses the older 802.11g standard rather than the newer, faster 802.11n. If you're trying to run HD video from your PC to the Xbox, make sure that both have a cabled connection to your router.

Want to keep your PC in a separate room? Try powerline networking. A 200Mbps kit plugs into a socket and creates a connection between either PC and router or Xbox 360 and router.

Build your own media empire

Five things to include if you're making your own media PC

GRAPHICS CARD If you go for an Nvidia or AMD graphics card, their latest chips support HDCP and are capable of decoding HD video without troubling the PC. AMD cards natively support HDMI too, for the best TV connection.

A GOOD CASE There are plenty of well designed Windows Media Center cases on the market, and many have displays to let you know which channel you're tuned to. The majority come in mini-case designs or DVD-styled slimline cases.

REMOTE CONTROL Get a wireless keyboard and mouse – you don't want cables lying around. Ideally, get a Windows Media Center remote – this has all the controls you need for using your PC as a set-top box.

If you don't own an Xbox 360, or want to play HD DVDs from PC to TV, you'll need to connect your PC directly to your TV. This isn't as tricky as it sounds. Most modern TVs offer a variety of signal inputs that should work with your PC. The first is the VGA port. Despite its age, and the connection being analog, you should get a good picture by setting the desktop resolution to 1,280x768. If you accidentally change the resolution to one your TV can't display, reboot the PC and press **F8** as it starts up. This will take you to Advanced Boot Options, where you can select **Enable low-resolution video** to take you back to a TV-friendly display.

HDMI ports

All you need to connect in this way is the DVI to VGA adaptor that came with your graphics card and an appropriate cable – but, because VGA can't carry an audio signal, you'll need a separate cable to connect your sound card to the TV or speakers. There is one big limitation to VGA cable, though. Encrypted content – like that on HD DVD or Blu-ray – requires a digital HDCP connection between player and TV; VGA isn't going to cut it.

The only digital input most TVs use is

QUALITY ENTERTAINMENT Enjoy hi-def TV with the help of Windows Media Center

the HDMI socket – many new graphics cards now offer these either directly or via an adaptor. Some, including the latest Radeon graphics cards (the HD series), will also send the sound signal through the HDMI port, so you only need one cable for movie playback. One of the benefits of using HDMI to connect to your TV is that your graphics card should adjust

itself to the correct resolution – either 1,920x1,200 or 1,280x768. It's important to use a 1:1 ratio for desktop to screen resolution – an attempt by the screen to guess at missing pixels will result in messy text. So why are the resolutions quoted slightly higher than the HDTV resolutions of 1,920x1,080 and 1,280x 720? Because there are often unused lines in the panel which your PC display will try to fill. If they don't work, try the HDTV standards.

Now use your TV controls to raise the brightness and lower the contrast and sharpness until the text on your desktop is readable. Right-click on your desktop and go to graphics options for extra settings.

Now you have two ways of interacting with your PC. The easiest is Windows Media Center. If you're feeling more ambitious, and want to surf the web or answer Windows Live Messenger while watching video, try these two tricks.
1 Click anywhere in the desktop area and hold down **Ctrl** while scrolling the mouse wheel – this will adjust the size of the desktop icons to make them easier to see.
2 Right-click on the desktop and choose **Personalize**. In the left-hand bar you'll see an option for **Adjust font size (DPI)**. This will allow you to smoothly scale the system fonts to a size that's easy to read on a large screen in high resolution.

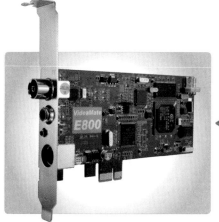

TV TUNER You'll want to make sure that you aren't reliant on pre-recorded media. Digital TV cards now come with one, two or four tuners on board so you can record several feeds at once, and use your PC's hard drive for pausing live TV.

A MICRO-ATX MOTHERBOARD If your case doesn't ship with a motherboard, there are a host to choose from. Pick one that's correct for your type of processor and potentially save money by picking one with on-board HDMI video output.

Your hi-def questions

High-definition? It's all too confusing... Well, here are answers
to your most burning questions about the successors to DVD

1 What is high-definition?
High-definition is a new way of recording and watching TV, video and console games. The picture is made up of a larger number of parts, which makes for greater detail and clarity. In technical terms, high-definition (hi-def or HD) is an increase in the resolution; in practical terms, pictures seem clearer, sharper – more vivid.

2 What is HD DVD?
HD DVD is a disc format based on standard DVD technology. A single-sided HD DVD disc can hold 30GB of data (15GB in two layers) – equivalent to 7,500 music files – more than six times the capacity of standard DVD. The HD DVD standard also incorporates features such as interactive content. You can buy an external HD DVD drive for your Xbox 360. (Although in February 2008, Toshiba – principle designer of the format – announced it would no longer continue to develop or manufacture the drives.)

3 What is Blu-ray?
Blu-ray Discs (BD) work in a slightly different way, offering higher capacities than HD DVD but higher production costs. The Sony PlayStation 3 plays Blu-ray as standard. The Blu-ray format can hold 25GB per layer; with the demise of HD DVD, Blu-ray is now first-choice for the high-definition optical disc format.

4 Do I need a hi-def TV to play high-definition discs properly?
Yes, your TV needs to be HD ready – fortunately, most new TVs are. When choosing a new TV, make sure that you get one with the 'HD ready' logo. This means the TV meets the hardware requirements to play high-definition videos and games.

MOVIE MAKER Windows Movie Maker can publish to various high-definition formats

5 Will my PC and monitor be capable of high-definition content?
Unless you bought your PC with specific hi-def hardware in mind, chances are you'll need to upgrade. Your monitor, for example, needs to be 24-inch widescreen to cope with HD videos at 1,080p. You'll also need an HDMI and possibly HDCP support, and if you want to watch discs as well as downloaded clips, you'll need a suitable HD DVD or BD drive. You'll also need a capable graphics card and modern processor with a good chunk of memory. Happily, Windows Vista was developed with HD in mind.

6 Can I make HD videos?
Yes you can – but it needs to be filmed in HD for the true hi-def experience, which means you need an HD camcorder. You'll also need editing software for your Windows Vista PC – see question 8.

7 Does Windows Media Player play Blu-Ray/HD DVD discs?
The way HD films are stored requires additional software so you'll need a third-party program; ideally, try to get one that supports both formats. Bear in mind, though, that if you buy an HD DVD or Blu-ray drive it may very well come with the appropriate software anyway.

8 What hi-def stuff can I edit with Windows Movie Maker?
You can edit and publish high-definition videos using Windows Movie Maker in a variety of formats. These output profiles are called Windows Media HD and are available in the Windows Vista Home Premium and Ultimate editions of Windows Movie Maker.

9 Are the discs just for videos?
No – though it will be the most common use. Both types can be used to store data, in much the same way as a USB flash drive, external hard drive, or a standard CD or DVD. The difference is that both formats can store much more. A Blu-ray disc has potentially enough space for a full system backup.

10 What do I need to stream hi-def from my Windows Vista PC to my Xbox 360?
This can be done wirelessly, but it's advisable to do it via an Ethernet cable – a wired network connection. So you'll need a Home Premium or Ultimate Windows Vista PC, appropriate software, an Xbox 360, an HDTV and an HD DVD or Blu-ray disc drive.

11 What about drives to make and record my own hi-def discs?
You'll need a drive capable of reading and writing whichever format you want to use. That means buying either a Blu-ray or HD DVD recorder, with appropriate software. Once you do this, you'll not only be able to watch your HD videos on your HDTV but also be able to make data discs.

12 What are HDMI and HDCP connections?
HDMI (High-Definition Multimedia Interface) is a connector that enables the

hi-def audio and video signals to travel from, for example, an HD DVD player to an HDTV, in a similar way to an S-video lead and socket. Your monitor and graphics card or motherboard will need to have HDMI ports or an adaptor to convert the more common DVI connection.

HDCP (High-bandwidth Digital Content Protection) makes an encrypted connection between the source and the destination display hardware before a video can be played. It's intended as a form of copy protection designed to protect the video during transmission, and all the hardware involved needs to support this standard to correctly play the video.

13 Where can I download high-definition content from?
You can download hi-def television programmes and movies through your Xbox LIVE service. You can also download sample clips from www.microsoft.com/windows/windowsmedia/musicandvideo/hdvideo/contentshowcase.aspx.

What to watch...

OK, so you've gone HD, but where do you get the programs to watch?

1 OPTICAL ILLUSION Now you've got your PC up and running, what on earth are you going to watch? The largest selection of HD media is still on optical disc, but you'll need a Blu-ray or HD DVD drive for that.

2 MOVIE DOWNLOADS Head to http://movies.msn.com for all the latest high-definition movie trailers and for links to download sites, such as www.cinemanow.com, which are becoming increasingly popular.

3 ONLINE MEDIA You'll find a number of premium content digital download channels in the Online Media section of Windows Media Center. Just fire it up from the Start menu and navigate to **TV + Movies ➔ More TV**.

4 STANDARD DEF If it's standard definition TV you want, the MSN TV portal offers clips and full episodes to stream alongside features and news. Head over to http://tv.msn.com/tv to browse the all the latest TV programs.

5 XBOX LIVE Microsoft is already offering the best new movies in HD format as downloads via the Xbox Live Marketplace, and it won't be long before other PC providers catch up. Make sure your PC and TV are ready.

Make your own cell phone ringtones

Don't waste money on downloads – you have all the music you could ever want sitting there in your CD collection

Even if you ignore half the features in your mobile phone, the ringtone is one thing that's always worth changing. At the very least, you want to avoid being one of those people patting their pockets when the default ringtone is heard in a crowd. At best, you want a tune that makes you glad to receive a call. While the tones that come with your phone won't necessarily fit the bill, it's easy to create something that does by turning one of your CD tracks into a ringtone.

The process is more straightforward than you might think. Finding a track is simply a matter of copying it from a CD and saving it as an MP3 file – the format that nearly all polyphonic phones support. You don't need to download any specialist software to do this – Windows Media Player is fine – but it's worth spending a bit of time picking a suitable tune before you start.

Choose something distinctive but tolerable; remember that particularly rich sounds aren't going to sound very impressive on a small phone's tinny speakers. Also, try to pick a few bars that won't sound too 'cut off' when you answer the call. It's a small thing,

but it can be surprisingly wearing to keep cutting off a track mid-melody every time you pick up the phone.

The only practical consideration then is how to transfer your MP3 from your phone to your PC. There are a number

of ways that this can be carried out. Most phones now come with a USB cable that connects the handset directly to your PC. Alternatively, you can use an infra-red or a Bluetooth connection to carry out the transfer, but to use either of these methods your laptop or PC will require the correct adaptor or built-in hardware – consult your computer manual for more details. To show you just how easy this is to do with different phones and connections, the following pages look at three common ways in which various cell phones connect to and work with Windows Vista... ⊞

Rip your CDs and create new ringtones

Set bit rate
There's no point using the highest audio quality for a phone's tiny speakers – and a lower rate means a smaller file.

Transfer files
If you want to use infra-red, you may need to activate the connection on your phone before you can use it. If your wireless transfer fails, make sure that there's enough capacity on the destination device.

Transfer type
Transfer the new ringtone file using cable, Bluetooth or infra-red. Cable offers the fastest transfer speeds, but will not always be the most convenient. You may need to download the software utility for your phone.

Rip tracks
Your CD collection can double as your personal ringtone store. Use Media Player to rip tracks ready for transferring to your phone. Tag information can be used on some phones as well, so make sure this shows the correct details.

Edit down your audio files

If you want to edit tracks before uploading them to your phone, you can download software from the internet. You'll find that some music

editing software is free, and you'll be able to trim songs to just the best sections, and reduce the bit rate to take up less space.

Phone specific software

Certain cell phones come with their own custom software

1 Click to add
This handset comes with its own software utility, called Disc2Phone, which enables you to get the track from PC to phone in just a few clicks.

2 Choose audio
Click **My Music** and select the location where your track is stored – this can be a CD. Click on the remove button to stop selected tracks being transferred.

ADDING RINGTONES The process of adding a new tone can vary between devices; check your phone manufacturer's web site to see if there's software utility you can use.

3 Connect your phone
Choose the bit rate for the transfer – the higher the rate, the bigger the file. Using the supplied USB cable, attach the phone to the PC.

CD INFO When grabbing audio tracks directly from a CD, wait until the disc has been recognized by the audio database – this will ensure that track and artist information is displayed.

THE CORRECT RATE Bit rate affects the output quality as well as the size of the file. Don't select a particularly low rate unless you're really low on space.

TONE COLLECTION
Ringtones and music files are one and the same on many phones, so stored tracks can be set as tones.

5 Select the tone
Go to **File Manager** on the handset, open **Music**; find and select the track. Click on **More**, go down to **Use as** and choose **Ringtone**.

4 Transfer file
On the handset you'll see USB connection on the display. Select **File transfer**; once the transfer is finished, close the software on the PC and disconnect the USB cable.

BE SELECTIVE You don't have to import the entire contents of a CD. Select those tracks you don't want to use and click on **Remove selected tracks**

Windows Mobile phones

The most Windows-friendly option

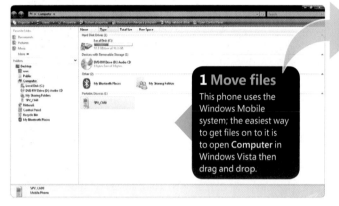

1 Move files
This phone uses the Windows Mobile system; the easiest way to get files on to it is to open **Computer** in Windows Vista then drag and drop.

2 Choose file type
As this set accepts Windows Media Audio format, if you rip from a CD using Media Player you can switch between WMA and MP3. Go to the Rip Music tab in Options.

SHARE YOUR DATA Use the Windows Mobile Device Center to synchronize the files on your PC with your mobile device. Outlook contacts, calendar and email can all be kept up to date.

SPACE RACE You can use MP3 files if you like, but the WMA format does have the advantage of taking up less space in your phone's memory.

An example of a phone that incorporates the Windows Mobile operating system

KEEP LISTENING If you want to be able to listen to your ringtone as an audio track it's a an idea to copy it to the My Music folder. MP3 or WMA will be OK.

3 Browse your phone
Connect your set to the PC with a USB cable. The set will appear in Computer, and you can browse its contents as if you were using another drive.

SYNC OR SWIM Sync your phone automatically to keep information up to date. Alternatively, just open Computer and take a look

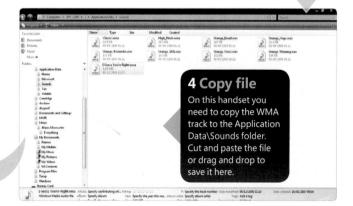

4 Copy file
On this handset you need to copy the WMA track to the Application Data\Sounds folder. Cut and paste the file or drag and drop to save it here.

5 Select your newly-added tone
Click on **Start**, browse to Settings and select **Sounds**. Under Ring tone scroll through the list of sounds and you'll see that your track has been added. Click to select, and you'll hear a preview of it.

SOUND FILES Although your ringtones can be in MP3, WMA, MIDI or WAVE audio formats, for notifications or reminders you are restricted to WAVE (.wav) and MIDI (.mid) files.

Using a Bluetooth connection

Wireless transfers can make life a lot easier

1 Try Bluetooth

Although your phone may come with a cable, there's nothing to stop making use of other types of connection. If your PC has Bluetooth capabilities, you can also use this to transfer your tracks.

GET CONNECTED If your PC doesn't have Bluetooth built in, you can purchase an inexpensive USB adaptor. You can also use Bluetooth across a home network to share files and devices.

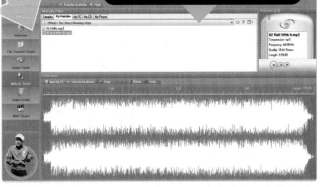

2 If you want to edit a track

Not only can this model make use of MP3s, to save you converting, it even comes with a utility called Multimedia Studio, which can be used to edit your MP3 files.

YOUR TUNE Your average audio track lasts about three minutes, but a phone will only ring for a fraction of that time. Edit your track so that the ringtone plays the best part of the tune.

3 Cut here

If you want to use the chorus, click on **Melody Studio** then choose the MP3 file. Select **Crop** to save the section of the song you want.

READY TO SEND Bluetooth and infra-red may be convenient transfer methods, but the speeds won't be as fast as they would if you used a USB 2.0 cable.

You may find it convenient to use Bluetooth

MP3 RINGTONES Many phones now double as MP3 players. Import your playlists from your media player and they'll be available as your ringtone selection as well.

4 Begin the transfer

For Bluetooth transfer, use the settings on your PC to pair up with your phone. Once you've done this, send the file across. Make sure you use the same PIN on the handset and your PC.

5 Finally

Select **Multimedia** then **Multimedia Finder**. Browse to the folder where you received the file from the PC. Locate it, click on **Options** and select **Apply As Ring Tone** to use it.

TWO'S COMPANY Once you've paired two Bluetooth devices you won't have to enter the PIN again. This information can be saved to make future transfers run as smoothly as possible.

Get fit using your PC

Getting fit used to be about blood, sweat and tears, but now your computer can take some of the strain

 James Stables, Staff Writer on *Windows Vista: The Official Magazine* wanted to see if Windows Vista – and some techno gadgets – could help to improve his fitness levels...

My feet would barely lift off the ground, my legs ached and my heart felt as though it was about to burst out of my rib cage. That was the last time I took up running in a bid to get fit. As you can imagine, my new regime didn't last long.

If, like me, you feel guilty about the amount of exercise you don't do but lack the motivation to do anything about it,

there's good news. A mass of new technologies can make battling the bulge more enjoyable, and get even the most inactive of us off the sofa. To prove this, I set a mission to use my PC as a training aid to get fit in six weeks. I was scientifically assessed before and after the six-week period with the aim that, by sticking to my training schedule, the second round of tests would show some improvement in my overall health.

I chose three products that link with the PC to help me change my slothful ways. The first was the humble dance mat, already a champion with eight-year-olds everywhere, but anyone who has used

one knows it to be a demanding activity. The second, a product called the PCGamerBike – a USB exercise bike that doubles as a games controller. The third was the Nike + iPod, which links your trainers to your iPod nano and maps your runs online. In addition, I used a Polar Heart Rate Monitor to see what impact each device had on my heart rate levels.

Plan of attack

My personal training plan was as follows: running using the Nike + iPod on Mondays, Wednesdays and Fridays; 45-minute dance mat and pedal game sessions on Tuesdays and Thursdays; rest

TESTING On the treadmill, and connected to a machine that will tell it like it really is!

Fit favorites

Work up a sweat with these...

LCD Soundsystem 45:33
As the title suggests, this is a 45-minute mix by one of the most respected producers around – James Murphy. The ups and downs are designed to keep you motivated, with a peak around 25 minutes to give an extra boost.

The Crystal Method Drive
The first 45-minute mix made specifically for running, designed to transfer the energy of the dance floor into your exercise.

Rage Against the Machine Self-titled
If steady beats aren't your cup of isotonic liquid, the renegades of funk can provide an alternative. Angry lyrics, blistering guitars and anti-establishment rants will get you pumped.

Queen Greatest Hits
With songs such as *We are the Champions*, *Another One Bites the Dust*, and *Bicycle Race*, Queen are the undisputed kings of music to work out to.

and recovery at weekends. If I was going to complete the mission, I would need some serious help. I met up with Gavin Reynoldson, a fitness and personal training tutor from a local university which specializes in health and fitness.

Gavin agreed to assess my health before and after my computer-aided fitness regime, so I could see if my new lifestyle was doing me good. He also checked over the merits of my equipment. The verdict on the dance mat was that it would improve the efficiency of the heart and lungs, in turn delivering more oxygen to the tissue; it should also improve flexibility in the muscles. ➲

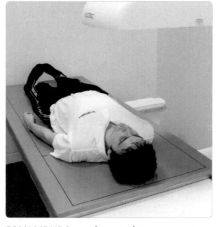

SCAN ME UP James lays on the scanner so the team can measure his body fat levels

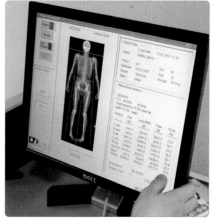

A QUARTER FAT The body scan reveals that James has a 25 per cent fat content

Gavin seemed impressed with the Nike + iPod; running provides a great aerobic workout, and the high impact training helps prevent osteoporosis.

In order to test how effective this exercise regime could be, it was essential to check my overall fitness, so I was checked over for blood pressure, body weight, standing heart rate, body fat and blood oxygen levels before and after the six-week period. Most of these tests are quite easy to perform at home. You can buy blood pressure monitors on the high street, and some pharmacies even check it for free. My blood pressure was 130/81 – a little high – 120/80 is normal and anything over 140 means medical advice may be needed.

To test your resting heart rate, it's important to be sitting comfortably for about five minutes to make sure the test is as accurate as possible. Locate the artery on the thumb side, underneath your wrist, and count the beats for exactly one minute. Gavin took three readings of my pulse, which averaged 70. Any reading between 60 to 80 beats is normal; anything over may indicate a medical problem or a need to embark on a tentative exercise regime.

Next I was subjected to a VO_2 test – this involves a body scan to determine the fat in my body and a run on a treadmill to

My aim was a reduction in body fat and an increase in oxygen uptake

assess my body's ability to deliver oxygen to my blood. The result showed my body was 25 per cent fat and my oxygen uptake was 38.8ml/kg/min, well below average for someone of my age. My aim was a reduction of body fat and an increase in oxygen uptake.

SOUND & STATS With the Nike + iPod you can play music and record your stats

How to set up Nike+ iPod

Put your best foot forward with this nifty device

1 CREATE ACCOUNT Sign up to Nike+ on the web site at www.nikeplus.com and create an account. After a workout, connect your iPod nano to your PC; Nike+ will store and display your data through its dynamic interface.

2 SET SOME GOALS Have an idea of what you want to achieve and use Nike+ to set some realistic goals. Aim to do a certain amount of runs per week; you can also access your own personal trainer with Nike+ Coach.

3 JOIN THE COMMUNITY Nike+ is community based... You can join in with forums and chat to other runners, purchase Powersongs to motivate or share routes with Map It. You can even pair up with others and set challenges.

Primed and ready for action, I headed out on my first run with the Nike + iPod. I set it for a 20-minute workout, which Gavin recommended as an introduction, and started running at a gentle pace. However, I'd already had to stop to catch my breath when the merciless woman who encourages you from your iPod informed me that I had been running for five minutes – it felt like days!

However, Nike+ does make the experience a lot less painful. I had chosen my playlist, and the iPod enables you to select a power song for moments of weakness, which drives you on for that extra mile. I hadn't yet travelled one mile, and I'm not sure the power song is designed to be used so early in the workout, but I needed it.

Back at home, plugging the iPod into my PC made the device come alive. It displayed the distance travelled, calories burned and a graph of my journey, showing every downturn in my

Keep fit kit

Everything you need to keep yourself in peak physical condition

Nike + iPod
A sensor in your trainer links to your iPod nano, recording time, distance, and calories burned.
Price $29 for the kit (+ iPod nano)
Web www.nike.com

Polar Heart Rate Monitor
This wrist watch/chest strap combo monitors your heart rate, enabling you to plot fitness charts.
Price $300 (models/prices vary)
Web www.polar.fi/polar/channels/uk

Logic 3 Dance Mat
The humble dance mat makes for a mean exercise machine. Sustained use is good for muscle flexibility.
Price $40
Web www.spectravideo.com

PCGamerBike Mini
This device replaces a button on your keyboard, allowing it to be the input device for most games.
Price $179
Web www.gamecycles.com

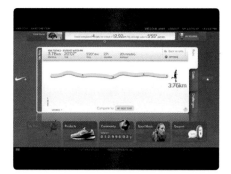

4 ADD YOUR RUNS When you plug in your iPod nano, your data will be automatically updated on the Nike+ website. It plots a line graph of your run showing your pace, distance, time and calories burned.

5 TRACK YOUR PROGRESS All your runs are listed together, and can be viewed by week or month. The chart shows how far you have run each time and the improvement achieved in your fitness levels.

Desk stretches

Avoid injury before exercise...

Before exercise it's important to warm up to steer clear of nasty injuries. Here are five stretches you can do at your computer desk

Calf stretch
Put one foot in front of the other. Put your hands on the desk and lean forward, bending your front knee so you feel tension in your back leg. Reverse and repeat.

Hamstring stretch
Stand up and put one foot on the desk, so it's perpendicular to your body. Point your toes back and try to touch them, holding the tension for 10 seconds.

Quads
Hold on to the corner of the desk and pull your feet back to touch your buttocks, keeping your knees together. Hold the stretch, swap and repeat.

Groin
Sit up straight in your chair, and bring your feet together between your legs by tucking your knees up to your chest. Push your knees apart, hold the stretch for 10 seconds, relax and repeat.

Elbow press
Sit up straight and pull your arm up and back over your shoulder, stretching it down between your shoulder blades. Put your hand on the point of your elbow and hold it here for 10 seconds, then repeat with your other arm.

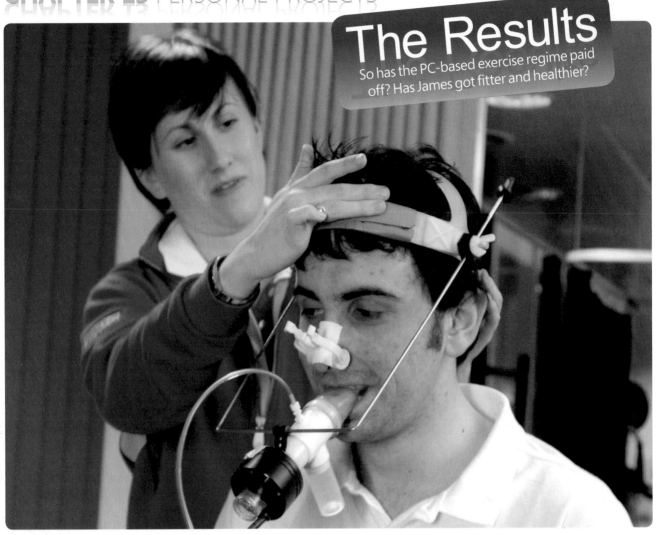

The Results

So has the PC-based exercise regime paid off? Has James got fitter and healthier?

performance like the crash of a stock market. Having a visual representation of my efforts made the aftermath seem a lot less painful, and it really does drive you to get out there and do it again. On my repeated outings to pound the pavements, I could see real improvement and, after four runs, the voices of Paula Radcliffe and Lance Armstrong congratulated me on my progress. I felt proud of my efforts.

While the assisted running was a high-effort activity, taking plenty of motivation to get out into the cold night air, the dance mat was one that could be done with relative ease. And it really is fun to use – in fact, it is really addictive.

Aerobically, it's OK; while it may not compare to a full run, a 20-minute session left me sweating and tired, and I can really see what Gavin meant about it helping a variety of muscle groups.

Rather helpfully, the Logic 3 Dance Mat also records your statistics, and tells you

Almost two per cent of the fat was lost, and my muscle mass increased

how many calories you have burned on each dance. My 20-minute session burned 110 calories, which sounded like a fair bit to me but turned out to count for little more than the packet of low-fat

chips I had eaten 10 minutes before I started dancing.

The PCGamerBike is a novel idea, guaranteed to have your mates crowded around you, begging for a go. You can use it to play any game that usually uses the keyboard, by assigning forwards and backwards to specific keys. However, the degree of success you achieve depends on the style of game.

The best games are racing ones, where one key command dominates your movement. You can then use the keyboard, which is quite awkward, or a joypad to control lateral movement.

The bike enables you to change the resistance and therefore vary your workout and, like the dance mat, does leave you pretty exhausted. An on-board

What you can achieve
The benefits of training with technology

TORSO
Over the six weeks there was a massive increase in muscle mass, coupled with a slight decrease in fat. You can expect a decrease in fat levels after muscle has been built up; this was prevalent in the torso and legs.

HEAD
Other than the physical benefits of fitness activity, those who exercise regularly report better sleep and eating patterns and improvement in general wellbeing.

HEART
James's overall resting heart rate was decreased and, while exercising, the heart rate was significantly lower at higher speeds; showing that the heart is working less to get oxygen to the muscles.

LEGS
Regular high-impact activity, such as jogging, is good for the bones and can help avoid diseases such as osteoporosis. Low impact activity, such as a dance mat, can also improve muscle flexibility.

BLOOD
After the six-week programme, James's blood transferred significantly more oxygen to his muscles. This was coupled with a decrease in lactate levels, which is the acid that makes your muscles hurt when exercising.

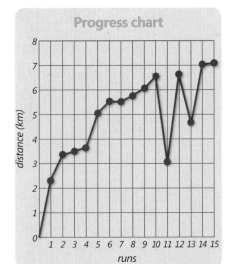

computer also records the distance pedalled, time spent and calories burned – and all this effort, while playing your favorite PC games.

And after six weeks...

Six weeks later and the fitness program has definitely improved my wellbeing. I've only lost one per cent in terms of body fat but that's actually equivalent to about half a kilogram, and my oxygen levels are up, too.

The PC peripherals may not transform me into a marathon runner but they are a fun way of exercising without the 'slog'. Getting fit will always require effort, but involving the computer means you can work out indoors or track your results. Every little bit helps...

Progress chart

(line graph: y-axis "distance (km)" from 0 to 8, x-axis "runs" from 1 to 15)

FRIDAY NIGHTS James found the odd Friday night out seriously affected his performance

The verdict
Do exercise gadgets work?

Nike+ iPod
Having some way of tracking your performance and setting goals helps you improve, and makes the experience more enjoyable.
Rating ★★★★★

Logic 3 Dance Mat
A fun back-up exercise tool. The dance mat provides an opportunity for indoor exercise.
Rating ★★☆☆☆

PCGamerBike
While the PCGamerBike is fun-based, extended and regular use will provide positive effects.
Rating ★★★☆☆

Polar Heart Rate Monitor
Serious equipment for athletes, or for those who are focusing their fitness for specific events.
Rating ★★★★☆

Create your perfect patch

Yes, your computer can turn your fingers green and help you make the most of your backyard!

The prospect of transforming your backyard can seem daunting. You have to know what to plant, when to plant, how long your seedlings will take to grow, and so on. Fortunately, there's a veritable orchard of fruitful sites on the internet, where you'll find no end of useful information.

A rich resource for learners and experts alike is the easily customizable and handy Windows Vista Sidebar, where you can install a web feed to suit your exact requirements and levels of expertise; some gardening sites offer users a constantly updated live feed, to tell you about new hybrids and

remind you when to plant your bulbs.

There's also an abundance of software that will help you to design, organize and understand your garden. One such example is Garden Organizer Deluxe (http://www.primasoft.com/deluxeprg/goodx_try.htm), and this gives you all the elements you need to start and maintain your garden in a freely downloadable demo (see the walkthrough opposite).

Manage your garden

Once you've figured out how it all works, you're going to need to start planting. The calendar in Windows Vista makes it easy to organize and manage your horticultural chores; helping to ensure

that you don't overuse one patch of soil from year to year, and that you vary your colors if you have a more floral garden.

If you want new seeds or bulbs, or need to replace that dodgy trowel, you'll find many web sites offering everything you need, from plants to pitchforks, only one mouse click away. Alternatively, you can chat with, be inspired by, or even just watch the daily lives of other gardeners as they muddle on through, by reading their gardening blogs. A great place to start is MSN Groups, which are user-built communities of people with similar pursuits or interests; head to http://groups.msn.com to get started and look under the Home & Families section.

PLANNING AHEAD There are iCal calendars online that can remind you to do regular tasks or you can create your own

ONLINE FRIENDS Communities online can help provide you with invaluable help, support and ideas for your new garden

Tips and tools from Garden Organizer Deluxe

Plan, budget and maintain your garden

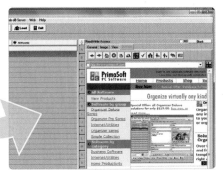

1 ACCESS WEB RESOURCES Using Garden Organizer Deluxe, you can make a list of, and then access, all of the various web resources you think you might need. You can also customize the layout to suit your requirements.

2 STORE PLANT INFORMATION All the plant data that's relevant to your planning is stored in the cleverly laid-out spreadsheet, which covers everything from plant type to weather and soil condition to eventual size.

3 PLAN AND BUDGET YOUR IDEAS The Project Data section helps you to list not only the scope but all of the costs of any garden project. It also enables you to look at before-and-after shots of your projects.

4 PLAN ACCORDING TO THEME The Idea Data section helps you to plan and allot a themed garden of your choice, such as a water garden, alongside all the relevant web applications you might need to access for the project.

Home & garden

Windows Vista and a download can help you get so much more from your garden – but you needn't stop here. All aspects of your home life can be enhanced by using Windows Vista and Microsoft software, learn more at www.microsoft.com/athome.

Five tips for great greenery

And there's more you can do to landscape to your liking

1 PC-SAVVY PACKETS Look at the downloads listed on some seed packets to populate your electronic calendar instantly. You'll also get access to plant photos and links to more detailed instructions and pre-formatted, printable plant labels.

2 SHOOT A SHOOT Whenever you take a trip to a garden center or show, make sure you take a camera or camera phone along with you, so you can photograph the various plants and – as importantly – their labels to make sure you can remember what you need to do at home.

3 TIME LAPSE By either setting up a spare webcam or taking photographs from the same vantage point you can not only build up a fascinating timelapse of your garden as it grows over the year but you can use the footage to track how well your displays are working, enabling you to move plants over the winter.

4 SEED POD TO PODCAST Listen to gardening podcasts on your MP3 player – type in 'gardening podcast' into Windows Live Search and it will list the latest ones that various gardening organizations have on offer.

5 SEARCH FOR INSPIRATION If you're short of inspiration make full use of the Windows Live Search, use the Image link to track beautiful shots of all sorts of gardens and displays.

Learn a language - in a fun, flexible way

Forget dull textbooks – if you want to learn a language, your computer can make the experience accessible, informative and fun

Vacations, eh... Sun, sea, surf, and struggling with the language – two weeks not understanding a word! While the world is getting smaller, with cheap flights and accommodation, the difficulty in furthering your travel experience is the language barrier.

For those of us whose language lessons are distant memories, learning a foreign

tongue is often associated with dull rules about grammar and tenses, or the packs of CDs that promise to 'teach you a language in just 15 days', when all you achieve is a nervous tension associated with the monotonous voice that tells you to repeat the same phrase over and over.

Luckily, the days of *écoutez et répétez* are over. In the last few years, computers and the internet have revolutionized the way we learn languages, making the experience a lot more fun.

Pod patois

Central to this brave new way is podcasting. Before, language lessons had a knack of sounding boring and lifeless. Now, though, technology has enabled a whole host of people to record their own

versions, injecting personality and humour as they do so. One such service is JapanesePod101, which specializes in making learning a language into an engaging experience, so students become interested in the language they're studying and want more.

It's a technique that's proven popular. By making shows that can be downloaded to an MP3 player, people can listen on the way to work, at the gym, or even while lying in bed. And because the shows are entertaining, 'students' are more inclined to pop the headphones on.

These services come with other benefits, too. Vibrant communities usually flock to engaging podcasts, made up of people from all nationalities who come together to help one another.

Three to try

Popular language podcasts

JapanesePod101.com
With a different character set, Japanese is one of the hardest languages to learn. Thankfully, the hosts of this podcast liven it up with sheer enthusiasm and scenario-based learning.

learnfrenchbypodcast.com
The hosts of this podcast take simple phrases and break them down into basic components, so you understand exactly what you're saying, instead of repeating passages verbatim.

spanishsense.com
The great thing about SpanishSense is the way the hosts complement each other. The 'teacher' delivers the majority, but the 'pupil' intervenes when he needs some clarification.

Learn a new language

See how Encarta can help you learn languages

1 SELECT A LANGUAGE Open http://encarta.msn.com/encnet/features/worldwide.aspx in your web browser and select a language. Then select a topic, preferably one you're familiar with.

2 FEELS LIKE HOME From previous trips to Encarta, you might be surprised by how much you instinctively understand, simply by knowing what should be there, like the 'Welcome to Encarta' element.

Dos and don'ts

What to do and what to avoid when learning a lingo

Do

1 Practise every day; even if it's only 10 minutes, it will help the language stay fresh in your mind.

2 Get into the culture; make the language feel real, rather than just an academic means to an end.

3 Visit the country. Even a short visit can be of real benefit – you have to really try to make yourself understood, but it's fun to try, too!

Don't

1 Try to literally translate every word. Languages often work differently, so try to be flexible.

2 Practise your language late at night. By the evening, your brain rarely wants to digest anything new.

3 Feel like a failure if it doesn't come easily. Learning a new language is like rewiring your brain, so it's not an 'overnight' process.

Taking the idea of community-based learning one step further are web sites like DailyFrenchPod. As well as regular services such as a forum and community blog, the Paris-based group provides the community with interactive exercises, grammar tutorials and listening lessons to support the podcast content.

Interactive gaming

Offline, a whole range of software has been developed to make languages easier. One such course is produced by Linkword Languages, which specializes in improving your ability to remember foreign words by associating them with phrases and pictures you can remember.

So, for example, to remember what a hedgehog is in French – *herisson* – it would ask you to 'imagine your hairy son' looking like a hedgehog. A novel approach, but one that's working for some who were previously struggling.

Existing software and games can also be modified to help teach languages, or rather, software can be downloaded to modify them. One creative post-graduate, Ravi Purushotma, spent part of his thesis research finding ways to modify both *The Sims* and *The Sims 2* to help players learn French and German.

The keen gamer noticed that many of the tasks in the game contained the same words as the German homework he had

Playing games in another language can help improve your vocabulary

been given to complete. By switching the language settings to German, he found his familiarity with the game allowed him to pick up German words. Since then, a whole host of full language customization tools have been released for games and multimedia applications in general. See www.langwidge.com for more details.

Total translation

Your computer can help develop existing knowledge of languages, too. One way to improve vocabulary is to browse regional web sites. Even for someone quite unfamiliar with the language, layouts are often quite formulaic, so it's surprisingly easy to work out at least the gist of what's being said. Of course, if you're really struggling you can use MSN Live Translator (http://translator.live.com) to translate an entire web site.

Unfortunately, though, computers don't always understand the vast nuances of languages and can get it wrong. In these circumstances, the Systran Windows Sidebar gadget comes in useful. By pasting a chunk of text into the gadget, it will not only translate it, but display the original text by the side for reference.

3 BREAK IT DOWN Select a page you'll be familiar with and copy the web address. Head to http://translator.live.com, select the language conversion and paste the address in the web page box.

4 COMPARE AND CONTRAST Once it's done, you will be able to compare between the original and the translation. While the direct translation will be formal, it's a great entry point.

5 TRICKY LITTLE WORDS Occasionally you'll get a word that doesn't quite make sense. It's worth trying the word translator by going to http://encarta.msn.com and clicking the Dictionary link.

Create a paperless home with Windows Vista

Households throw out masses of paper every week – most of that could be saved by using your Windows Vista PC to its full potential

Is a paperless existence really still a distant pipe-dream? Or can we clear the clutter and save the rainforests at the same time?

Opt for online billing

Getting up to a pile of bills at breakfast is never fun. Increasingly, though, credit card and utility companies allow you to switch to online bills or statements. Many companies even discount your bill if you go for this option.

Bank online

With so many payments now made by card rather than in cash, money is more virtual than ever. That's why online banking is so important. It's a secure, accessible way to keep an eye on your cash and, with daily

updates, you can budget more effectively. You may never get another warning letter from your bank again – saving both paper and money.

Scan your documents

With some companies your only choice is a paper bill. Our advice? Once paid, scan bills and important letters. Save the scanned image as a PNG file, giving the document an explanatory name. You now have an electronic copy of your bill or letter that's easy to find. With Windows Photo Gallery, you can even add tags to the image. As for the paper original, put it in storage or shred it.

Email everything

Almost any correspondence can now be sent by email. Letters to friends and relatives, queries to your bank, complaints to the local government.

READ ALL ABOUT IT It's quicker and easier to get your news online – and less messy, too

Just occasionally, you may get asked to fax a form or photocopied document to someone. Ask them if they have an email address – you can scan in any document and send it as an attachment using Windows Mail instead. And why not send greetings cards by email? Great for the environment, cheaper for you and far more personal for the recipient. Add text to your own photos to turn them into electronic postcards.

Transferable text

Printing off a word-processed document for a friend? Give them an electronic copy instead. Rather than saving in your word processor's format, save as an RTF. Standing for Rich Text Format, this Microsoft file type is readable on almost any computer – and maintains your formatting and text styles.

Ditch the address book

Windows Vista features Windows Contacts integrated directly into Windows Explorer. The quickest way

ADDRESS BOOK Windows Contacts enables you to export contacts from your old PC

to get to Contacts is to go to your user folder and open the **Contacts** subfolder. Add a new contact by right-clicking and choosing **New → Contact**. You can export contacts to transferable formats in Windows Contacts, too.

Read papers online

With expert content and in-depth features, magazines and books give tangible value that the web can't compete with, but when it comes to news the net is far faster and will save you from the scourge of inky fingers. All the major newspapers have their own web sites now, and you'll find a plethora of gossip-based pages, too.

Create PDFs

Adobe PDF (Portable Document Format) files are the best cross-platform format for moving digital documents. They

FIRST POST Windows Mail is the replacement for Outlook Express, built into Windows Vista; use it to send scanned-in documents

preserve formatting, text styles and fonts and can even include embedded images – and the reader is free so everyone you send them to should be able to view them. If you use Microsoft Office, you can download a PDF converter as a free add-in. Go to www.microsoft.com/downloads and search for 'Save as PDF', then download and install Save as PDF or XPS.

Digitize your notes

Stop scribbling on envelopes and scraps of paper – take notes on your computer instead. Windows Notepad is ideal for quickly jotting down the odd telephone number, shopping list or appointment. You can then add the information to Windows Contacts or Calendar at your leisure – or transfer lists to your mobile phone. Need to insert today's date into Notepad? Just hit **F5**.

Opt out of junk mail

From your letterbox straight to the bin – junk mail accounts for a large percentage of paper waste, and the plastic address windows in those envelopes mean they're difficult to

recycle. Opt out instead, by visiting an online mail preference service; register your postal address at one of these service sites and you should see a substantial reduction in the number of unsolicited advertisements landing on your mat.

Share photos

Don't print out your digital pictures – share them online instead. Sign up with Windows Live Spaces (spaces.live.com) and click **Share photos** to add digital images quickly and easily to online albums your friends can access.

Shred and recycle

Windows Vista helps you protect user accounts with passwords and secure your data using advanced encryption. And yet, many of us still throw paper documents containing personal information straight in the bin. Bank letters with our account numbers, new PINs, invoices and receipts – they all contain data that identity thieves can use. Invest in a shredder and make sure you destroy all personal information before putting it in the recycling bin.

Make your own must-see movie

Turn your fun day out into a film you can share with friends and family, using Windows Movie Maker

"Wow" Output for DVD

Windows Vista offers one-click access to Windows DVD Maker from within Windows Movie Maker. Open the Tasks pane and click **Publish to DVD**

Not only are digital camcorders more affordable than ever, making a recording can be a simple case of pointing and shooting. The difficult part is turning the results into a professional-looking movie. Fortunately, Windows Vista comes bundled with Windows Movie Maker – an easy to use video-editing package that can help you turn a day out into a mini-masterpiece.

Editing is more than just assembling clips into sequence. Turning a collection of events into a coherently told story is both an art and a craft. You'll find practical tips for using Movie Maker on the following pages. Then, with the craft taken care of, the art is up to you.

With digital video, it's a painless process transferring footage to your PC. Windows Movie Maker has a built-in 'Import from digital camera' wizard that holds your hand every step of the way.

Start editing

Windows Movie Maker detects transitions in your footage and creates clips from your video. This means you can begin your editing in the default Storyboard view though, if you want, switch between the Storyboard and Timeline views by hitting **Ctrl** and **T**. Drag-and-drop clips from the Collections pane onto the storyboard to build a narrative sequence.

Be selective, though. Click on **Clips** in the Collections section window and hit

the space bar to preview before placing them in the storyboard. Much of the footage you shoot won't be needed – so you can bin many of the clips.

You won't even need all the material in every clip that you do use. For example, a 30-second shot of ducks paddling might easily be reduced to 10 or even 5 seconds. Getting rid of this 'fat' is the first stage of editing. Use the Split tool to cut down your clips. ➡

With digital video, it's a painless process transferring footage to your PC

Import video to your computer

Use the video import wizard in Windows Movie Maker to transfer clips

1 CREATE A COLLECTION Click the **Show or Hide Collections** icon next to the **Location** dropdown, then **File ➡ New Collection Folder**. Give the folder a relevant name such as 'Day-trip footage'.

2 READY TO LAUNCH Make sure your DV camcorder is connected to your PC by FireWire or USB 2.0. Click **Show or hide tasks ➡ Import ➡ From digital video camera** to launch the wizard.

3 FORMAT AND DESTINATION It's best to save your video footage to a separate, clean partition or hard drive if possible. Select **AVI** as the format if your video is destined for DVD playback.

How to shoot great footage

Top tips that will make your final footage good enough for the silver screen

Look for movement

This isn't photography, so outside of the odd establishing shot you want to have change in every frame. Take video footage of things that are moving (people, animals, water) or pan the camera across the scene.

No great shakes

Don't worry too much about keeping steady; a little movement adds energy and reality to a shot. Many modern cameras have built-in sensors that reduce shake anyway.

Don't zoom

When you're watching TV, how often do you see zoom shots? If you need to get a close-up, move closer. And bear in mind that camera shake increases as you zoom in.

Keep shooting

Shoot more than you need. You may have to video for a minute to get the four or five seconds you want.

Look for the light

You can't always control the lighting in the real world – but you can make sure you don't shoot directly into it. Ideally, you should have a light source behind you, not your subject.

Three to try

A range of camcorders fill the market, all with different abilities

High-end hard drive based camcorders offer hours of recording time, high-def resolutions and are perfect for people who want semi-pro results from their home videos.

For ease of use, many people still enjoy camcorders that can record directly to optical discs in one of the many DVD or CD formats. These are convenient to use but can be limited on the record time.

The latest generation of digital camcorders are compact and lightweight. These use flash memory cards to record video and, while this can limit the overall record time, these are generally a lot more affordable.

4 CUE THE TAPE Click **Next ➜ Import parts of the videotape to my computer ➜ Next**. The buttons control your camcorder and enable you to find and cue up the right section of tape.

5 CAPTURE THE VIDEO Hit the **Start Video Import** button. To stop capture, click **Stop Video Import**, then **Finish** to commit the capture to disc and import it into the selected collection.

A 30-second shot might easily be reduced to 10 or even 5 seconds

To start, add a clip to the storyboard, then hit **Ctrl** and **T** to switch back to the timeline. Position the playback head so it's in the approximate spot where you'd like the clip to begin. You can fine-tune by hitting **Alt** and the arrow keys to advance the play head back or forth a frame at a time. When you're happy, hit **Ctrl** and **L** to split the clip at that point. Select the part you want to remove and hit the **Delete** key.

Clip your clips

Once you've got a rough-cut, you can tweak this in the timeline using the most powerful editing weapon in Windows Movie Maker – the Trim tool.

Start by playing back your rough cut. Some sections will seem too long, others won't follow on well from the footage that precedes them. Click on any clip that needs tweaking in the timeline and hover your cursor over the start of the clip. You can click and drag

the clip, adjusting its start point. You can trim the end point of any clip in the same way. If you need a bit more precision, move the playback head to the start or end point you'd prefer and hit **O** to trim the beginning of the clip or **I** to trim the end.

One clever aspect of Windows Movie Maker that's easy to overlook is that you can visually edit to an audio track. Click the **Expand video track** icon in the timeline. It looks like a '+' symbol next

to the Video track label. This opens the **Audio and transition** tracks. Next, hover your cursor over the edge of the **Timeline** panel – your cursor should change to a double-headed arrow.

Click and drag to resize the timeline vertically. This causes the audio track to grow and the waveform becomes visible. When editing footage with dialog in it, you can use this expanded view to position the playback accurately before trimming or splitting a clip. ⊞

In real life...
Making better movies

Nick Odantzis, Technology Writer, offers the following insights:

1 Have fun! Editing will be as much fun as you want to make it. Either edit raw footage into a great home movie or try and film a movie from scratch to your own script.

2 Less is more People have a tendency to leave every second of footage in, don't. Long shots are usually dull and unnecessary, cut back to what gets the message across.

3 Keep it simple While a good transition or effect can help lift a shot or smoothly cut between two, stick to one type and don't throw every different one at your movie as it will end up looking messy.

4 Use narrative Even in a holiday movie you're telling a story, make sure you have a beginning, middle and end, told out through your shots.

5 Try everything Remember this is digital media, you can experiment as much as you like and still start again from scratch at the end.

Transitions and effects

Some finishing touches to give your movie a professional feel

1 DON'T GO OVERBOARD Don't make the mistake of throwing every effect you have at your clips: not every edit needs transitions or effects. Use them sparingly when context demands.

2 FADE IN In this example, the first scene comes in from a black fade. This comes straight after the titles and 'tells' the viewer the action is beginning. Go to **Effects ➜ Fade In, From Black**.

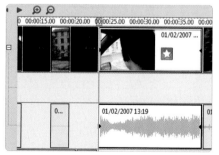

3 APPLYING EFFECTS Dragging and dropping an effect to a clip adds it immediately. A small star icon is added to the clip. To edit or change the effect, right-click on it and choose **Effects**.

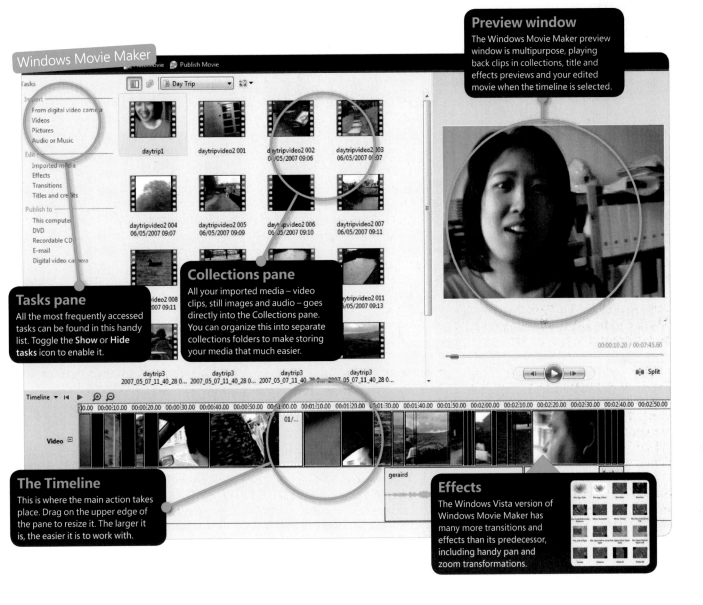

Windows Movie Maker

Preview window
The Windows Movie Maker preview window is multipurpose, playing back clips in collections, title and effects previews and your edited movie when the timeline is selected.

Collections pane
All your imported media – video clips, still images and audio – goes directly into the Collections pane. You can organize this into separate collections folders to make storing your media that much easier.

Tasks pane
All the most frequently accessed tasks can be found in this handy list. Toggle the **Show** or **Hide** **tasks** icon to enable it.

The Timeline
This is where the main action takes place. Drag on the upper edge of the pane to resize it. The larger it is, the easier it is to work with.

Effects
The Windows Vista version of Windows Movie Maker has many more transitions and effects than its predecessor, including handy pan and zoom transformations.

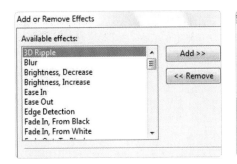

4 MASS EFFECT The Effects box allows you to remove the current effect or add further effects. To add effects, select from the column on the left and chose **Add** (but remember, less is more).

5 SMOOTH PASSAGE Transitions are placed between the end of one clip and the beginning of the next. These are useful to smooth jarring changes, where a normal jump cut would be too harsh.

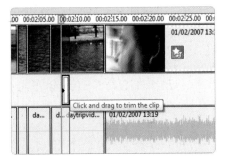

6 TRIM TO LENGTH Expand the video track in the timeline and you'll see any transitions there on their own track. You can shorten or lengthen them in the same way you trim normal video clips.

Shoot and share

Unleash the creative power of your digital camera and Windows Vista to capture great memories

There's no more rewarding time to take photographs than during a vacation. With children constantly excited and adults in high spirits, it's a magical time for the whole family, no matter if it's summer or fall. During winter, the crisp mornings and the possibility of snow make the most perfect picture-postcard landscapes – irresistible to anyone with a digital camera. While during the summer, blue skies and lush scenery make a stunning backdrop.

If you've invested in a new digital camera or Windows Vista PC and you're itching to test them – whether you're a longstanding photographer or just opening the box and plugging in for the first time – creative help and finishing touches aren't far from your fingertips.

You've been framed

Every great image begins with the incentive to press the shutter and take the picture. The golden rule is to keep your camera with you at all times, with batteries fully charged and space on your memory card, as photo opportunities constantly appear in front of your eyes.

Spontaneity may be key, but it doesn't hurt to think ahead. Think of all the great occasions when the entire family gets together – events like Halloween, Thanksgiving and Christmas make for perfect photo opportunities.

Take Christmas morning when the kids open their presents... Frame them in the LCD and press the shutter halfway to focus. Wait till they gasp in delight – or

have a tantrum in disappointment – then fully press the shutter to capture that critical moment. Keep shooting, too. Switch your camera to a continuous shooting mode and take a few; you can always use Windows Photo Gallery to whittle out the bad ones later. If you can, turn the lights on and open the curtains to let more light in the room, as using your flash will kill any festive atmosphere, counteracting any subtle lighting. Give your zoom finger a workout and fill the frame with their faces to really capture those expressions of happiness on Christmas morning.

During quieter periods, why not grab a sneaky shot of grandpa sleeping off his dinner in front of the TV, or children frowning in concentration as they get to

HELP YOURSELF If you have Microsoft Word 2007 you have access to a library of templates

"Wow" Photo Swap

A great new feature in Windows Live Messenger is MSN Photo Swap. This enables you to share photos with any of your Messenger Contacts: just click the **Activities** button to get going!

"I've trashed my photos!"

What to do when it all goes badly wrong...

There are few things more precious than those special moments caught on camera. Losing or ruining them doesn't bear thinking about. However, it can happen, and you'll need to know what to do if it does.

A major benefit of fixing your photos in Windows Photo Gallery is that you can crop and adjust images in the knowledge you can revert back to the original file at any time – even years later! Simply open your

photo in Fix and click the **Revert** button to go back to the original.

Pictures that have disappeared from your PC or memory card take longer to fix, but it's not impossible. The usual culprit is accidentally formatting a memory card or hitting delete by accident. Don't worry, there are programs that can usually find and recover data from memory cards and hard drives even if it's corrupt, been deleted or formatted.

SAVE ME Changes made through the Windows Photo Gallery can be reverted

GREAT SNAPPER Take a few shots in succession to be sure of at least one winning pic

grips with their new toys? What about posing the whole family around the Christmas tree? It's easy. Pull a comfy chair in front of it and get older family members to sit in the chair, keep the taller adults behind and get the kids on the

When the kids open their presents capture the delight or disappointment

floor. Don't forget yourself, either. Use a tripod or place the camera on a table and use the self-timer.

And why not try for a creative macro shot you can use to make thank you cards? Switch your camera's Macro mode

on (indicated by a flower symbol) and close in tight on some colorful tree decorations or festive food. Focus on a bright area of interest in the frame, such as a fairy light, hold the shutter halfway, recompose the shot so it's off centre and fire off the shutter.

Get out!

Remember that macro photos aren't just for indoors, either. Think of all that sparkling winter frost covering fallen leaves and branches, just waiting to be turned into stunning photographs and creative images. Zoom in a little and try to get as close as possible to pick out the frozen detail. Alternatively, if there's snow around, make sure you make the most of it and head out to the country to capture some winter wonderland scenery. If your camera has a snow scene mode then use →

Perfect pics
Top tips for spot-on shots

1 For a cosy family winter shot get the clan huddled together. Use a tripod and timer to make sure you're in the photo, too!

2 Be ready – keep your batteries fully charged and memory cards empty.

3 Give your landscapes a more dramatic feel – take them when the light is at its best in the early morning or at sunset.

4 Avoid dark, underexposed landscapes by switching your camera to Scene mode and choosing the Landscape setting.

5 When out and about, concentrate on details such as leaves and flowers by using your camera's Macro mode. ›

6 For party pics packed with energy, switch the flash on and select the Night Portrait mode.

7 Capture dusky evening cityscapes by setting your camera on a tripod, using the self-timer and shooting as the sun sets.

8 Over Christmas, shoot a 'fairy-light portrait' of a loved one by positioning them near the tree and turning the camera flash off.

9 Switch your camera to Macro mode and take lots of close-ups of seasonal decorations – great for decorating cards.

10 Capture the delight on kid's faces as they open presents by switching to Continuous shoot mode and taking lots of pictures.

DIGITAL FREEDOM The latest digital cameras offer amazing levels of details and features

it to capture bright white snow rather than dull gray slush. Compose with a frozen puddle or frosty bench in the foreground for maximum impact.

Easy editing

When you're back from your walk, get the camera's batteries on charge as you'll definitely want it ready for action at all those parties. Remember to switch your camera into a night party mode. Any low-light mode will get you great pictures, but to be sure of the best results – with plenty of color and movement – turn the flash on and select the night portrait setting.

Don't worry too much if things don't go to plan on the night as Windows Live Photo Gallery can help. Download Windows Live Photo Gallery from get.live. com to get the latest editing tools and the most from your shots. Use **Fix** to sharpen blurry images, create amazing panoramas and increase the color saturation and contrast with precision for photos that scream impact. Remember to use the full power of the program to organize your images, too. Use star ratings to identify all your favorites and be sure to tag your shots with relevant keywords so you're able to dig out all of those wonderful memories for many years to come.

Share your photos with everyone
Show off your holiday snaps with friends online

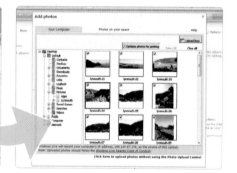

1 GET SPACE To share photos online, try putting them on MSN Live Spaces – it's free and easy. Browse to http:// spaces.live.com. If you have an MSN Messenger account you can sign in with this, otherwise create a new account.

2 SET LIMITS Once signed in, click **Share Photo**, click **Add Album** on the next page. Before adding images, click **Permission** to restrict who can view the images – everyone, MSN Messenger contacts, MySpace friends or just you.

3 UPLOAD Click **Add Photos**. You'll need to accept the security prompt to install an ActiveX control before this will work. Browse to your photos and click the top-left tick box in each image you'd like to upload, then click **Upload**.

4 SHARE The uploading will take a few minutes depending on how many photos you're uploading and how fast your connection is. Once done give the album a name and click **Save**. Depending on your permission settings, friends and family will now be able to view and enjoy your photos.

You can restrict who can view the images to everyone, select contacts or friends, or just you

Happy holidays!

Ditch the e-card and use your images to send out stylish greeting cards

1 Download a favorite photo to your mobile phone and send it out with a personalized message.

2 Use an editing tool to caption photos and send by email.

3 Use your web site to send out holiday greetings by uploading your best pictures to your blog.

4 For an extravagant gift why not send a loved one some of your best photos on a digital photo frame?

5 Use Windows DVD Maker to put your pictures on DVD and spice them up by adding music and text.

6 Upload your best holiday photos to an online gallery.

7 Print your best shot and use your home printer to make a bespoke and traditional style Christmas card.

8 Download Windows Live Photo Gallery and publish your images directly to Windows Live Spaces.

9 Create a calendar with pictures from relevant times of the year.

Use your photos to create stunning cards

A home-made card implies lots of effort, but it's actually really easy!

1 WHERE TO START You can create your own cards by using an art package, a word processor or online template. For inspiration office.microsoft.com has a range of projects to try.

2 WORD IT Here's how to make a card using Microsoft Office Word 2007. Create a new document, choose **Layout → Orientation → Landscape**. You may want to zoom out to see the whole page.

3 INSERT By selecting **Insert → Picture** you can choose an image to add. Right-click this and choose **Text Wrapping → In Front of Text**, so you can resize and move the image at will.

4 FLIP & MOVE Hover the mouse over the green handle to rotate the image 180 degrees. Size it and move it to the top-left corner; once the paper is folded into four this will be the front of the card.

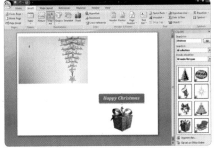

5 ADD TEXT Select **Insert → Text box** to add a text message bottom right. You may want to do the same on the back, but flip this again to match the image. Add in any other images.

6 PRINT OUT Adjust the print options and check the alignment of the images on the page. Try a black and white draft print to check before the color version, and then your card is done.

Take the hard work out of homework

Windows Vista has an array of features to help your child with schoolwork – they might even enjoy their next project!

Windows Vista can help make studying a whole lot easier for your child; whether it's organizing work, researching, creating and listening to podcasts, or completing assignments, Windows Vista has the tools to help.

Writing an essay or compiling a project means pulling together information from a variety of sources and preparing it all to a set length. Thankfully, children no longer have to rely on textbooks from the local or school library. Instead they have access to millions of sources on the internet. But then there's almost too much information to tap into and digest! By the time your child's finished researching, they may well have thousands of random snippets scattered randomly on your PC's hard drive, and won't know where to start to collate it all.

Fortunately Windows Vista provides some very useful tools, even for the terminally disorganized. At its simplest, the Instant Search function enables your child to find all references to a topic. Quotes can help narrow the search (for instance 'dinosaur' AND 'carnivorous') to weed out all the references to the herbivore kind. There are a whole series of other filters you can apply to narrow searches further, whether it's the size of the file, when it was created or what program was used (see more on this in the Files and Folders section on p52). In Windows Vista you also get Natural Language Search – a flexible search that doesn't require brackets, inverted quotes or capital letters. To turn on Natural Language Search, click **Start**, then **Control Panel**, **Appearance and Personalization**, and select **Folder Options**. Click the **Search** tab and select **Use natural language search**.

Having found the files they want, your child can keep them as a Saved Search by clicking the button on the Results toolbar. This is very useful when it comes to

All their own work...

The thin line between research and plagiarism

Computers have made plagiarism much easier; it's just a matter of a quick cut and paste job. There are even web sites selling essays, ready to be downloaded and passed off as a child's own work.

Of course, teachers aren't stupid. When the school truant suddenly turns in a well written assignment, somebody is going to smell a rat. And, be warned, the technology that makes it easier to steal work can also help to catch the cheats.

So how can your child avoid plagiarism? Journalists often say: "Stealing from one source is plagiarism; stealing from many is research." There's an element of truth in that – no piece of work is 100 per cent original. The best essays take ideas from a number of sources and say clearly where the information has come from; a process made easier using Office Word 2007's Source Manager. The student should then organize those arguments logically and reach a clear conclusion based on them. Most marks are awarded on the basis of how many specific points

REMEMBER ME Never forget another source thanks to Microsoft Word 2007

relevant to the question are included in the essay. It's often useful to see how other students have answered similar questions. Some web sites are dedicated to coursework, and you can search for and analyze existing work.

The internet is a valuable research tool and that's exactly how it should be used. Make sure your children source facts and information, but also that they reflect on what they've learned and inject their own individual 'spin' on their work.

revision as it keeps all references to a particular topic in one handy place.

Another way of keeping track of files is by using tags. Your child may, for instance, use the tag 'geography project' to keep together all text documents, pictures, video clips and sound files that they need.

Word to the wise

For day-to-day work your child will doubtless use Microsoft Word. Be sure they know about all its functions. There are research options available when you right-click on a word; synonyms, available in the same way, can help make an essay read better by reducing repetition, and

the same goes for Microsoft Word's grammar and spelling checks.

Microsoft Office 2007 is competitively priced; if you're not a business user, you can buy a copy of the Home and Student edition for about a third of the Standard edition price. Both suites include Office Word, Office Excel and Office PowerPoint.

The Home and Student edition has a copy of OneNote in place of Office Outlook 2007. OneNote offers a way to gather and organize information in a variety of formats – whether it's text, pictures, handwriting, audio or video recordings and more, into one place on your computer. ➲

Seven ways to better grades

Philip Collie, managing director of Schoolzone (www.schoolzone.co.uk), one of Britain's largest educational resource web sites, gives his advice on how your child can achieve academic success

1 Use the Track Changes feature in Office Word when studying or using revision notes. They'll gain confidence from seeing how their understanding of a subject is changing. It allows for notes to be added and hidden from classmates and teachers.

2 Create revision aids in Office PowerPoint and share with friends.

3 Use Office Excel to keep a record of test or homework scores and track progress or identify areas of weakness.

4 Create audio files of revision notes as podcasts. Groups of study friends may want to divide up a set of notes and do a section each, then share online.

5 Use MSN, Bebo and Facebook to share ideas and help each other with homework and school projects.

6 Find titled videos, for instance, 'chemistry experiment', 'photosynthesis' or 'Tudor England' on YouTube. They can then write a revision guide based on the clip to use in class.

7 Use Windows Calendar to create and share revision timetables, then they can log their success at meeting targets.

"I love using the computer"

Now the children are even teaching their parents...

The Moran family have been using Windows Vista since 2007. "The biggest issue is kicking the kids off when I need to work and don't have my laptop," says Mark, father of Lisa (nine), Michael (seven), Jamie (five) and Beth (four).

"The eldest two are pretty savvy when it comes to using the PC," he says. "Lisa has loads of projects from school, and they all seem to involve Office PowerPoint 2007 and loads of references from Wikipedia. She's actually started teaching me stuff, which is pretty scary. I thought I had at least another couple of years of being top dog."

"I love using the computer," enthuses Lisa. "It's really cool changing all the wallpaper and pictures. I love making projects for school in Office Word and Publisher. I always get great photos from our camera or by downloading them from the web. I like having a password so Michael can't touch my stuff. I also use it to chat to friends. We have classes in school about using computers and it's dead easy as I can do it all at home."

Michael's also on his way to being

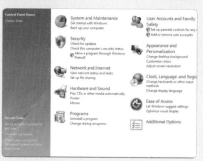

SAFETY FIRST Use the Parental Controls to restrict your child's access to web sites

a techie: "I love playing games on the internet and doing competitions as well. I love drawing things using the mouse."

Of course, dad Mark has some concerns about safety for the children: "We do use the Parental Controls available in Windows Vista to protect the kids. They're very simple to use and only take a couple of minutes to set up. We haven't bothered with additional programs such as Net Nanny because the Parental Controls seem more than adequate at the moment."

For more details on using the Parental Controls to protect your children turn to page 48.

OneNote is a great feature for students. References and handouts can be copied or scanned and dragged into OneNote and organized in sections, pages and sub-pages. Then, as your child searches the web, useful information, links and pictures can also be dropped and stored in OneNote notebooks complete with personal annotations. Everything can, of course, be searched, shared online and is

You can download thousands of useful podcasts on various school topics

automatically backed up. The information can also be reorganized and restructured to fit the way the project is developing.

Then, because OneNote is part of Office 2007, it's easy to export the results into Word or PowerPoint. One of the many improvements in Microsoft Office 2007 is that it makes producing attractive documents a lot easier – it's easy to alter formats and access the huge number of templates that are available.

The only disappointment if you use OneNote with an ordinary desktop or notebook PC is that you miss out on one of its coolest features. Tablet PCs have a microphone and, if your child takes notes while a teacher is lecturing, it will tie the text to the audio so they can check to hear exactly what was said, rather than what they wrote at the time. Having said that,

WORD PERFECT The 2007 Microsoft Office system has many tools for perfect projects

some relatively inexpensive MP3 players now have a recording function, and you can save anything that's been recorded as a sound file to your computer.

Pod project

In an ideal world you'd then be able to convert that sound file to text using the voice recognition function in Windows Vista. Unfortunately, the software still has to be trained to recognize an individual's voice using a process of reading and correcting the results. There is, however, a trick: stick one ear bud in your ear so you can hear the recorded speech, then speak the words into the mic attached to your PC and you'll change the spoken words into text without having to type. Simple.

Of course, you could think of the original lesson recording as a sort of podcast. In fact, if your child wants to create a useful revision tool he could make his own podcast using sound editing software such as the free program Audacity (from audacity.sourceforge.net).

They would, however, need to use other software if they wanted to publish the podcasts online. A less powerful, but easier to use, free alternative is WildVoice (www.wildvoice.com). You can also publish direct from this software.

Cool tool

Get an online revision buddy

For instant answers to homework and other questions, add encarta@botmetro.net to your Windows Live Messenger contacts. Type in your query and the bot will open up the appropriate Microsoft Encarta encyclopaedia page for you in a chat window.

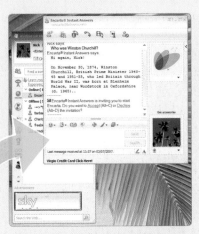

ENCYCLOPAEDIC KNOWLEDGE Encarta will make a useful contact – especially for those last-minute revision panics

There are thousands of useful podcasts available to download, usually for free, on all sorts of study topics. To find out what's available, go to your favorite search engine such as Windows Live search, type in, say, 'podcast US & World History SAT' and see what comes up.

Many podcasts are created by teachers, but don't let that put you off! After all they do know how best to present a topic to make it easy to understand. It's surprising how hearing familiar topics discussed by different people can make them easier to understand and remember. Podcasts are great for when the dreaded revision time comes and they don't want to waste a moment – they can revise when walking to school or waiting at the bus stop.

Smart study aids
Gadgets that look good and help!

LAPTOP
With Windows Vista-capable laptops now as affordable as budget desktop systems these make the perfect choice for your child's education.

DIGITAL AUDIO PLAYER
Not just handy for enjoying music, many models now offer microphones so they're perfect for recording and listening to lectures and podcasts.

POCKET PC
Have the best of all worlds in the palm of your hand. Many Pocket PCs offer phone, audio features and Microsoft Office support in a tiny package.

How to get the best grades

With help from Windows Vista, getting a good result can be as easy as a click of the mouse...

Take charge of how well you do in your next exams by using the technology that your PC and Windows Vista puts at your disposal. While there's no magic formula for studying, there are some sure-fire ways of getting yourself into the top stream.

The first method is to schedule effectively. A good schedule helps you to allocate realistic units of study time. The Windows Vista Calendar can alert you minutes, hours or days ahead – either on a one-off or recurring basis. Many universities offer the iCalendar format, with which Windows Vista is compatible, listing exam times, podcasts and more.

Should you want to tailor your reminders, you'll find various examples of downloadable software on the internet that you can add to your Windows Vista Desktop Sidebar. Some of these even offer a speech function so that your reminders are read out loud and, if your concentration span is limited, you can set a number of prompts to

beep at regular intervals during your study, just to keep you alert!

If you can, go to a café or a park when reading through material – a relaxed environment can help you absorb information. This is when a Tablet PC can come in handy. And Windows Live Messenger (get.live.com/messenger/overview) is perfect for linking up with fellow students to test each other, or you can use a webcam for a video chat.

Many colleges offer free podcasts, enabling you to revisit lecture themes. These are a good way to revise when your eyes are too tired to carry on reading.

The Windows

Vista Innovation Café also gives you online access to the British Library . You've scheduled, prepared and dug in when you realize that you are missing one of the most important study ingredients: pizza. You don't have to leave your study zone – make use of the fact that Windows Vista is the securest system yet and order some thin and crispy inspiration online! Although, make sure the padlock icon is there when you enter your details, and don't start studying the menu instead of your homework.

"Wow" Windows Meeting Space

Studying can be lonely but this fab tool enables you to work face-to-face with up to nine Windows Vista users over a network

ONLINE RESOURCES A host of online reference libraries make research easy

Keep to the agenda
Get on top of your revision schedule

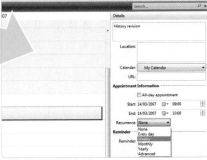

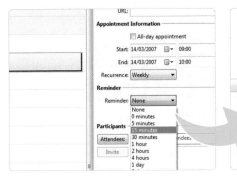

1 GET STARTED Type 'cal' into your Start menu search bar and click **Windows Calendar**. Use the date viewer in the top left corner to find the appropriate date for when you plan to start revising for a particular test.

2 ADD APPOINTMENT Right-click a time slot in the calendar and select **New appointment**. You can give it a meaningful name and alter the time for this piece of revision on the right-hand side of the calendar.

3 RECURRING EVENTS To save you having to add a repeat entry every week, you can set a recurrence – for example, every Wednesday at 9am it's history revision, with a 15-minute reminder beforehand.

4 FINISH UP Keep going, adding your various revision slots, choosing how often they should recur and whether you want a reminder for each one. Don't forget to schedule in breaks for rest, recuperation, refuelling or game playing.

Get some new gadgets!

Tired of studying? Feel like the walls are closing in? Well, Windows Vista is just as good at giving you a break as it is in helping you to get your studies going.

Go to gallery.live.com and immerse yourself in a multitude of toys, gadgets and Sidebar fun. My

Mood-Clock is a nifty little number. No matter how happy, sad or grumpy you feel, you can let everyone know. It helps you to express your mood to your visitors on Live.spaces and you'll find yourself enjoying glaring back at it when the mood takes you.

Five top tips
Improve your revision online

1 Make full use of all your study aids and not just the obvious ones. Your most precious resource is time – use online tools such as Windows Live Calendars to create study schedules and stick to them. As they're online you can access them anywhere – in the library or even your cell phone – and have them send you reminders via text message or email.

2 The simplest way to get the most from your lectures – if permission is granted – is to record them. This enables you to listen to them whenever required, catch that vital point you missed or relive them months later. Many MP3 players and cell phones now come with mics and enough storage for hours of audio.

3 Store research, papers and your own essays online with tools such as Microsoft Office Live Workspace. This will enable you to access them wherever you may be as long as you have an internet connection and web browser.

4 Use online research tools with intelligence. Resources such as Google and Wikipedia are great as a starting point but do not quote from one source alone, always research the original source of the information used and attribute these in your work.

5 Explore and use the rich and ever increasing number of academic journals that are supplying helpful RSS feeds and podcasts. They're out there to be used so it would be foolish not to take full advantage of them.

Never forget anything again

Our lives are getting more hectic, but there are ways to organize your life cheaply and simply

Everyone forgets things from time to time, and the busier you are, the more easily it can happen. There are lots of 'tried and tested' methods for reminding yourself of important events: bits of paper, knots tied in handkerchiefs, notes on the back of your hand, and so on... The trouble is that a piece of paper can get blown off a desk, you wash your hands, and what was that knot for again?

By using your Windows Vista PC you really can make sure you never forget anything again. It's a bold claim, but there are some great free services out there, and they really work.

The first step on your path to total recall is Windows Calendar. This ships

with Windows Vista, and for a basic free program it's rather good. You can set up multiple calendars for each aspect of your life, and subscribe to a variety of online calendars. And you can download calendars online, and load them into Windows Calendar. These could include schedules for the Major League baseball season or release dates for upcoming PC games – there's a huge range to choose from. Just head to www.icalshare.com to find locations of online calendars, or if your PC spends a lot of time offline, download them as .ics files.

Keep connected

As you will appreciate, using calendars is all well and good but having your appointments stored in one place is

no good when you're on the move. Life is busy, and when you need your calendar most, you're likely to find it's stuck on your home PC.

Microsoft has launched a service called Windows Live Calendar, which takes organization to the next level. It is 100 per cent web-based and, like Windows Calendar, you can import your existing calendars using .ics files. You can also subscribe to web-based sources, and if you decide to make it your main calendar, it's easy to automatically link content to other calendars. This means that as long as you have access to an internet connection, no date will be able to escape you.

Of course, as we all know, calendars have several major weaknesses. The main

Keep your diary up to date

Subscribe to a sharing calendar to transfer important dates

1 SHARE Use www.live.com to search for an iCal calendar that you want to download. This could be for your favorite baseball team, TV series, or anything else that interests you.

2 SUBSCRIBE Download the calendar as an .ics file and import it into Windows Calendar. It won't automatically update your calendar, so press **Subscribe**, and copy the link.

3 REMEMBER In Windows Calendar click **Subscribe**, then paste in the link. The new dates will be added to your calendar, and you can toggle them on or off in the left-hand pane.

BREAKING POINT
Don't give in to chaos! Use your PC to get organized

Your own virtual PA

7 ways to use I Want Sandy

1 ONE-OFF
Remind me I have a marketing meeting on 3/14 from 1-2pm

2 EVERY WEEK
Remind me about my yoga class on Tuesday, 8-9am @weekly

3 TO DO LISTS
Write a business report @todo

4 ANNUAL DATES
Remind me Mom's birthday is January 13th @yearly

5 CONTACTS
Remember Paul's number is 555 1000

6 REMIND YOUR FRIENDS
TO: Keen, Charlie
CC: Sandy
SUBJECT: Remind us to call Uncle Peter on Sunday

7 TOTAL RECALL
Look up this week's to-dos

problem is that you have to remember to write on them, and if you're prone to forgetfulness, that won't work. Secondly, not everywhere is online so relying on web-based calendars does have its own inherent weaknesses.

Thankfully, a new internet service called I Want Sandy (www.iwantsandy. com) gives you your very own virtual personal assistant, on hand to remind you about anything, at any time.

When signing up to the service you are given a unique email address to communicate with Sandy. Simply copy Sandy into emails and give her orders, and the service will deliver like any good

PA. Sandy is designed to respond to real-life speak, without the need for complex codes or buzz words, and responds well to human turns of phrase. Just start a sentence with "Remind me to go to a meeting at 10am on Monday" and you'll get an email 15 minutes before. Check the guide (right) for ways to use Sandy.

The beauty of I Want Sandy is the diversity of help it provides, and the ease with which it fits into your existing organization. You can have alerts sent to your mobile as a text message, and Sandy also sends open format .ics files with every email, so you can update your calendar easily. ➡

ONLINE CALENDAR The Windows Live Calendar lets you take your life online

Using Microsoft Live Labs Listas

Five steps to keeping all your favorite URLs in order

1 SIGN IN Head to http://listas.labs.live. com and sign in using your Windows Live ID. Download the Microsoft Listas toolbar, which will appear at the top of Internet Explorer 7. Normally toolbars are a pain, but this one makes your life easier.

2 FIND OUT MORE Now you can search lists to get a flavor of the kind of things the community are interested in. Use the community panel to start exploring the most active users, or the search tab to look for specific material.

3 ADD YOUR OWN Go to the My Lists tab and choose **New**. A blank page will be displayed, where you can give your list a title, tags and content. Choose to make it public or private, or whether the community can make amendments.

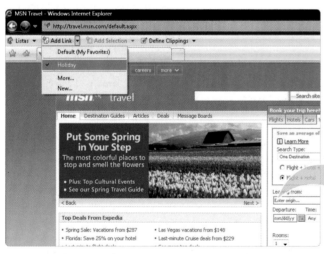

With Microsoft Listas you'll be able to create and share lists, view other lists and contribute to online communities

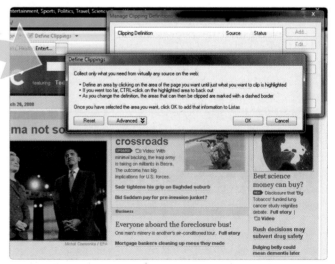

4 ADD CONTENT Writing endless lists can be tedious, so this is where the toolbar comes in handy. If you're researching a holiday, start a list called 'Holiday'. Then, when you come across useful web sites, click **Add Link** on the toolbar and choose which list to add it to, and it will be instantly updated.

Microsoft labs

If you find Listas interesting you can learn more, and join in with other innovations from Microsoft, from its labs site at http://labs.live.com. Here you'll find the latest technologies being developed and tested.

5 CUTTINGS If you just want a snippet of information, the cuttings system can really help. Just click **Define Clippings**, and areas of the page will be broken up into sections. Click the article or paragraph you wish to clip, and click the **Add** button in the corner. The cutting will be pasted into your lists.

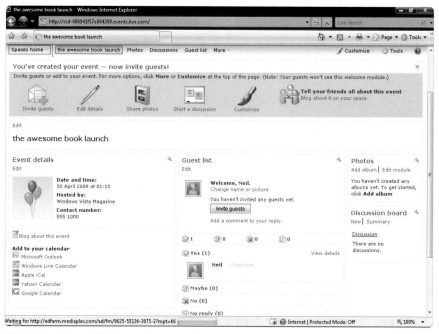

MAKE IT PERSONAL Windows Live Events lets you create a customizable invitation page

Links and Listas

While the Favorites Center in Internet Explorer 7 is very useful, it can become a bottomless pit of links, that you simply save and forget. The information held is often tiny too, so if you do remember to retrieve a page, finding the relevant snippet is virtually impossible.

A new service from Microsoft promises to revolutionize the way we browse the internet. It's been dubbed Microsoft Live Labs Listas and, at the time of writing, is in the early Preview stage. The grand idea is to be able to create and share lists, view other people's lists, and contribute to online communities. This is all very Web 2.0 and slick, but if you're not into the community aspect, there are features of real personal value, too.

If you're researching buying a new car, make a 'New Car List' and store a series of URLs on to it. When you're done researching, you can go to the list, which will now be complete with all your information. Microsoft Listas will even break web pages into 'cuttings' which you can save to your lists like an online scrapbook. This makes it easy to save small parts of information. Microsoft Listas is an online service, so all the lists

you create are available on the internet. While it's currently in the early stages of development, the improvements that could be made, in terms of mobile access, are endless.

Another new service from Microsoft is Windows Live Events. This is a similar service to the successful feature in Facebook, where you create an event and send invitations to your friends. Windows Live Events offers added versatility, as it doesn't rely on your contacts using Windows Live.

Simply go to the events tab and you can create an 'event' page with times, dates, venues and any comments you wish to make. Then you can start inviting people using your Windows Live contact list, or manually type in people's email addresses, who will then be sent an invitation. They can view the event and download .ics calendar entries so there's no way your event can be forgotten.

By making your PC work for you, rather than allowing information to stagnate in calendars, forgetting things becomes virtually impossible and, with so many products on the market that can sync with Microsoft Office Outlook, you'll always be organized.

In real life...
Windows Live

Jo Wickremasinghe, Windows Live Product Manager

1 Organize and manage events with Windows Live Events – a free event management service that integrates with Windows Live Hotmail, Windows Live Spaces, and Windows Live Messenger. Design invitations, customize pages and share photos.

2 Keep large files organized with Windows Live SkyDrive, a free storage and sharing service on the web with 5GB capacity. Go to skydrive.live.com to find out more.

3 With Microsoft Office Outlook Connector you can check your Windows Live Hotmail account in Microsoft Outlook; in addition, any changes made to Hotmail from Outlook are synchronized to your Hotmail account.

4 Organize photos and videos with Windows Live Photo Gallery. Import photos from your camera and Windows Live Photo Gallery will organize them based on date and time. Create panoramic photos and use the editing tools to improve shots.

5 Finally, get quick and easy access to all your Windows Live services at http://home.live.com. Whether it's accessing your mail on Windows Live Hotmail, viewing your friends' updated Windows Live Spaces profiles, or sorting out OneCare protection, the all-new home.live.com home page lets you access all your Windows Live services from one convenient hub.

Host the ultimate party with a firework finalé

If you really want a party to end with a bang, you've got to put some preparation in before the big night

Arguably, the greatest asset of Windows Vista is the ability to use it to help you have fun! Yes, your home computer can help you to prepare for a great party. So why not go all-out with a firework display?

First things first, before you even think about equipment, you want to make sure you have an audience for your show. Obviously, you could just text your friends, but there's a much easier way.

Put the date of your party in the Windows Calendar (find Windows Calendar in the Search menu). If you've not already created your own calendar, click on **File ➜ New Calendar**. To add a new event, scroll to the appropriate area on the left, select a date and time, and

select **New Appointment** from the menu above. From here you can give the event a name and a location.

Now you need to add your friends to your contact list. In the top menu, click

Check out your party purchases by watching videos before you buy

on **View ➜ Contacts** and, in the window that pops up, create your new contacts. Make sure you add their email addresses, so that you can send your invite out. Once this is done, add **Attendees** to the

Participants list and click **Invite**. This will attach your calendar to the email, so that when your friends open it, the event will be added to their Windows Calendar.

If you've got 2007 Microsoft Office software, you can download some great-looking templates that will make your invitation really stand out. If you go to office.microsoft.com/en-us/templates and search for either 'party' or 'celebration' you'll find a few to choose from. Download the template (usually a Microsoft Word document) and simply change the bits of text you need to, like the name of the party and where it's being held. Then just attach this to your invitation email by clicking on **Insert** in the top menu and selecting **File attachment** from the drop-down menu.

Bang, flash, what a party!

If you've got a firework finish planned, capture the moment

1 FLASH
Don't use flash – it won't reach far enough to light the fireworks that you're launching skywards.

2 SHAKE
If you turn off your flash, your camera may try to compensate by slowing the shutter speed; consider using a tripod to keep your camera stable, and your pictures sharp.

3 EXPOSURE
If your camera allows for such an adjustment, increase the exposure to make pictures look brighter (although if you increase it too much, they will look blindingly bright). If your camera is a little more basic, flick the mode to night setting, and it will automatically increase the exposure for you.

4 BRIGHT LIGHT
Don't take shots next to a bright source of light because it will interfere with your pictures.

WHOOSH! If you put on a pyrotechnic display, make sure you record the moment

5 MULTIPLE SHOTS
When the fireworks display takes off try to take as many pictures as you can; with something so unpredictable you'll find many shots don't come out too well. By taking as many shots as possible you will increase your chance of getting at least one really good shot. Make sure you have plenty of batteries and a spare memory card.

Wireless sound

Get music in your backyard

FAR OUT! Make sure your guests can enjoy your party mix in the backyard

So you want your music outside, too? Thankfully there are many portable, weatherproof outdoor speakers ready to entertain you. There's a raft of basic, highly-portable systems that will work with an MP3 player; typically battery-powered these are easily carried around, though aren't usually too loud. For a more meaty sound try something specifically designed for outdoor use. If you want something easier to install, try a wireless outdoor speaker, most will stream music direct from your wireless laptop!

Before people start turning up, you'll want to be prepared. One consideration is the weather. However, if you use a weather gadget from gallery.live.com, you can try to pick the best looking day within the appropriate week.

Party poppers
If you do want to end your party with a firework display there are a number of things to take into consideration...

When it comes to purchasing fireworks, consumers have until fairly recently been subject to a bit of a lottery. Forgetting quality issues, you also have to choose from some pretty random – and boastful – firework names that don't necessarily translate to the actual display at the point of ignition! Fortunately,

there are now web sites dedicated to all things pyrotechnic – you can even see examples in action, by watching the streaming videos, before you buy.

You must also be confident that any fireworks you buy are safe to use. Go to a dedicated firework safety web site to get details of the different sorts of fireworks to look for, and how to prepare your display safely. You will also be able to find information on making sure your family pets are looked after.

Sights and sounds
Ready? Not quite. No party – as visually impressive as it might be – is complete without a good selection of tunes. Fortunately, you can now get speakers that you can put in your back garden

to pump out the sounds. You'll need to couple these speakers with a media extender, such as an Xbox 360, to access all the songs stored on your PC. Obviously, if you're really clever you'll arrange the music to complement the display! Also, as you will be displaying such a visual feast, your friends will be taking photos of the evening; make sure you get all the shots downloaded to your computer, ready to share with everyone else over the internet – you can tag them in Windows Photo Gallery so that you know which party they're from, and who's taken them.

Until then, why not get yourself in the party mood by making your party mix or downloading a 3D fireworks screensaver from the internet?

Create a killer résumé – and bag that dream job

In the market for a new job? Then make sure your résumé is looking its best – a polished introduction is essential

Employment is a buyers' market, so it pays to sell yourself with a high-quality résumé. There are various styles you can choose from, ranging from ultra-simple to stylized formats. The two most common types are chronological and functional. The former should start with details of your current or previous employment. Functional documents are geared towards the position you hope to attain and focus more on your skills and experience. These look better if you're hoping to change your type of employment, or if you're entering the market for the first time or after a break.

There are certain items that must be included, and some things that should be left out. The latter is particularly important, as your curriculum vitae should be no longer than two pages. The first things to include are your personal details. These should include your name, date of birth, postal address and phone number, and also your email address. Think about emailing your finished application as an attachment to a prospective company, as well as posting.

Making the grade

Further content should include a list of your qualifications, as well as when and where you attained them, starting with your most recent. If your grades aren't particularly notable then it's a good idea to simply list the subjects you passed. Another essential is a detailed list of your most impressive work achievements, especially where they have a bearing on the position you're applying for. If there are no formal achievements as such, you could give details of challenges you've faced and how you overcame them. It's also a good idea to include a brief list of any hobbies and pastimes, especially where they're relevant to the job. Finish off with the name and address of both a personal referee, and a reference that's a current or recent employer.

Simplicity works best, but that doesn't mean your résumé should look dull. Tables are easy to set up and format in Office Word, so making use of them for education and employment history can give a clear, neat look to certain areas of your personal profile.

Organize your résumé with tables

With a deep breath and a coffee in hand, it's time to take the plunge...

1 GET PERSONAL To make the résumé more accessible, it's a good idea to use tables. To convert the text you want into a table, first highlight it and then click the **Insert Table** icon in the toolbar.

2 ADDING IN Here, the basic table has the right number of rows but only one column. To add extra columns, highlight the table and right-click, then select **Insert columns to the right**.

3 SPLIT AND MERGE You can give your table a neater look by merging and splitting cells as required, by right-clicking individual or groups of cells and using the relevant pop-up commands.

Create a great résumé
Use your PC to put together a profile that's easy to read, visually interesting and informative

Daniel Collins

Age 23, born 1 February 1985.
One Microsoft Way, Redmond
orson@widgets.msn.com

Education:
2006: Graduated from Maple University with a BA degree in Multimedia Journalism.

Areas Covered by BA Multimedia Journalism:
- News: I wrote many stories involving local news, and interviewed councillors a~~~~~~~
- Features: I wrote a wide range of features, from an interview with a foreign co~~~~
- Dissertation: I conducted a study into political spin and interviewed political i~~~~
- I have passed Law and Ethics, Public Affairs, Newspaper Journalism and N~~~~ Handout exams and I am currently working towards 100wpm shorthand.
- Television: I filmed a 10-minute TV package about bovine TB. I interviewed, le~~~~ farmers and welfare activists, which led to me being nominated for a journalis~~~~

Professional Experience:
I was the news editor of a full color newspaper with a readership of 15,000 students at Maple University. Under my editorship the news section uncovered poor conditions of t~~~~ accommodation.

I have completed three weeks' work experience at the Adventure Works.

In summer 2005 I worked for two weeks at School of Fine Art. I interviewed sen~~~~ police officers and former football manager Noel Asuncion. I also made packages about a local girl band and the top ten Christmas accidents countdown.

Work Experience:
I worked for two years at Fourth Coffee from 2001 until 2003 and took no sick days. I helped customers, and eventually ran the warehouse single-handed on weekends. The store would take in excess of $30,000 a day in peak season. From 2004 until 2006 I worked as a mentor at a scheme called Playing for Success, where I helped children with confidence, learning and behavioral difficulties with their literacy, math and computer skills. I organized the children to make their own newspaper as a literacy exercise.

Hobbies and Interests:
In my spare time I play baseball, and golf with a poor handicap.

Music is one of my passions, and I am always trying to discover new artists. I attended the Elm Festival in 2004 and 2005 and Maple 2002. I have been to countless gigs and shows, and regularly travel to club nights.

Stand out
Use eye-catching fonts and styles, and be consistent throughout. Different colors will break up the page and make reading your boasts much easier. However, if it resembles a Picasso it will go straight in the bin.

~~~eak it up
~~~ bullet points to break ~~~ong paragraphs. This ~~~ make your document ~~~ to read and get the ~~~ntion of even the ~~~iest employer. White ~~~ce is easy on the eye ~~~ looks good, too.

Things to avoid
Make sure you check the spelling throughout. With checkers built into most word processing software, there's no excuse for mistakes. Don't add flowery borders or a picture of yourself – make sure you keep it simple.

Be concise
Don't forget, the document is a summary of your experience, not a draft of your forthcoming autobiography. Two pages are OK, but one is better.

~~~etails
~~~her than simply listing ~~~ past jobs, tell the ~~~ployer what you learnt ~~~e. If you worked in ~~~urger joint then talk ~~~ut people skills and ~~~omer service. It all ~~~nts. Employers are ~~~king for skills so ~~~e sure to sell these.

Go get 'em champ
If you're struggling, 2007 Microsoft Office system has downloadable templates where you can edit generic résumés. However, a CV should be unique, so try to add your own edge to it.

Show a rounded person
Talk about your hobbies and outside interests, as well as employment. An employer wants an impression of you as a whole, not just your work.

Take your office with you using Windows Vista

With Windows Vista your office is no longer a place; your work can move with you. All you need is a PC and an internet connection

Where's your office? With Windows Vista it could be in a room at home, or at a local café using a latte-splashed PC, or absolutely anywhere with a wirelessly-connected laptop. The internet enables you to share files, access resources and use all the programs you use at work every day. You could be waiting for a train, sitting in a library or lying on the beach – no one need ever know you're not at work.

The first step in taking your office out on the move with you is to make sure you have the right tools at your disposal. Your office software – word processor, spreadsheet and task scheduler – should be available on whichever machine you choose to use. You could spend money on second copies of all your software. Having all the same programs (and same versions) you use at work is the only way to guarantee compatibility; this also works out as an expensive option.

Think alternative

Another route is to use an online, web-based office suite when you're away from work. The advantage here is that you can access the same programs on any computer – including machines you can't install software on. This has been a boom area lately, with a number of tools to choose from. Look for packages that work well with Microsoft Office – with spreadsheet and presentation applications, alongside word processing tools – preferably with the ability to import Word documents from your work machine. The best thing about these web suites is that they're absolutely free.

Make contact

With web mail services like Windows Live Hotmail (www.hotmail.com), you can access your email from any connection – even some mobile devices. (Some people are reluctant to use a free web mail service for their work address, as it can appear unprofessional, and it's probably not advisable to put a Hotmail address on your business cards.) However, there's a quick fix to make it look like you're accessing your mail from the office. Hotmail lets you change the 'Reply to' address so that replies appear to come from your office or any email ➜

Meeting in Windows Live Messenger

Need to have a meeting while you're out of the office? This can help

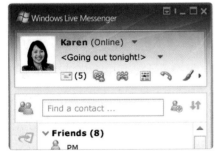

1 ONE-TO-ONE Why bother picking up the phone for that quick query when your colleague is just an instant message away? It's quick, free and easy to use – as long they haven't got you blocked!

2 GET TALKING Turn your one-to-one chat into a meeting by inviting other contacts to join in. Go to **Actions ➜ Invite a contact to this conversation.** You'll get a list of all your online contacts.

3 SHARE FILES Windows Live Messenger 8 lets you set up shared folders. Click **Share files ➜ Create a sharing folder.** A new window will appear for you to drag and drop files to.

HARD AT WORK
One of the best things about working from home: casual dress

I've just popped out for a coffee...

Seven ways to convince your colleagues that you're in the office when you're not

1 BE RIGHT BACK Leave your jacket on the back of your chair.

2 SOUNDS GOOD Record yourself typing. Leave it playing while you nip to the shops.

3 OFFICE SUPPLIES Call your mate at work and ask to borrow a stapler. Then, before he brings it, call to say: "It's OK, I've got one."

4 ON HOLD Re-route your office phone direct to your mobile.

5 KEEPING COOL Cover yourself in factor 40 sunscreen as you sit by the pool for that office pallor.

6 HAPPY BIRTHDAY Get a friend to pass a card round. Sign your name with that day's date.

7 TIME FOR A DRINK Turn up at the end of the day, then head to the bar like you were there all along.

4 VOICE CONFERENCING Sometimes it's quicker to talk than type. To start a voice call in the current conversation, click **Call a contact** and then **Call computer**. Don't forget the microphone!

5 CALL THE OFFICE Need to check in with the boss? You can call him directly from Live Messenger. Click **Call a contact → Call a phone**. Hit **Learn more** to find out how to prepay for calls.

6 VIDEO MEETINGS For face-to-face communication, you'll need a webcam connected to your computer. Then, just click the **Start or stop a video call** icon when you're in a conversation.

Pocket office

Not working from home, but sitting on the beach or in a bar instead? Then you need Windows Mobile 6

Windows Mobile 6 is Microsoft's new operating system for PDAs, handheld computers and mobile devices. With mobile versions of Microsoft Office Word, Excel and PowerPoint it gives you an office in your pocket. Of course, these are scaled down versions of their bigger siblings, but they're still jam-packed with enough features to make sure you can create and edit documents on the move.

When you've finished working with a file, you can deliver it in a number of ways. Synchronize your PDA with a PC to transfer documents across or synch with another user's mobile device to send a file direct to them. You can also email files to any account using Office Outlook or Windows Live Hotmail.

Microsoft Outlook is the email and scheduling tool that comes as part of Microsoft Office. The Windows Mobile version will synchronize with

EMAIL MOVER If you plan to write a lot of emails on the move, the HTC S710 offers a full integrated keyboard for rapid typing

Office Outlook on your main machine, importing and exporting contacts in a variety of ways. One recent innovation is Direct Push technology – which sends new emails, calendar and contact updates direct to your phone. You no longer have to specifically connect

OFFICE PHONE The HP iPAQ 514 Voice Messenger lets you take your entire office on the move along with your office applications

to the internet to check your mail.

Windows Live Messenger is included in Windows Mobile 6, too – so even when you're out and about, you can hold virtual meetings with work colleagues, exchanging instant messages, files and images.

you choose rather than Hotmail. In Hotmail you do this in **Options → More Options → Send and receive mail from other e-mail accounts**.

Of course, if you're on the move you'll need access to all your contacts, too. If you use Microsoft Office Outlook, there's a simple way to synchronize your online address book. You'll need a Windows Live Hotmail email account and an add-on for Microsoft Office Outlook called Outlook Connector. You can download the latter from http://office.microsoft.com/en-us/outlook/HA102225181033.aspx. Once this is installed on your main machine, you'll be prompted to create a connection to your Hotmail account. When you restart Outlook, you'll have access to the

Hotmail account – including your inbox and contacts – from Outlook. Now you can simply drag and drop your work contacts from Outlook to your Hotmail account, so you can access them anywhere.

SKYDRIVE Send files off to the file-store in the sky with Microsoft Live SkyDrive

So far, you can access office tools anywhere, keep track of your contacts and send email from your desk when you're not even there. What about all the important files that are already on your work machine? What you need is some storage – a place to keep those files so you can always get to them. There are several possible solutions to that particular problem; just take your pick.

Online storage

Online file storage and sharing services are an easy way to make your documents available on any internet-connected machine. Simply sign up for an account and upload the files you want to store. Then you can access your files and choose whether uploaded

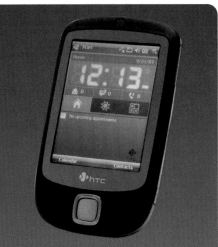

TOUCH ME The HTC Touch interface makes it a compelling device; a phone call is possible in just a few fingertip moves and it offers full Wi-Fi and a 2MP camera

GRID TO GO You can even check your spreadsheets with the mobile Office Excel

documents should be private or shared. With shared files, you can send a web link to anyone via email. They can download the file direct from the link you give them. Most of these sites also let you store pictures and you can post the links on message boards or in blog posts. While these services are good for the occasional picture or memo, what if you need access to all your files? In this case, you'll need to create an online back-up of all your files. An online back-up means you can access your files – using the relevant software – from your internet-connected PC as though it were another hard drive. These services are fast and easy to use, working in the background to save documents as you update and change them. This also

means you'll never lose a file again. This much peace of mind costs though – so compare subscription rates before making your decision.

Microsoft offers the Live SkyDrive service, which not only enables you to access your own files online but enables you to make them available to other users, if you so choose. The great news is if you already have a Hotmail or Windows Live account then you already have access to 5GB of online storage via Live SkyDrive, just browse to http://skydrive.live.com and click the **Get Started** button or else create a fresh Windows Live account and get going.

The interface lets you easily upload documents, music, pictures and videos, along with making files available to specific Windows Live users or to all users. When sharing files it's possible to specify people as Editors or Readers – a helpful shorthand for those with full or just read-only access to the files that you upload to the new folders.

Online file storage is an easy way to make your work available on any PC

The easiest way to keep your files accessible everywhere is to just carry them around with you in your pocket. USB flash drives, or USB keys, used to be novelty devices. Now you can purchase drives that will store as much as 4GB of data – enough memory for a thousand songs in Windows Media Audio format or tens of thousands of text files. The beauty of these is that you can plug one into the USB port of any computer to instantly access your files – your PC will recognize it as another drive attached to your system. For extra peace of mind, keys can also be password protected for extra security.

Use a combination of the facilities mentioned here, and you'll be ready to take your office on the move.

Being there

How to directly access resources on your work PC when you're away

TAKE CONTROL Remote Desktop allows you complete control of your work PC

Remote Desktop
Take control of your work PC from afar. Go to **Control Panel → System and Maintenance → System → Remote settings** and click **Allow Remote Access** on your work PC and your own machine. To connect to the work PC, launch **Remote Desktop**, then enter its IP address.

MEETING UP Make sure you're all on the same page with Windows Meeting Space

Windows Meeting Space
Collaborate with colleagues using Windows Meeting Space. Built into Windows Vista Ultimate, Home Premium and Business, it gives you shared access to applications on the host PC. Type 'Meeting' in Start search, then launch it and click **Start a new meeting**.

Childproof your home office

While working from home is convenient, it can be hazardous. Keep your kids – and your PC – safe

For parents, working from home can be a blessing – but all your office paraphernalia can be hazardous to children, and children can certainly be hazardous to your precious work documents and computer hardware.

That's something Linda Jones had to learn the hard way. "I'm naturally an untidy person, but I had to be really organized while working from home.

I was concerned about the number of cables and switches for little hands to get hold of or trip over; when my daughters Emily and Melissa were toddlers, they were never allowed in my 'office' unattended," she recalls. Despite this, Linda originally let her daughters sit on her lap now and again as she worked – and her computer ended up the casualty.

"Every time an exasperated computer repair man came to see us, he'd say 'don't have drinks near the computer!' and we'd smile, nod and say "OK" before counting the days before something else ended up over the keyboard." After a year of crumbs and drink spillages, Linda's PC finally gave up the ghost entirely.

Eventually, Linda decided that working from home and children didn't mix, and she hired a separate office... Something Jake Ludington considered when his son Wyatt crumpled up a crucial contract he'd left on his desk. But instead of giving up, Jake decided that 'something should be done'! He embarked on a quest to make his home office childproof – and he's helpfully

Identify dangers – explore your office from toddler level

published his advice online at www. jakeludington.com/child-safe-home-office. As Jake discovered, it is possible to make a childproof office – but it does take a bit of work first.

Home office hazards

One of the easiest ways to identify potential dangers in your work room is to 'do the crawl' and explore your office from toddler level. If something can be pulled, poked, prodded, bashed into or tripped over it probably will be, and doing your own personal crawl is a good way to spot the risks.

"Once you get past the obvious

Child-friendly Windows Vista

Use Parental Controls to protect kids from net nasties

The most obvious concern about mixing computer equipment and young children are the physical risks but, of course, there are other risks, too. It's all too easy to encounter objectionable material – or people – online, and if your kids are playing with an unrestricted PC they could see inappropriate content. The other risk is that they'll mess with things they shouldn't, such as work files. While Windows Vista makes it easy to recover files, it's easier to prevent damage from occurring at all.

The answer is found in User Accounts and Parental Controls. By giving each family member their own password-protected account, you can set up Parental Controls to filter their web browsing or prevent them from running specific

programs. Best of all, the controls can be different for each account – so while you might block almost everything for young children, you can give older kids more leeway. Setting up User Accounts and Parental Controls is easy: just log in on an administrator account, open Control Panel and follow the walkthrough on p204.

PARENTAL PASSWORDS There's no point in creating separate user accounts if your own account isn't password protected

Moveable monitor
If your fragile, and heavy, screen can be accidentally pulled off the desk, then it probably will be.

Unlocked drawers
Guaranteed to trap fingers, and if you're keeping sharp stuff or consumables in there, the contents can be risky, too.

Wired peripherals
A trip or a tug on your keyboard could send your whole system crashing to the floor, damaging the computer, your child or both.

Desk with sharp edges
Many desks are the perfect height to dent a child's head. Fit corner 'cushions' if you're worried.

Trailing cables
Trailing cables are far too easy to catch with a foot or hand, unplugging your kit or tripping your kid.

Power points and plugs
Sockets are too easy to explore. Fit covers and, where possible, block plugs from inquisitive fingers.

Paper mountain
Filing things away doesn't just remove the risk of the kids turning them into confetti – it makes you more organized.

Shredder
The combination of whirring blades and probing fingers is never a happy one.

things like keeping sharp objects out of reach, making light sockets unavailable, storing toxic substances appropriately and so on, most of what's left is keeping your working environment safe so you don't have reasons to get mad for what really boils down to carelessness," says Jake. Of course, there are many other elements of office equipment to be aware of – paper shredders, paper cutters, electrical cables and plugs, etc. Thankfully, Jake's online advice covers everything from putting covers on sockets to choosing a chair without adjusters that a child could bang into.

Isn't there a danger that paranoid parents will go over the top though, or is it prudent to imagine worst-case scenarios? "It's prudent... but I wouldn't go overboard with it," Jake says.

No, no, no
Jake's key advice is to create a 'yes' environment. He explains: "A 'yes' environment is basically a place where you aren't constantly telling your child no. If you're going to exist in a home office with your kids, you need things they can do because they are going to want to be where you are. Telling them 'no' to the point where there's nothing in the room they can do is not productive, and it's not really healthy for the kid, either.

"Providing solid alternatives," continues Jake, "like a small table where your kid can draw on paper – and other age-appropriate materials makes all the difference between getting work done and spending all your time giving a child negative attention."

Happy home working
Many forward-thinking companies are more parent-friendly these days, and a large number of employees are electing to become homeworkers when their little darlings arrive. We spoke to three parents and homeworkers: Patricia Kenar, Lynn Cormack and Alison Schillaci. So how do they cope?

Lynn's children – Cameron (10) and Natalie (8) – are older, so "no childproofing was really necessary, ●

Case study: toddling traumas

The home set up – and the changes that have to be made...

When Pete Boston joined web design agency Headscape (www. headscape.co.uk), working from home was entirely new to him. Fortunately, it now means Pete can spend more time with his daughter Rachel. Although Pete didn't do any childproofing to the office before she arrived, he had to make a few changes once Rachel began to assert her independence – and her curiosity.

"My main concerns are all the wires and plug sockets under my desk, which Rachel always heads for as soon as she crawls into the office," he says. "So I've made sure monitor cables are out of reach."

Pete will also be moving his halogen heater, which he quite sensibly uses instead of heating the entire house when he's cold and home on his own in the winter." The heater is a sensible economic choice but of all the things in Pete's office, this is probably the biggest potential hazard. So it's not just desk drawers and cupboard doors to worry about...

So is a home office more dangerous than any other room in the house? "Yes and no," Pete says. "It's more hazardous than a bedroom, but less than a kitchen – especially when I'm not there and the door is left open." For Pete, the best solution is simple: "Keep the door closed if you aren't in there!"

as my kids are at the age where they know better – most of the time," she says. There haven't been any disasters – that is, other than "the usual screaming fits while you're trying to talk to customers and the doorbell's ringing and the dog's barking..."

"The smart answer is to say 'keep them out of the office', but that isn't always possible," says Patricia Kenar. "I don't allow four-year-old Neco in my office when I'm working, but if

"I've bought Neco a little phone and he sits and copies me!"

I'm doing paperwork, or whatever, we play a game where he isn't allowed to talk to me and he'll sit quite happily with paper and crayons."

Patricia also recommends a baby gate "so you can see them but they can't get in to touch anything"; this kind of arrangement echoes Jake Ludington's comments about providing child-friendly alternatives. "I've bought Neco

Keep your kids safe when they're online
How to set up Parental Controls in Windows Vista

1 CONTROL Go to **Control Panel ➔ User Accounts and Family Safety ➔ Set Up Parental Controls for any user**. Once you've chosen the child's account, you'll see the screen shown here. Click **Parental Controls: On** to start making the account child-friendly.

2 WEB In addition to blocking access to programs, Windows Vista includes a web filter. Click on **Windows Vista Web Filter** and you can restrict or block internet sites. If you check **Only allow websites which are on the allow list** you can enter a specific list of safe sites.

3 TIME From the main Parental Controls screen click on **Time Limits** and you'll see a grid dividing each day into hour blocks. Use your mouse to color the grid – blue means that your PC is off-limits – if your child tries to log on Windows Vista will turn them away.

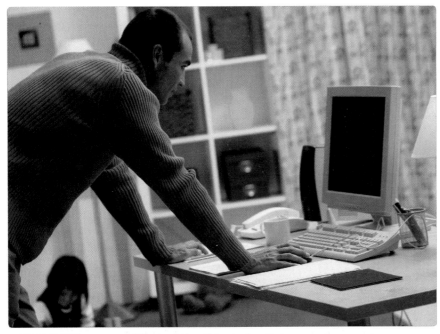

WORK & PLAY Keep your child occupied, and they're less likely to upset your work

a little phone and he sits and copies me," Patricia laughs. "It's hysterical."

"We use cable tidies, and while we have a shredder we have warned both Luke (7) and Isaac (4) how dangerous it is," says Alison Schillaci. "We let them shred unwanted documents, junk mail and so on with supervision, and they don't seem to feel the need to play with it... we did tell them that they would lose a finger and it would never grow back. Shocking I know, but we find it works to be dramatic if the consequences could be dramatic."

"Children always seem to want what they can't have," Alison notes, so when Luke was three she introduced him

GIVE AND TAKE It's an idea to show your children how dull office equipment really is!

to Paint and another child-friendly website. "He doesn't touch anything – modem, wires, etc – because he's more interested in what he can put up on the screen." She found the same approach worked with other equipment: "I just demonstrated what it was and fed their appetite to play with something new, and now they don't seem to bother."

A 'yes' environment

Like Jake Ludington, Alison found that creating a 'yes' environment for your children is one of the most effective ways of childproofing.

"Feed and respect your child's curiosity," she says. "Show them how things work and give them their own time, supervised at first, on the computer, let them send a fax – it soon gets boring – and watch them learn new skills. We feel that when Luke and Isaac learn and respect what things are for and how they work, their curiosity is significantly reduced. When they don't try to go behind your back, you don't worry about their safety." So, it seems, that with a bit of forward-planning and good observation skills, a parent can work from home!

Child-friendly

Top tips for a child-safe office

1 DO THE CRAWL Explore your office on your hands and knees. Look for things that can be pulled, prodded or crashed into.

2 CUT THE CABLES Wireless keyboards and peripherals aren't tied to your PC, so grabbing hands won't pull your entire system off the desk. More expensive to start with, but could save you a fortune in repair bills.

3 TIDY THE REST Some cables – power, video and so on – are necessary; use cable tidies to keep them out of sight and reach.

4 PUT LOCKS ON Childproof locks for drawers and doors are cheap, easy to fit and prevent kids from getting their hands on dangerous or irreplaceable items.

5 COVER THE PLUGS Plug covers stop curious fingers getting into electrical sockets. Consider covering power strips and plugged-in cables to prevent accidental unplugging too.

6 MOVE YOUR PC To children, CD and DVD drives are perfect places to put toast. Move your desktop case – and monitor while you're at it – out of reach.

7 GET A LID Put a lid on your wastepaper bin to prevent potentially painful bits and bobs being grabbed.

8 MAKE SPACE Creating a kids' area in your home office will hopefully provide enough distraction to stop your little darlings tugging at power cables.

Liven up your PC with Windows DreamScene

DreamScene Ultimate Extra brings life to your desktop by converting or creating movies to be used as animated wallpaper

If you've got Windows Vista Ultimate, you can download DreamScene via Windows Update – and it couldn't be easier to use. Once running, go to **Control Panel ➜ Change Desktop Background** and you'll see the Windows DreamScene option.

Initially, you have five movies there – including running water, flames and rain. To add another, open its location in Windows Explorer and drag the file into the box. Provided that it's in MPEG or WMV format, it should be imported.

Creating new DreamScene content couldn't be easier in theory but, in practise, it takes time to get the right balance of factors to make a good desktop. Most importantly, while it's nominally a video desktop, you don't want to run lengthy videos. The higher the resolution – the size of the movie on your screen – the greater the strain it will put on your computer.

Equally, the more movement you have, the more annoying the movie becomes. Move the camera or start panning or zooming around and it won't be long before you make the viewer feel ill.

Making movies

With the camera fixed, you need to film a clip that lends itself to being looped continuously – 30 seconds is a good length. The biggest problem comes at the end, as the world doesn't tend to be so repeatable. Film 30 seconds of running water and it's likely to be a close enough match, but do the same with sped-up footage of clouds and there's a noticeable 'click' every 30 seconds as it restarts. If another position gives you a smoother transition, don't feel locked to that 30-second suggestion.

You may also be able to do a few tricks with your footage, such as duplicating the initial clip, cutting it down to its opening frames and cross-fading between it and the final clip, smoothing out the reset. However, this depends on the footage you're working with.

DeskScapes and DreamMaker

You could create something that everyone wants on their desktop

If you've never heard of Stardock (www.stardock.com), it's the company behind WindowBlinds and many other Windows customization tools. DeskScapes is the latest, with the ability to do more than just play video – it also creates background content automatically and alters it on the fly according to triggers. For example, you could have the background change from day to night as time progresses.

Even better news is that at the time of writing DeskScapes v2 is under development and will extend animated desktops to all the editions of Windows Vista. In the meantime, DeskScapes v1 and DreamMaker serve two functions – managing downloaded Dreams from dream.wincustomize.com and

DREAM TIME Impressive Dreams are only going to get more interesting over time

packaging up videos you make for other people to download. You'll also find plenty of downloads at the site if you want to take advantage of the technology without having to invest in a high-resolution camera.

DREAM ON Looking for more Dreams? WinCustomize has plenty to choose from

Dream a better dream

The easy way to create animated backgrounds

1 CAMERA CHOICE The first thing you need is a recording device. Digital cameras can record video but you need something with more oomph to get quality and resolution – ideally an HD-ready camcorder.

2 PICK A SCENE Pick your subject carefully. This image is of daffodils in a garden. The movement comes from the wind in the grass and the movement of the trees, both easily looped.

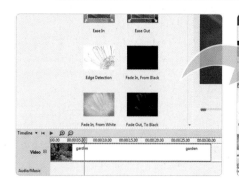

3 EDIT FILM Import your footage into Windows Movie Maker (or any other video editor). Apply any necessary effects and cut your raw footage down to your desired length. As mentioned, a good guide time is around 30 seconds.

4 NEW RESOLUTIONS DreamScene can stretch video, but export the MPEG/WMV file in as high a resolution as you can without the bit rate slowing your machine to a crawl. Microsoft recommends a bit rate of 4,991.

5 FILM DISTRIBUTION Try the background out by dragging the movie into the DreamScenes window. If it works well, why not package it up using DreamMaker so that other people can enjoy the fruits of your labor?

Appendix

If this book has whet your appetite but you're yet to make the change, these pages will help you prepare

Installing Windows Vista

Choosing the right edition

Whatever your needs, there's a version of Windows Vista that's perfect. Which one is best for you?

Microsoft has made not one version of Windows Vista, but four main editions (as well as a 'starter' version for emerging markets, one for global organizations, and special '64-bit' versions of each for heavyweight PCs!). Whichever edition you go for to start with, you can actually get all of them: Microsoft has put every version on the same disc, so if you decide you want a more powerful edition you don't need to trek to the shops. Instead, just contact Microsoft, pay for the upgrade and unlock a more powerful version instantly.

Over the page you'll find details of the four main Windows Vista editions, along with a rundown of the specific features.

Home Premium is the best version for most people, but then the all-singing, all-dancing features of the Ultimate Edition are difficult to resist...

Decision time

Windows Vista was one of the most ambitious computing projects of all time. Originally codenamed 'Longhorn' and intended as a minor upgrade for Windows XP, development started in 2001 with a planned release date of 2003. However, Microsoft decided a minor upgrade wasn't enough: the next version of Windows was to be a major new interpretation with a brand-new look, stacks of improvements and a huge number of features. The Longhorn project was rebooted in 2004, and ➔

> The next Windows was to be a major new interpretation

In real life...
Upgrade advice

Paul Douglas, Editor, *Windows Vista: The Official Magazine* If you are worrying about upgrading from Windows XP, the good news is that Microsoft has foreseen the concern and produced the Windows Vista Upgrade Advisor. This handy program (available from www.microsoft.com/windows/products/windowsvista/buyorupgrade) will scan your PC and provide a detailed breakdown of potential problems, so that you can buy and upgrade in complete confidence.

UPGRADE The move from Windows XP to Windows Vista is usually very smooth

Entertainment
Windows Vista Home Pemium
If you enjoy gaming, videos and music then the Home Premium Edition is perfect, as it offers full Media Center capabilities

"Wow"
Service Pack 1
Now available via Windows Update –
and in the latest editions in shops –
this first Windows Vista Service
Pack 1 offers a huge range of
performance, security and
stability updates

Office
Windows Vista
Business Edition
If you're running a home office or small
business then this is the best option for
you and all your business needs

Office & Entertainment
Windows Vista
Home Pemium
For the user who wants everything this edition
takes all the features of the others and then adds
in a little more to make it truly ultimate...

APPENDIX INSTALLATION

CLEAR VIEW You can turn off transparency, but why would you when it looks so good?

three years later, Windows Vista was the result. As you'll discover, it's similar enough to Windows XP that you won't feel lost when you use it, but there are some major new features, new programs and new tools designed to make your PC more powerful, more productive and more in tune with your life. It's an impressive achievement.

Windows Vista is an operating system, which means its job is to act as a middleman between your PC's hardware and software – so when you want to print a document from your word processor, Windows Vista tells the hardware what to do; when you need to find a file, Windows Vista searches your hard disk, and so on. However, it's more than just an interpreter...

Full of features

Windows Vista comes stuffed with software that enables you to do all kinds of useful things without shelling out for extra programs; web browsing and email, home entertainment, DVD burning, photo editing, video editing and much more. It also comes with a range of security tools, although you'll still need to invest in an anti-virus program. So what's new in Windows Vista?

The Windows Vista user interface strikes you as soon as you hit the on switch. The familiar green Start button has morphed into a blue orb and the Start menu itself is organized differently. The Desktop still sports a taskbar with a Notification Area to the right and an

Windows Vista comes stuffed with software

optional three-icon Quick Launch area next to the Start button, but that's where the similarity ends. Icons are now high resolution and 3D; the taskbar is semi-transparent, as are the borders of windows, and you'll find a bunch of 'gadgets' nestled in a strip running vertically down the right side of the

Windows Vista – the four main editions compared

So what are the differences between each edition of Windows Vista? Here are the salient features...

Features

	Home Basic	Home Premium	Business	Ultimate
Manage your kids' access to the PC using Parental Controls	✔	✔	✘	✔
Back up files to a network device	✘	✔	✔	✔
Stay secure with Windows Defender and Windows Firewall	✔	✔	✔	✔
Find documents with Instant Search	✔	✔	✔	✔
Browse the web with Windows Internet Explorer 7	✔	✔	✔	✔
Enjoy the new look Aero desktop and Flip 3D	✘	✔	✔	✔
Get on the move with Windows Mobility Center and Tablet PC support	✘	✔	✔	✔
Share documents with Windows Meeting Space	✘	✔	✔	✔
Use your PC as an entertainment center with Windows Media Center	✘	✔	✘	✔
Protect against hardware failure with business backup features	✘	✘	✔	✔
Business networking and Remote Desktop	✘	✘	✔	✔
Protect against data theft with Windows BitLocker Drive Encryption	✘	✘	✘	✔

desktop. The overall color scheme is subtle, soft and very easy on the eye.

As you'd expect, virtually everything in Windows Vista is customizable. More surprising, perhaps, is that some familiar tools and shortcuts have moved. For instance, if you right-click the desktop in search of the Properties dialog box – as you might do to adjust screen resolution, change the wallpaper and tweak the graphics driver settings – you'll find no such menu. Instead, there's a Personalize option that fires up a hefty Control Panel-style window comprising seven main headings, a separate 'task' list and some links to related features.

There's plenty to discover about Windows Vista, and the elements covered in this book should help you to enjoy the benefits that the new operating system has to offer. However, if you've yet to upgrade, the most important question is which of the different editions is best for you. The chart below will give you an idea; the feature breakdown on the previous page will help, too. ⊞

Which edition is for me?

Follow the chart to discover your Windows Vista

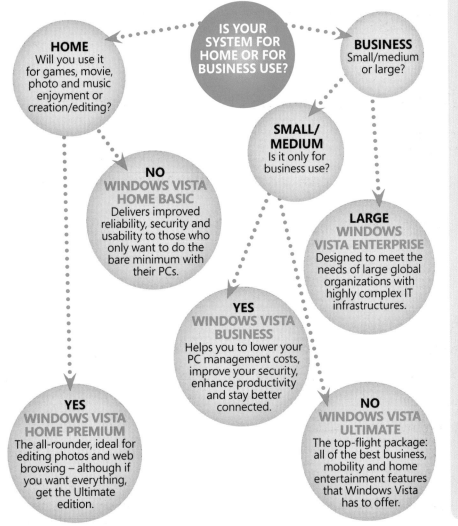

IS YOUR SYSTEM FOR HOME OR FOR BUSINESS USE?

HOME
Will you use it for games, movie, photo and music enjoyment or creation/editing?

BUSINESS
Small/medium or large?

SMALL/ MEDIUM
Is it only for business use?

NO WINDOWS VISTA HOME BASIC
Delivers improved reliability, security and usability to those who only want to do the bare minimum with their PCs.

LARGE WINDOWS VISTA ENTERPRISE
Designed to meet the needs of large global organizations with highly complex IT infrastructures.

YES WINDOWS VISTA BUSINESS
Helps you to lower your PC management costs, improve your security, enhance productivity and stay better connected.

YES WINDOWS VISTA HOME PREMIUM
The all-rounder, ideal for editing photos and web browsing – although if you want everything, get the Ultimate edition.

NO WINDOWS VISTA ULTIMATE
The top-flight package: all of the best business, mobility and home entertainment features that Windows Vista has to offer.

Solid security

Iron-clad protection for your PC

Bolstered security is arguably the most important innovation in Windows Vista. For instance, the Windows Firewall is now two-way, monitoring outbound and inbound network communications (previously it was inbound only). Windows Defender, Microsoft's anti-spyware tool, is turned on by default, offering real-time protection against malicious software. Similarly, Internet Explorer runs in a 'protected' mode that forces you to grant permission for every action that could be construed as suspect, such as downloading and installing software.

Windows Vista includes a clever security feature called User Account Control, which pops up whenever Windows is about to perform a process that could be damaging or at least far-reaching. The screen goes black, then freezes, and up pops a dialog box that forces you to choose between continuing or cancelling. For newcomers to computing, this may be alarming; for old hands, it can be a little frustrating. However, if you really can't live with the intrusions, the answer lies in simply modifying the User Account privileges.

NEW SEEKERS Every folder has a search box and there's one in the Start Menu

Take precautions before you install

If you're upgrading to Windows Vista, you're probably worried that something will suddenly go wrong. A little preparation is a good idea...

Imagine being seconds away from finishing an installation and the worst happens – a power cut, lightning strikes your house, aliens land on the roof or, more mundanely, your hard drive fails. No matter how unlikely it is that anything will go wrong, you should never risk all your photos, emails and other mementos on the chance, particularly when it's so easy to protect them using Windows Backup. You'll find this in **Start ➜ All Programs ➜ Accessories**, though if you're running Windows XP Home, you

need to install the utility first – you'll find it in the VALUEADD\MSFT\NTBACKUP folder on the installation CD.

If you want an even easier option, dumping My Documents and any personal folders on a single DVD or CD takes less than half an hour.

Fight the temptation to tidy up My Documents before backing up – just be selective when you restore the data. Check where more obscure programs store files by checking their **File ➜ Save** menu, and don't forget any save points for games; they're usually in their own folders in Program Files. If you've bought

online applications, grab the keys and passwords for these as well (and the actual files). And, if other members of your household use the same machine, you need to do all of this for each account. Other areas you should take note of are your internet favorites, email account settings and web site passwords. It's also worth taking note of the programs in the Start Menu, because it's easy to lose more obscure utilities.

Easy transfers

The manual approach isn't the only choice, though. Windows Vista introduces Windows Easy Transfer, a new program that makes it really easy to copy all the important settings over. While you can use it to get files off an old PC and on to your new Windows Vista machine – either by connecting their USB ports with an Easy Transfer cable or connecting them both to a home network – you can also use it to back up a computer before installing Windows Vista on it.

It doesn't support every program, and you'll still need to reinstall lots of stuff once you've got your new system in place, but it's a lot easier than painstakingly tracking down long-forgotten set-up details.

"Wow" More stable

Service Pack 1 has been designed to remove up to 75 per cent of all reported system failures from crash reports that relate to Windows Vista, helping to make it even more stable

HELPING HAND Forget a laborious manual approach – let the Backup utility take the strain

And if you're migrating to a new PC...

Using Windows Easy Transfer really is easy

1 GETTING STARTED Place the Windows Vista disc in your old system, wait for the Install Windows screen, and click **Transfer files and settings from another computer.**

2 TO TRANSFER Click **Next → Close All** to close running programs. Choose how to transfer data; an Easy Transfer Cable is best, but this example uses Use a CD, DVD or other removable media.

3 PICK A DRIVE Easy Transfer can use USB flash drives or a network drive. If you don't have either, click **CD**. Pick a CD or DVD writer from the list, and password-protect your files.

4 WHAT FILES? You can click **All user accounts, files, and settings** to transfer the lot, but that requires lots of space (say, a network drive). If using DVDs, click **Advanced options**.

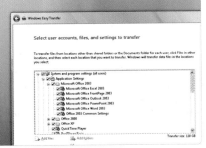

5 WHICH SETTINGS? You'll see a tree of every group of files and settings that Easy Transfer can move, with the size displayed. Browse the list, clearing check boxes for entries you don't need.

6 BURN DATA Place a blank, writeable CD or DVD in the drive specified, and click **Next**. Windows Easy Transfer will copy the checked files and settings – prompting you to replace it as required.

7 AT THE NEW PC Put the first disc in a drive. Click **Start → Computer**, choose the drive containing your disc; double-click on the **Migration store** file it contains to import the transferred data.

8 NAME CHECK Your PC may not have the same user account names as your old one, so you'll be asked which new accounts should be used for each old one. Pick an account and click **Next**.

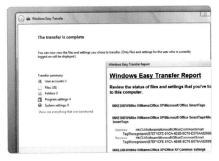

9 LET'S DO IT Click **Transfer** and switch discs as prompted. When complete, click **Show me everything transferred** for a list of every file and Registry setting added or changed. Otherwise click **Close**.

APPENDIX INSTALLATION

Consider the power of your PC

You need to check a few things before deciding which upgrade is best for you, and you need to maximize performance...

If you're upgrading a computer that's running Windows XP, you can save money by opting for an upgrade rather than the full version of Windows Vista. However, you can't necessarily perform an 'in-place' or 'over-the-top' upgrade; sometimes you have to perform a clean installation of Windows Vista, which means backing up and reinstalling all your current programs, folders and files. The table shows where an over-the-top upgrade is possible.

In practise, a clean install means a fresh start, and anything short of this can potentially carry over all manner of problems from your old, cluttered version of Windows XP. Strictly speaking, when Windows Vista installs itself over Windows XP, it actually does perform a clean install and then imports all the old settings. This should help prevent problems and can even, in principle, carry through hardware drivers that can't be installed under Windows Vista

From/To	Windows Vista Home Basic	Windows Vista Home Premium	Windows Vista Business	Windows Vista Ultimate
Windows XP Home	Yes	Yes	Yes	Yes
Windows XP Professional	No	No	Yes	Yes
Windows XP Media Center	No	Yes	No	Yes
Windows XP Tablet PC	No	No	Yes	Yes

Is your PC powerful enough to install

Don't upgrade in haste and repent at leisure – look before you leap

1 CHECK THE SPECS Get the Upgrade Advisor from snipurl.com/1tqwo. As the opening screen recommends, connect as many of your external devices as possible, including hard drives. Initiate a scan and leave alone for a few minutes.

2 NO ROOM When the scan concludes, click **See Details**. This report tells you whether you can install Windows Vista – or, if you can't, why not. It may be that a simple upgrade in the graphics or memory department is all that's needed.

3 DECLARE INTEREST You'll see recommendations about which version of Windows Vista is best for your PC, in this case Home Basic. Click **Other versions** and the program tells you about specific issues in relation to each.

	Windows Vista Capable	Windows Vista Premium Ready
Processor	At least 800MHz	1GHz or better
RAM	512MB	1GB
Graphics	Supports DirectX 9, 32MB RAM	Supports DirectX 9, WDDM driver, 128MB RAM

itself. However, a truly clean install is obviously the recommended option.

If you're buying a new PC with Windows Vista pre-installed, you should have nothing to worry about with regard to performance. It will be at least Windows Vista Capable and possibly Windows Vista Premium Ready. The difference is one of hardware capability, particularly in the graphics department. A Windows Vista Capable computer can run all core features of Windows Vista, including the enhanced search and security frameworks, but may not be able to handle the three-dimensional transparency and live thumbnails at the heart of Aero Glass.

A Premium Ready computer is rated to handle anything that Windows Vista can throw at it (see the guidelines listed above). The reason for the hefty system requirements is that DirectX, Microsoft's

graphics engine, is no longer used just for games; it's used throughout Windows Vista to deliver the Aero interface. Virtually all recent graphics cards are DirectX-compliant, but it's worth checking that WDDM (Windows Vista Display Driver Model) drivers are available. If your graphics card isn't up to speed or WDDM drivers aren't available for it, Windows Vista defaults to the Classic gray interface.

If the graphics card is compatible, does have the right drivers but doesn't have quite enough horsepower, Windows Vista displays the Aero theme but skips the transparency effects.

Windows Experience Index
If you're not entirely happy with the performance of Windows Vista on your PC, particularly following an upgrade from Windows XP on an older machine,

check out Microsoft's on-board system performance monitor. The Windows Experience Index rates the processor, memory and hard drive speeds, and checks the graphics processor's ability to render the Aero desktop theme and the demands of 3D gaming. The result is a base score of somewhere between 1 and 6, potentially going upwards as new hardware develops and is released.

The idea is that all Windows Vista-compatible programs will carry a base score rating. If a box says that a base score of 4 is required (or recommended), expect sluggish performance on a PC that scores below 3. However, if this is the case it may be that just a single component, such as the memory, needs upgrading to improve performance.

To rate your hardware in Windows Vista, just click **Control Panel → System and Maintenance → Performance Information → Tools.** Use the View and print details option for the full low-down on your system spec.

Of course, it would be nice to know whether your hardware is up to the mark before installing Windows Vista, and that's what the Upgrade Advisor is for. See the steps below for details.

and run Windows Vista?

4 POTENTIAL PROBLEMS To run Home Premium, this PC needs a new audio driver, a TV tuner and a new graphics card; Home Premium ships with Media Center, but Home Basic doesn't – hence the earlier recommendation.

5 OTHER ISSUES Upgrade Advisor flags up any devices connected to your computer that it doesn't have drivers for. It's worth checking that Windows Vista drivers are available from the manufacturers before you upgrade.

6 DOWNLOAD UPDATES Finally, visit the **Task List** tab for a summary of what to do and what you should expect to have to do post-installation. A visit to Windows Update can help keep devices working after you install Windows Vista.

Starting the install...

It may seem a scary thing to do but replacing the operating system of a PC isn't anywhere near as difficult as it used to be. In fact, it just takes a number of easy steps to get the job done

There's every possibility that you'll first encounter Windows Vista when buying a new PC, but you may well be upgrading from an older system. If you aren't buying a brand new PC with Windows Vista pre-installed, there are three ways to upgrade your PC to Windows Vista:

1 An 'in-place' upgrade of an earlier version of Windows. This preserves your old programs, files and settings.

2 A clean installation over the top of an existing version of Windows. This erases your previous version and all of your old files, favorites and settings.

3 A clean installation on a new or freshly formatted hard disk or hard disk partition, with or without a dual boot environment.

Option 1 is not recommended as there are four main concerns. First,

there's no way back, so if you don't like Windows Vista or if it doesn't perform as you expect, that's just tough. Second, there's a risk, however small, that the upgrade will fail at some point and you'll lose your data. Third, any existing problems on your PC may be carried through, potentially including viruses and spyware. And finally, your current system may well be performing at less than peak performance due to internal clutter and conflicts, and this could affect your post-upgrade performance. There's simply nothing like a fresh, clean installation to get the best out of Windows Vista.

So which of the other options is best? Well, option 2 is fine so long as you make absolutely sure that you've backed up everything you could ever need from your old version of Windows. Windows Vista formats (wipes clean) the hard disk

during installation, so your data will be gone for good. You emerge with a pristine installation of Windows Vista that's free from the performance and security issues inherent in option 1, but you have to install all your old software again. Windows Easy Transfer makes it much easier to configure your new version of Windows like the old one.

Option 3 is easier still. That's because Windows Vista doesn't have to delete the old version of Windows; it simply installs alongside it in a different location. If you only have one hard disk, you can either install a second disk – an easy hardware upgrade – or you can split it into two (or more) partitions. A partitioned hard disk has separate sections that behave just like physically distinct hard disks. This way, you can leave your previous version of Windows on one partition while installing

It's only 15 steps to installation heaven

Just to prove how easy it is to install, here's every major step

1 MAKE SPACE If you intend to install on a hard disk partition next to Windows XP, create the partition using a third-party tool. If you have a second hard disk, you don't need to worry.

2 NO MESS The installer gets straight to the point. If you haven't already run the Upgrade Advisor (see page 216 for further details) you can do it from this screen; otherwise, click **Install Now**.

3 GET UPDATES It's best to enable checking for updates. Even something as simple as a new device driver could make an important difference post-installation.

In real life...
Quick and easy

Paul Douglas, Editor, *Windows Vista: The Official Magazine* We've installed Windows Vista on a lot of different PCs – for ourselves, friends and family, and for readers. The general consensus on the magazine is that Windows Vista is the smoothest Windows upgrade we've experienced. However, when problems do occur it's never fun; in our experience these issues have been linked to old hardware without drivers. It really is advisable to use the Upgrade Advisor before making a decision.

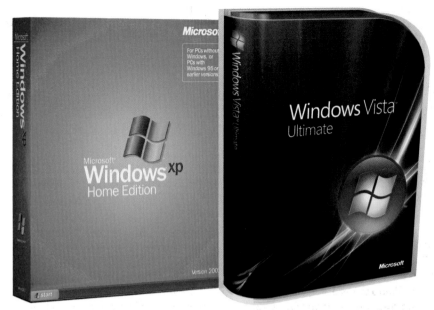

MOVING ON UP Moving from Windows XP to Windows Vista is a smooth and easy process

Windows Vista cleanly in the other. You can also use your old version of Windows whenever you like simply by selecting it from a menu when you reboot. You can launch the Windows Vista set-up routine either by accessing the DVD from within Windows XP or by booting directly from the DVD.

The walkthrough below looks at option 3, accessing the DVD from within

Windows XP. There is a point about partitioning that needs to be taken into consideration. If your hard disk isn't already partitioned, Windows Vista can't do it for you without erasing your existing data. So if you have a PC with a 100MB hard disk and you ask Windows Vista to split it into two 50GB partitions – one for Windows XP and one for Windows Vista – you get two 50GB

partitions. Unfortunately, the Windows XP one will be completely empty.

There are two ways around this. You can either install a second hard disk, which removes the need for partitioning altogether, or you can invest in a third-party disk partitioning program. If you use such a tool to partition your hard disk, make sure you choose the NTFS file system option and not FAT32.

4 UNCHECK ACTIVATION Before going any further, the installer prompts you for the license key. Consider unchecking the automatic activation box, in case you need to reinstall Windows Vista later on.

5 CHOOSE METHOD If you launched from within Windows XP, either select **Upgrade** to replace Windows XP or **Custom** to install to a separate hard disk or disk partition.

6 UNHAPPY INSTALLER To illustrate the importance of formatting a new drive or partition, here's what happens when you don't or when the partition is formatted with the older file system. ➡

Installation heaven...

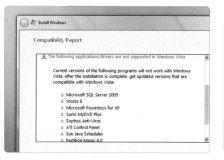

7 SAFE THAN SORRY By way of another illustration, here's what happens when you try to perform an upgrade without first remedying compatibility issues identified by the Upgrade Advisor. There's no way forward here so retreat.

8 GET ON Pitfalls aside, Windows Vista should now install smoothly with no further intervention from you for a while. Your PC will reboot a few times. When you see the **Press any key to boot from CD** option during a reboot, don't do this.

9 CHOOSE PASSWORD You'll be asked to specify your regional settings – Windows Vista defaults to US settings – and thereafter to create a User Account. This is the master account that Windows Vista will use by default.

10 NAME THIS KIT Give your PC a name. This will become important if and when you connect to a network. Choose a name that's not already on any network that this computer will join. You can also select a desktop background.

11 PLAY IT SAFE Now specify some basic security settings. It's best to go for the default **Use recommend settings**, because this turns on the Windows Firewall and configures automatic updates.

12 WHERE AM I? You'll be asked to review your international time settings and to specify how the computer will be used. This is to help with your Windows networking settings, although you can adjust the Network setup later.

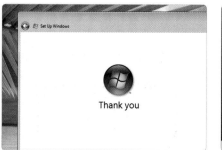

13 READY TO ROCK And that's that. All that remains now is to hit the **Start** button to run some final automated configuration. Your PC will reboot and, if you have upgraded Windows XP, fire up Windows Vista for the first time.

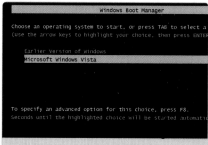

14 WHICH WINDOWS? If you selected a separate hard disk or hard disk partition (step 5), you will be presented with a boot menu. The 'earlier version of Windows' is Windows XP. Use the **arrow** and **Enter** keys to select.

15 HERE WE GO Finished! Your new desktop appears on your screen for the first time, displaying the wallpaper you chose in step 10. Welcome to the world of Windows Vista. Is it a wonderful world? You'll soon find out....

Common queries answered
Having a few problems? Check these fixes...

Q My software doesn't install. What can I do to make sure it does?

A If you put an install CD in the drive and nothing happens, right-click on it in Computer and choose **Explore**. Right-click on the installer program itself (usually called Setup or the name of the program) and choose the **Run as Administrator** option.

Q What do I do if my software installs, but doesn't work?

A Go to **Control Panel → Programs → Use an older program with this version of Windows** and pick the program. Follow the steps to make it think it's running an old version of Windows. You can also manually set compatibility options by right-clicking a program, choosing **Properties → Compatibility**. Choosing **Windows XP (Service Pack 2)** should work, and you can tick boxes as required.

Q My software isn't working properly – what should I do?

A Make sure that you're running the latest version. Many programs need to have updates installed to work in Windows Vista, and some won't work at all – check the official web sites for their respective details.

Q Why am I having difficulties trying to import backed-up files?

A This can happen if you've transferred your files from DVD and they're set to **Read-only**. Simply select the files, right-click them, and choose **Properties** – and make sure that the **Read-only** attribute is not checked.

Q How can I get my incompatible hardware to work?

A Unfortunately, not all hardware devices and components will immediately work with Windows Vista. You'll need to look for a Windows Vista-compatible driver at the manufacturer's web site, or try installing a Windows XP driver instead.

Q How can I get my really old games to run in Windows Vista?

A If you've got any really old software (particularly in gaming) that requires DOS, then it won't work in Windows Vista. However, this can be sorted. You need to install DOSBox from Dosbox.sourceforge.net in order to run your old games on your new system.

Q Why is my PC now running so slowly?

A If your computer only has a small amount of RAM, then it's going to struggle when it comes to running Windows Vista. If you can't add any more, plug in a USB2 ReadyBoost-compatible memory stick and choose **Speed up my system** from the menu that appears.

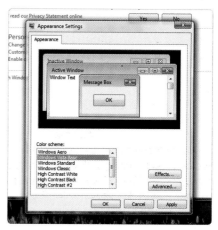

Q Why is Windows Vista taking so long to appear?

A Windows Vista is more demanding on your computer and your graphics card. Search for **Aero** in the **Control Panel**, click **Enable or disable transparent glass** then **Classic appearance properties**, then select **Windows Vista Basic**.

Index

Index

What do you think of this book?

We want to hear from you!

Do you have a few minutes to participate in a brief online survey?

Microsoft is interested in hearing you feedback so we can continually improve our books and learning resources for you.

To participate in our survey, please visit:

www.microsoft.com/learning/booksurvey/

... and enter this book's ISBN-10 number (appears above barcode on back cover*). As a thank-you to survey participants in the United States and Canada, each month we'll ramdomly select five respondents to win one of five $100 gift certificates from a leading online merchant. At the conclusion of the survey, you can enter the drawing by providing your e-mail address, which will be used for prize notification only.

Thanks in advance for your input. Your opinion counts!

*Where to find the ISBN-10 on back cover

ISBN-13 000-0-0000-0000-0

ISBN-10 0-0000-0000-0

No purchase necessary. Void where prohibited. Open only to residents of the 50 United States (includes Distrtict of Columbia) and Canada (void in Quebec). For official rules and entry dates see:

www.microsoft.com/learning/booksurvey

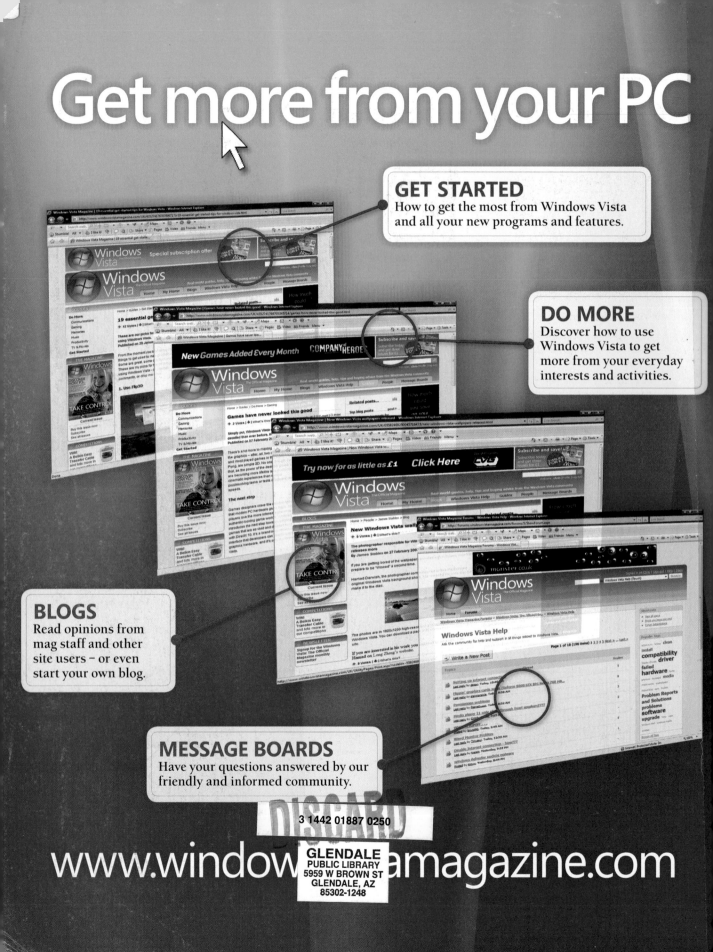

Get more from your PC

GET STARTED
How to get the most from Windows Vista and all your new programs and features.

DO MORE
Discover how to use Windows Vista to get more from your everyday interests and activities.

BLOGS
Read opinions from mag staff and other site users – or even start your own blog.

MESSAGE BOARDS
Have your questions answered by our friendly and informed community.

www.windows...amagazine.com